MariaDB 11 Essentials

MariaDB 11 Essentials

ISBN-13: 978-1-965764-17-6

Rev: 1.0

https://www.payloadbooks.com

Contents

Table of Contents

Table of Contents

1. Start Here

Databases are the foundation of applications like websites, mobile apps, and large-scale enterprise systems. MariaDB is one of the most highly regarded database management systems in use today. MariaDB 11 Essentials provides a concise guide to MariaDB, covering fundamental concepts, advanced techniques, and best practices.

The book begins by installing and configuring MariaDB on Windows and Linux before outlining the fundamentals of relational database management systems.

Beyond the fundamentals, this book covers advanced MariaDB features such as indexing for performance optimization, automation with triggers and events, and database modeling.

In addition to covering the command-line tools provided with MariaDB, several chapters introduce the phpMyAdmin and MySQL Workbench tools, which offer user-friendly graphical interfaces for database management.

By following this book, you will learn how to:

- Install and configure MariaDB on Windows and Linux.

- Use MariaDB client tools and graphical interfaces like MySQL Workbench and phpMyAdmin.

- Design efficient database schemas and relationships.

- Manage databases using the Structured Query Language (SQL).

- Optimize database performance using indexing and query optimization techniques.

- Automate repetitive database tasks using triggers and scheduled events.

- Secure MariaDB databases by managing user privileges and access controls.

This book explains each topic in detail and includes practical examples that provide hands-on experience. The chapters also contain quick-reference summaries highlighting key points for easy review.

By the end of this book, you will have the confidence to build and manage MariaDB databases.

1.1 About MariaDB

The History of MariaDB began in 1995 when MySQL AB, a Swedish company founded by David Axmark, Allan Larsson, and Michael Widenius, released the MySQL Server database management system. In 2000, MySQL Server became an open-source project.

In 2008, MySQL AB was acquired by Sun Microsystems, and in 2009, Oracle purchased Sun Microsystems. MySQL continues to develop and evolve and holds a significant share of the relational database market.

In 2009, MySQL co-founder Michael Widenius, concerned that Oracle might focus on the commercial aspects of MySQL at the expense of the open-source community, created MariaDB. MariaDB is derived from the MySQL source code (a concept known as a "fork" in open-source parlance). Originally intended as a fully compatible alternative to MySQL, MariaDB has started to diverge from MySQL in recent years, but the two systems remain highly compatible.

MariaDB continues to evolve and increase in popularity and is considered to be faster and more scalable than MySQL. K1 Investment Management acquired the company behind MariaDB, and like MySQL, MariaDB is available in free community and subscription-based enterprise editions.

The name MySQL comes from a combination of "My" and "SQL." In this context, "My" is a proper noun rather than a possessive adjective and is named after My, the daughter of Michael Widenius. SQL stands for Structured Query Language, the language used for managing databases. MariaDB, on the other hand, is named after Widenius' younger daughter Maria.

1.2 Downloading the database snapshots

Many chapters in this book assume that you have completed the steps from previous chapters. If you would rather not read the chapters in sequence, you can import database snapshots at the beginning of each chapter using the snapshot files available for download at the following link:

https://www.payloadbooks.com/product/mariadb11/

1.3 Importing the database snapshots

To import a snapshot, open a terminal or command prompt, navigate to the directory that contains the sample files, and run the following commands:

```
mariadb-admin -u demo -p drop sampledb
mariadb-admin -u demo -p create sampledb
mariadb -u demo -p sampledb < snapshot_file_name.sql
```

1.4 Download the Color eBook

Thank you for purchasing the print edition of this book. Your purchase includes a color copy of the book in PDF format.

If you would like to download the PDF version of this book, please email proof of purchase (for example, a receipt, delivery notice, or photo of the physical book) to *info@payloadbooks.com,* and we will provide you with a download link.

1.5 Feedback

We want you to be satisfied with your purchase of this book. Therefore, if you find any errors in the book or have any comments, questions, or concerns, please contact us at *info@payloadbooks.com.*

1.6 Errata

While we make every effort to ensure the accuracy of the content of this book, inevitably, a book covering a subject area of this size and complexity may include some errors and oversights. Any known issues with the book will be outlined, together with solutions, at the following URL:

https://www.payloadbooks.com/mariadb11_errata

If you find an error not listed in the errata, email our technical support team at *info@payloadbooks.com.*

1.7 Find more books

Visit *https://www.payloadbooks.com* to view our complete book catalog.

2. The Basics of Databases

The chances are that if you have ever logged into a website or purchased an item on the internet you have interacted with a database in some way. Anything that involves the retrieval or storage of information on a computer system is most likely to involve a database. In fact, databases are the core of almost every application that relies on data of some form to complete a task. In this chapter, we will introduce the basic concepts of databases.

2.1 Database vs. DBMS

The first step in learning MariaDB is understanding the difference between a database and a database management system (DBMS). The term database refers to the entity that stores the actual data (such as ID numbers, names, and addresses, for example) in a structured way. A database management system (DBMS), on the other hand, refers to the software used to store, access, and manipulate the data stored in the database. All interactions with the database are performed via the DBMS.

Modern databases and database management systems are not restricted to storing just text. Today, databases store such items as images, videos, and software objects.

2.2 Client-server databases

MariaDB is classified as a client-server database management system (DBMS). This type of DBMS consists of two main components. The server, which usually resides on the same physical computer as the database files, is responsible for all interactions with the database. The second component is the client, which sends database requests to the server. The server processes these requests and returns the results to the client.

There are several key advantages to using a client-server architecture for a database management system (DBMS). First, the client does not need to run on the same computer as the server. Instead, clients can send requests over a network or internet connection to a server located on a remote host. This setup makes the database accessible to a large number of clients. In large-scale enterprise environments, it also allows for fault tolerance, high performance, and load balancing to be implemented effectively.

Second, separating the client from the server allows a wider range of client types to be used to access the database. Typical clients include MariaDB tools, desktop and mobile apps, web-based applications, web servers, and even other database servers:

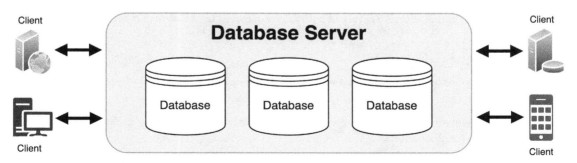

Figure 2-1

2.3 What is a database server?

The term "database server" can be somewhat misleading as it can refer to different concepts. One definition relates to the computer system hosting a Database Management System (DBMS) and other applications and services. However, in this book, we will specifically refer to the software component of a DBMS responsible for executing database operations on behalf of clients and returning the results. In the context of MariaDB, this role is fulfilled by MariaDB Server.

A database server can contain multiple databases, each containing one or more tables.

2.4 Understanding database tables

Database tables provide the most basic level of data structure in a database. Each database can contain multiple tables, each designed to hold information of a specific type. For example, a database may contain a customer table containing the name, address, and telephone number for all the customers of a particular business. The same database may also include a product table that stores the product descriptions with associated product codes and pricing for the items the business sells.

Each table in a database is assigned a name that must be unique to that particular database. A table name, once assigned to a table in one database, may only be re-used within the context of a different database:

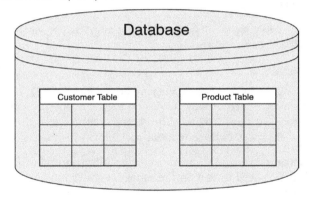

Figure 2-2

2.5 Introducing database schema

Database schemas define the characteristics of the data stored in a database table. For example, the schema for a customer database table might define that the customer name is a string of no more than 20 characters in length and that the customer phone number is a numerical data field of a specific format.

Schemas are also used to define the structure of entire databases and the relationship between the various tables in each database.

2.6 Columns and data types

At this stage, it is helpful to begin viewing a database table similar to a spreadsheet, where data is stored in rows and columns.

Each column represents a data field in the corresponding table. For example, a table's name, address, and telephone data fields are all columns.

Each column, in turn, is defined to contain a specific data type, which dictates the type of data it can store. Therefore, a column designed to store numbers would be defined as a numerical data type.

2.7 Database rows

Each new record saved to a table is stored in a row, which consists of the columns of data associated with the saved record.

Once again, consider the spreadsheet analogy described earlier. Each entry in a customer table is equivalent to a row in a spreadsheet, and each column contains the data for each customer (name, address, telephone number, etc.). The individual columns within a specific row are referred to as *fields*.

When a new customer is added to the table, a new row is created, and the data for that customer is stored in the corresponding columns of the new row.

Rows are also sometimes referred to as *records*, and these terms can generally be used interchangeably:

Table			
Columns			
customer_id	customer_name	customer_address	customer_phone
1001	John Smith	London	123-54355
1002	David West	Miami	424-09238
1003	Mark Wiliams	Paris	234-84509
1004	Sarah Parker	New York	768-30895

Figure 2-3

2.8 Primary keys

Each database table must contain one or more columns that uniquely identify each row. This is known in database terminology as the *primary key*. For example, a table may use a bank account number column as the primary key. Alternatively, a customer table may assign unique identifiers to each customer as the primary key.

Primary keys allow the database management system to uniquely identify a specific row in a table. Without a primary key, retrieving or deleting a specific row in a table would be impossible because there is no certainty that the correct row has been selected. For example, suppose a table existed where the customer's last name had been defined as the primary key. Imagine the problem if more than one customer called "Smith" was recorded in the database. Without some guaranteed way to uniquely identify a specific row, it would be impossible to ensure the correct data was being accessed at any given time.

Primary keys can comprise a single column or multiple columns in a table. To qualify as a single column primary key, no two rows can contain matching primary key values. When using multiple columns to construct a primary key, individual column values do not need to be unique, but all the columns combined must be unique.

Finally, while primary keys are not mandatory in database tables, their use is strongly recommended.

2.9 What is SQL?

As discussed previously, a database management system (DBMS) provides the means to access the data stored in a database. One key method for achieving this is via a language called Structured Query Language (SQL), which is abbreviated to SQL and pronounced "sequel".

SQL is a straightforward and easy-to-use language developed at IBM in the 1970s specifically to enable the reading and writing of database data. Because SQL contains a small set of keywords, it can be learned quickly. In addition, SQL syntax is identical in most DBMS implementations, so having learned SQL for one system, your skills will likely transfer to other database management systems.

Throughout this book, particular attention will be paid to explaining the key SQL commands so that you will be proficient in using SQL to read, write, and manage database data.

2.10 Reference points

The main points covered in this chapter are as follows:

- **Databases vs. DBMS**
    - A database stores structured data (e.g., names, addresses).
    - A DBMS (Database Management System) is software to access, store, and manipulate the database (e.g., MariaDB).

- **Database Client-Server Architecture**
    - Databases operate on a server, and clients (apps, web servers) access them locally or remotely via a network.
    - A database server may host multiple databases, each with one or more tables.

- **Database Tables**
    - Tables organize data into rows (records) and columns (fields).
    - Each column has a specific data type (e.g., numerical, text).

- **Database Schema**
    - Defines the structure of a database and its tables, including data types and relationships.

- **Primary Keys**
    - Unique identifier for rows in a table (e.g., customer ID).
    - Can be a single column or a combination of columns.
    - Strongly recommended to ensure reliable row identification.
    - Proper table structure and primary keys ensure efficient data management and retrieval.

- **SQL (Structured Query Language)**
    - The primary language for interacting with databases.
    - Used for querying, updating, and managing database data.
    - SQL is simple, widely adopted, and transferable across DBMS platforms.

3. Installing and Launching MariaDB on Linux

This chapter explains how to install and run MariaDB on Linux, including instructions for starting and stopping the MariaDB server and using the MariaDB client. The steps to install MariaDB will depend on the Linux distribution, of which there are many. Fortunately, most distributions support one of the two main package management systems, which will be covered in this chapter.

3.1 Installing MariaDB on Linux

Most Linux repositories include MariaDB packages that can be downloaded and installed using package management tools such as *dnf* and *apt*. However, these repositories often do not provide access to the latest version of MariaDB. For example, as of now, most Linux distributions and the Oracle repositories only offer packages for MariaDB 10. To ensure that we install the latest MariaDB packages, we can download them directly from the MariaDB website and install them manually. However, while this will provide us with the latest version of MariaDB, we will need to manually download and install newer versions as they become available.

The best way to install MariaDB on Linux is to do so directly from the MariaDB repositories. Not only will this install the latest version, it also ensures that newer releases are installed automatically when performing routine operating system updates.

3.2 Installing the MariaDB repositories

MariaDB provides a script called *mariadb_repo_setup* that adds the MariaDB repositories to most Linux distributions. To download the script on your system, open a terminal window, change to a suitable directory and run the following commands:

```
sudo dnf install wget -y
wget https://downloads.mariadb.com/mariadb/mariadb_repo_setup
```

After downloading the script, execute it using the following command:

```
sudo bash ./mariadb_repo_setup
# [info] Checking for script prerequisites.
# [info] mariadb Server version 11.rolling is valid
# [info] Repository file successfully written to /etc/yum.repos.d/mariadb.repo
# [info] Adding trusted package signing keys...
/etc/pki/rpm-gpg /home/demo/mariadb
/home/demo/mariadb
# [info] Successfully added trusted package signing keys
# [info] Cleaning package cache...
Updating Subscription Management repositories.
0 files removed
```

The script will detect the operating system type and CPU architecture, and perform the necessary steps to add the MariaDB repository to the system.

Once the repositories have been added, run the following command to install MariaDB on Red Hat-based systems such RHEL, CentOS, Fedora, Rocky Linux, and AlmaLinux:

```
sudo dnf install mariadb mariadb-server
```

After the installation is complete, use the *systemctl* command to start the MariaDB server service as follows:

```
sudo systemctl start mariadb.service
```

To check that the service started, run the following command:

```
sudo systemctl status mariadb.service
```

If you would like MariaDB Server to load each time the system boots, run the following command to change the default configuration:

```
sudo systemctl enable mariadb.service
```

To stop the server, use the following *systemctl* command:

```
sudo systemctl stop mariadb.service
```

3.3 Installing MariaDB on Debian and Ubuntu

The mariadb_repo_setup script can also be used to add the MariaDB repository to Ubuntu and Debian systems. To download the script, open a terminal window, navigate to a suitable directory and run the following commands:

```
sudo apt install curl -y
wget https://downloads.mariadb.com/mariadb/mariadb_repo_setup
```

After downloading the script, execute it using the following command:

```
sudo bash ./mariadb_repo_setup
# [info] Checking for script prerequisites.
# [info] MariaDB Server version 11.rolling is valid
# [info] Repository file successfully written to /etc/apt/sources.list.d/
mariadb.list
# [info] Adding trusted package signing keys...
# [info] Running apt-get update...
# [info] Done adding trusted package signing keys
```

The script will detect the operating system type and CPU architecture, and perform the necessary steps to add the MariaDB repository to the system.

Once the repositories have been added, run the following command to install MariaDB on Ubuntu and Debian systems:

```
sudo apt install mariadb-server
```

After the installation is complete, use the *systemctl* command to start the MariaDB server service as follows:

```
sudo systemctl start mariadb.service
```

To check that the service started, run the following command:

```
sudo systemctl status mariadb.service
```

If you would like MariaDB Server to load each time the system boots, run the following command to change the default configuration:

```
sudo systemctl enable mariadb.service
```

To stop the server, use the following *systemctl* command:

```
sudo systemctl stop mariadb.service
```

3.4 Launching the MariaDB client

Now that the MariaDB server is secured and running, we need a way to interact with it. The simplest option is to use the MariaDB client (*mariadb*). This tool connects to the server and provides a command-line environment for executing SQL statements on the stored data.

Since this is a new installation, the only configured user is the root user. We will explore how to add users to a MariaDB server instance in a later chapter. For now, to access the MariaDB server as the root user on Linux, you must launch the MariaDB client with superuser privileges. For example:

```
sudo mariadb
```

Once MariaDB has connected, the following output will appear:

```
Welcome to the MariaDB monitor.  Commands end with ; or \g.
Your MariaDB connection id is 6
Server version: 11.7.2-MariaDB MariaDB Server

Copyright (c) 2000, 2018, Oracle, MariaDB Corporation Ab and others.

Type 'help;' or '\h' for help. Type '\c' to clear the current input statement.

MariaDB [(none)]>
```

At the *MariaDB [(none)]>* prompt, enter the following statement to confirm that we are operating as the root user:

```
MariaDB [(none)]> SELECT CURRENT_USER();
+----------------+
| CURRENT_USER() |
+----------------+
| root@localhost |
+----------------+
1 row in set (0.000 sec)
```

Next, test the installation by entering the following SQL statement to generate a list of databases:

```
MariaDB [(none)]> SHOW DATABASES;
+--------------------+
| Database           |
+--------------------+
| information_schema |
| mysql              |
| performance_schema |
| sys                |
| test               |
+--------------------+
5 rows in set (0.001 sec)
```

To exit from the client, enter *exit* or *quit* at the prompt:

```
MariaDB [(none)]> quit
Bye
```

3.5 Reference points

The main points covered in this chapter are as follows:

- **Installation Overview**

  - MariaDB can be installed through Linux package managers (dnf/apt)

  - Default repositories may not have the latest version

  - Recommended method: Install from official MariaDB repositories

- **Adding Repositories**

  - Use the mariadb_repo_setup script:

    ```
    wget https://downloads.mariadb.com/mariadb/mariadb_repo_setup
    sudo bash ./mariadb_repo_setup
    ```

  - Works for both Red Hat-based and Debian-based systems

- **Installation Commands**

  - For RHEL/CentOS/Fedora:

    ```
    sudo dnf install mariadb mariadb-server
    ```

  - For Debian/Ubuntu:

    ```
    sudo apt install mariadb-server
    ```

- **Service Management**

  - Start service:

    ```
    sudo systemctl start mariadb.service
    ```

  - Check status:

    ```
    sudo systemctl status mariadb.service
    ```

  - Enable auto-start:

    ```
    sudo systemctl enable mariadb.service
    ```

  - Stop service:

    ```
    sudo systemctl stop mariadb.service
    ```

- **Using the MariaDB Client**

  - Connect as root:

    ```
    sudo mariadb
    ```

- Basic commands to verify installation:

```
SELECT CURRENT_USER();
SHOW DATABASES;
```

- Exit client: `quit` or `exit`

- **Key Points**

  - Always use official repositories for latest version

  - systemctl commands manage the service

  - The mariadb client provides command-line access

  - Root access requires sudo privileges

4. Installing and Launching MariaDB Server on Windows

This chapter will explain how to install and run MariaDB Server on Microsoft Windows. This will include instructions for starting and stopping the MariaDB server. Additionally, we will cover how to use the MariaDB client and explore various configuration options available for MariaDB on Windows.

4.1 Downloading MariaDB for Windows

MariaDB for Windows is available as a Microsoft Software Installer (.MSI) file. To download the latest version of MariaDB Server, open a web browser window and navigate to the following page:

https://mariadb.org/download/

On the download page, use the menu marked as A in Figure 4-1 to select the latest rolling release of MariaDB Server 11 and set the operating system menu (B) to Microsoft Windows. MariaDB Server is only available for 64-bit x86 systems, so leave the architecture menu (C) unchanged and set the package type (D) to MSI Package:

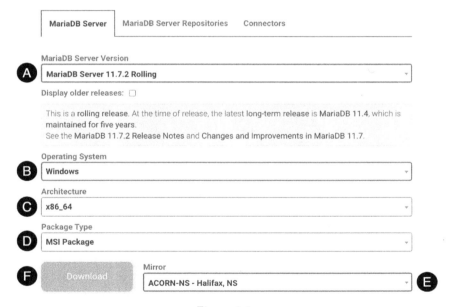

Figure 4-1

To download the MSI Installer, use the Mirror menu (E) to choose a download server within your geographic region before clicking the Download button (F). When prompted, save the MSI file to a suitable location on your local filesystem.

4.2 Running the software installer

Using Windows Explorer, navigate to where you downloaded the MariaDB MSI file and double-click it to begin the installation. Once the installer has loaded, the screen shown in Figure 4-2 will appear:

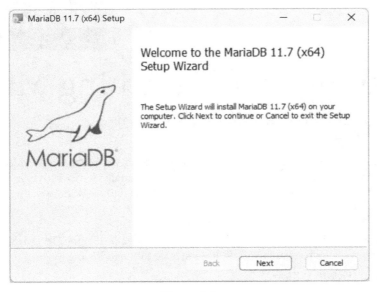

Figure 4-2

Click the Next button to review and accept the licensing terms before moving on to the Custom Setup screen shown below:

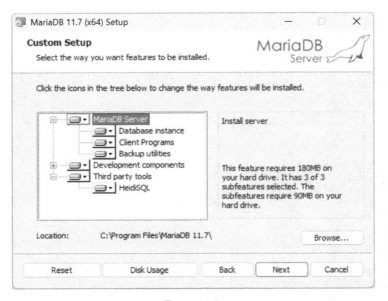

Figure 4-3

This screen allows us to choose which MariaDB features we want to install and will, by default, install all the available options. For the purposes of this book, leave the feature settings unchanged.

The standard installation location for MariaDB is follows (where <version> is replaced by the release number):

```
C:\Program Files\MariaDB <version>\
```

Although this book will assume that MariaDB is installed in the default location, a different destination can be selected by clicking the Browse button and navigating to an alternative destination folder.

Click Next to display the user settings screen shown in Figure 4-4, where we can specify a new password for the root user and change the directory into which MariaDB will store its database files:

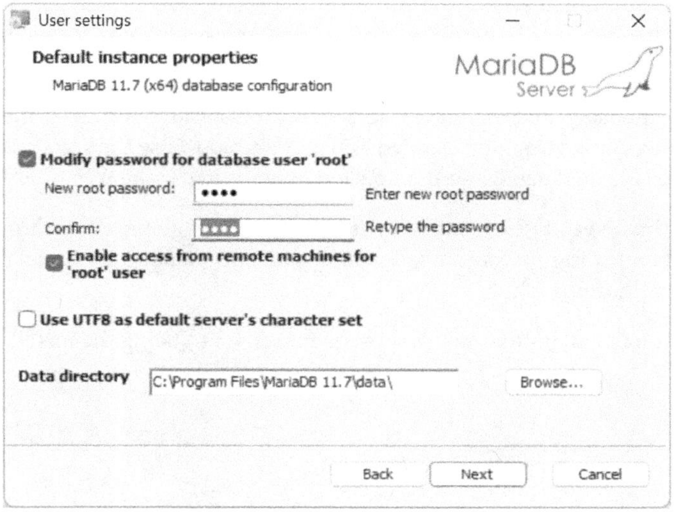

Figure 4-4

The root account functions as a "superuser," providing complete access and control over the databases managed by MariaDB. For this reason, it is crucial to select a sufficiently complex password. If you do not assign a password, anyone accessing the host system can access the MariaDB server instance.

You can also allow remote root access to the MariaDB server instance. Remote root access is not generally recommended. However, if you are accessing your Windows system remotely, you will need to keep remote root access temporarily until you have created at least one additional user account.

After entering a root password and making a remote root access appropriate to your situation, click Next to modify the database settings:

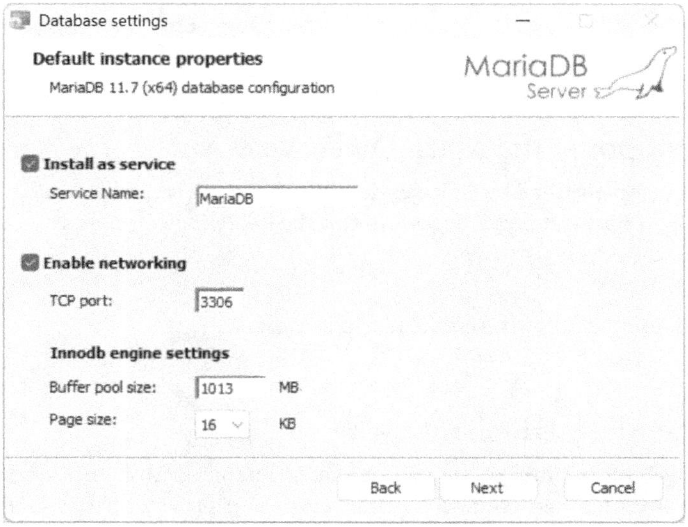

Figure 4-5

The database settings screen determines how MariaDB Server operates on the system. MariaDB can run as a managed Windows service or be launched manually by executing the mariadbd.exe file. However, launching the server manually involves additional steps and requires passing several command-line configuration options to mariadbd.exe. The Windows service option is recommended unless you have a specific requirement requiring manual execution.

The networking setting manages external client access to the MariaDB server instance. Since MariaDB is a client-server DBMS, networking is usually enabled and configured to use the standard 3306 TCP port. In later chapters, we will explore remote database access, so keep networking enabled.

The Innodb engine settings specify how memory is allocated and managed within the server. While these settings are essential when tuning performance for high-demand databases, the default values are more than adequate for the exercises in this book.

Click Next followed by the Install button on the subsequent screen to being the installation process:

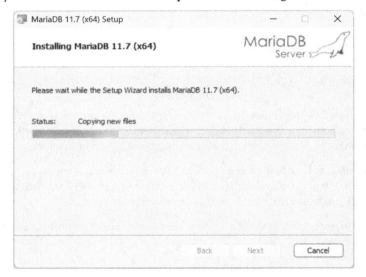

Figure 4-6

After MariaDB has been installed, click Finish to exit the installer. MariaDB Server is now installed and running.

4.3 Starting and stopping the MariaDB service

Once the installation is complete, the MariaDb service will start and is ready to use. To stop the service, open a PowerShell session with administrator privileges and run the following command:

```
net stop mariadb
```

If the service is stopped, use the following command to start it:

```
net start mariadb
```

4.4 Launching the MariaDB client

Now that the MariaDB server is running, we need a way to interact with it. The simplest option is to use the MariaDB client (mariadb). This tool connects to the server and provides a command-line environment for executing SQL statements on the stored data. There are several ways it can be launched.

When MariaDB Server was installed, two shortcuts were added to the Windows Start menu to launch the client.

The first is called MySQL Client (MariaDB 11.7 (x64)) and can be located and launched by entering MariaDB into the search box in the Windows taskbar and selecting it in the Start panel, as highlighted in Figure 4-7:

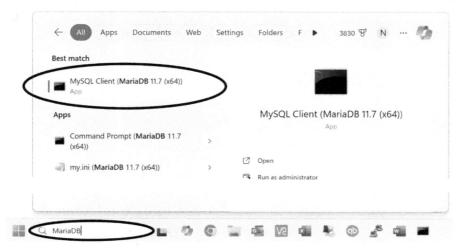

Figure 4-7

The shortcut starts the client and attempts to connect to the server as the root user. If you specified a root password during the installation, enter it at the prompt. Otherwise, press the enter key to establish the connection:

```
Enter password: ****
Welcome to the MariaDB monitor.  Commands end with ; or \g.
Your MariaDB connection id is 7
Server version: 11.7.2-MariaDB mariadb.org binary distribution

Copyright (c) 2000, 2018, Oracle, MariaDB Corporation Ab and others.

Type 'help;' or '\h' for help. Type '\c' to clear the current input statement.

MariaDB [(none)]>
```

The second shortcut opens a command-prompt window configured to allow you to run the MariaDB client manually:

Figure 4-8

Installing and Launching MariaDB Server on Windows

When starting the MariaDB client at the command prompt, you must provide a username and, if one was assigned, a password to access the server. Since this is a new installation, the only configured user is the root user, and you will use the password you specified during the installation. If you set a root password, type the following command in the MariaDB command prompt window and enter the root password when prompted:

```
mariadb -u root -p
```

If your root account is not password protected, omit the -p option from the above command:

```
mariadb -u root
```

Once the client has connected, the following output will appear:

```
Welcome to the MariaDB monitor.  Commands end with ; or \g.
Your MariaDB connection id is 8
Server version: 9.2.0 MariaDB Community Server - GPL

Copyright (c) 2000, 2024, Oracle and/or its affiliates.

Oracle is a registered trademark of Oracle Corporation and/or its
affiliates. Other names may be trademarks of their respective
owners.

Type 'help;' or '\h' for help. Type '\c' to clear the current input statement.

MariaDB>
```

At the *MariaDB [(none)]>* prompt, enter the following SQL statement:

```
MariaDB [(none)]> SHOW DATABASES;
+--------------------+
| Database           |
+--------------------+
| information_schema |
| mysql              |
| performance_schema |
| sys                |
+--------------------+
4 rows in set (0.021 sec)
```

To exit from MariaDB, enter *exit* or *quit* at the prompt:

```
MariaDB [(none)]> quit
Bye
```

4.5 Setting the PATH environment variable

To make the client and other MariaDB tools available within all command-prompt windows, it helps to add the path to these tools to your PATH environment variable. Assuming that you installed MariaDB into the default location, the following path will need to be added to your PATH environment variable (where *<version>* is replaced by the version of MariaDB that was installed):

```
C:\Program Files\MariaDB <version>\bin
```

To ensure this is included in the path whenever a Command Prompt or PowerShell is opened, right-click on the Windows Start menu, select Settings from the resulting menu, and enter "Edit the system environment variables" into the "Find a setting" text field. In the System Properties dialog (Figure 4-9), click the *Environment Variables...* button:

Figure 4-9

In the Environment Variables dialog, locate the Path variable in the User variables list, select it, and click the *Edit...* button:

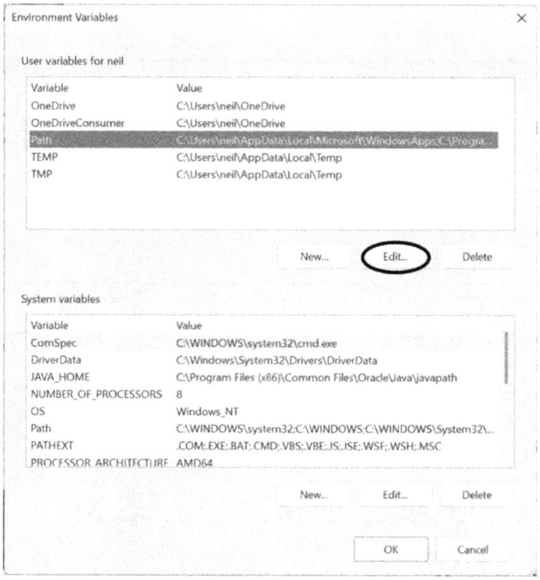

Figure 4-10

Using the *New* button in the edit dialog (Figure 4-11), add a new entry to the path:

Figure 4-11

For example, assuming MariaDB was installed into *C:\Program Files\MariaDB 11.7\bin*, the following entry would need to be added to the path:

```
C:\Program Files\MariaDB 11.7\bin\
```

Once the new path entry has been added, click OK in each dialog box and close the system properties control panel.

Open a Command Prompt window by pressing Windows + R on the keyboard and entering *cmd* into the Run dialog. Within the Command Prompt window, enter:

```
echo %Path%
```

The returned path variable value should include the MariaDB path. Verify that the path is correct by attempting to run the *MariaDB* client as follows:

```
mariadb --version
```

If the Path is correctly configured, you should see output similar to the following:

```
mariadb from 11.7.2-MariaDB, client 15.2 for Win64 (AMD64), source revision
80067a69feaeb5d
```

4.6 Reference points

The main points covered in this chapter are as follows:

- **Downloading MariaDB**

    - Download the MSI installer from *https://mariadb.org/download/*

    - Select:

        - Latest rolling release of MariaDB Server 11 (Menu A)

- Microsoft Windows OS (Menu B)

- 64-bit x86 architecture (Menu C)

- MSI Package type (Menu D)

- Choose a mirror server (Menu E) and click Download (Button F)

- **Installation Process**

  - Double-click downloaded MSI file to begin

  - Accept license terms

  - Default installation location:

    ```
    C:\Program Files\MariaDB <version>\
    ```

  - Can customize location via Browse button

  - Recommended to install all default features

- **Root User Configuration**

- Must set secure root password (superuser account)

- Option to enable remote root access (not recommended for production)

- **Server Configuration**

  - Recommended to run as Windows Service (default)

  - Networking enabled on default port 3306

  - Database storage directory can be modified

- **Service Management**

  - Start service (PowerShell as admin):

    ```
    net start mariadb
    ```

  - Stop service:

    ```
    net stop mariadb
    ```

- Using MariaDB Client

  - Via Start Menu shortcut "MySQL Client (MariaDB)"

  - Via command prompt:

    ```
    mariadb -u root -p (with password)
    ```

    - or

    ```
    mariadb -u root (no password)
    ```

  - Exit client: `quit` or `exit`

Installing and Launching MariaDB Server on Windows

- **PATH Configuration**
  - Add MariaDB binaries to system PATH:

    ```
    C:\Program Files\MariaDB <version>\bin
    ```
  - Edit via:
    - Windows Settings → "Edit system environment variables"
    - Environment Variables → Path → Edit
    - Add new entry with MariaDB bin path
  - Verify:

    ```
    mariadb --version
    ```

- **Troubleshooting**
  - Ensure service is running before connecting client
  - Verify PATH if commands aren't recognized
  - Administrator privileges required for service control

- **Key Points**
  - Always set root password during installation
  - Running as Windows Service is recommended
  - Client can be launched via GUI or command line
  - PATH configuration makes command-line tools accessible
  - Default networking configuration is suitable for development

5. The MariaDB Client

In the chapter titled *"The Basics of Databases"* we learned that MariaDB is a client-server-based database management system (DBMS). Along with the MariaDB server, MariaDB provides an interactive client that allows administrators to connect to server instances and execute SQL statements. In this chapter, we will explore the features of the MariaDB client.

5.1 The mariadb command-line tool

The MariaDB client is a command-line tool installed with the MariaDB package bundle. It can also be installed separately on non-server systems. From the MariaDB shell prompt, you can execute various commands on both local and remote database servers. This includes tasks such as creating and deleting databases and tables, searching for data, adding new rows, and much more. There are alternative client tools for interacting with MariaDB Server, including MySQL Workbench and phpMyAdmin, which will be discussed in later chapters.

Assuming MariaDB has been installed, the *mariadb* tool may be loaded at the operating system command prompt as follows:

```
mariadb -u <username> -p
```

The -p command-line flag indicates that the account belonging to *<username>* is password protected, prompting the client to request the password before granting access to the server:

```
mariadb -u demouser -p
Welcome to the MariaDB monitor.  Commands end with ; or \g.
Your MariaDB connection id is 36
Server version: 11.7.2-MariaDB MariaDB Server

Copyright (c) 2000, 2018, Oracle, MariaDB Corporation Ab and others.

Type 'help;' or '\h' for help. Type '\c' to clear the current input statement.

MariaDB [(none)]>
```

Note that the space between the -u and the username can be omitted when starting the client. The following, therefore, is also valid:

```
mariadb -udemouser -p
```

Another option is to specify the password on the command line, but this method is less secure because the password appears in plain text:

```
mariadb -u demouser --password='mypassword'
```

If the mariadb client is running remotely from the MariaDB server, the -h flag is used to specify the server host, either using the hostname or IP address:

```
mariadb -h <remote server> -u <username> -p
```

By default, access to MariaDB servers from remote clients is blocked for all user accounts, including the root account. Appropriate privileges must be granted to enable remote access for specific user accounts. This topic

The MariaDB Client

will be discussed in the *"MariaDB Users, Privileges, and Security"* chapter.

In the standard configuration, the MariaDB client and server communicate over TCP port 3306. If you need to connect to a server that is configured to use a different port, you should use the -P flag as follows:

```
mariadb -h <remote server> -P <port number> -u <username> -p
```

For example:

```
mariadb -h MyDBServer -P 3306 -u john -p
```

You can obtain a list of command-line options by running *mariadb --help* at the command prompt. Once MariaDB is running, you can enter commands at the MariaDB [(none)]> prompt. Typing 'help' at this prompt will display a list of commands supported by the MariaDB client.

The (none) entry in the MariaDB prompt indicates that no database has been selected within the client session, and will change to the database name when one is selected. The prompt can be changed from within the client using the *prompt* command. For example, the following command displays the current user name instead of the database name:

```
MariaDB [(none)]> prompt \N [\u]>
PROMPT set to '\N [\u]>'
MariaDB [root]>
```

Table 5-1 lists a subset of the options that can be combined to customize the MariaDB client prompt:

Option	Description
\c	A count of statements executed in the current client session
\D	Current date
\d	Current database name
\h	Hostname of the connected server
\m	Current time - minutes
\N	The name of the client (i.e. MariaDB)
\n	Newline character
\O	Current month (three-letter format)
\o	Current month in (numeric)
\P	Display am/pm
\p	Current TCP/IP port or socket file
\R	Current time (24-hour time)
\r	Current time (12-hour time)
\s	Current time - seconds
\t	A tab character
\U	Full user name (user@hostname)
\u	Current user name
\v	Version of the connected server version
\w	Current day of the week (three-letter format)
\Y	Current year (4-digits)

\y	Current year (2-digits)
_	Space character
\t	Tab character

Table 5-1

Use the following statement to return to the default prompt:

```
MariaDB [root]> prompt \N [\d]>\_
PROMPT set to '\N [\d]>\_'
MariaDB [(none)]>
```

Changes made using the prompt statement only apply to the current session and will be lost when the client exits. Steps to make persistent changes to the prompt will be covered in the *"Configuring MariaDB using the my.cnf File"* chapter.

5.2 Using the mariadb client

Once the client is running, you will see the MariaDB [(none)]> prompt where you can enter commands and statements. SQL statements typed at this prompt are executed interactively, and the results are shown in real-time. For example, the following statement will display a list of databases managed by the server:

```
MariaDB [(none)]> SHOW DATABASES;
+--------------------+
| Database           |
+--------------------+
| information_schema |
| mysql              |
| performance_schema |
| sys                |
+--------------------+
4 rows in set (0.05 sec)
```

SQL statements must end with a semicolon (;) or \G. If a command is not terminated, pressing Enter continues the current statement on the next line:

```
MariaDB [(none)]> SELECT *
    -> FROM myDB.customers
    -> WHERE account_status='active';
```

The output from SQL statements ending with a semicolon is formatted horizontally. Long output lines will wrap to the next line, making the content difficult to read. Consider the following output as an example:

```
MariaDB [(none)]> SELECT * FROM mysql.user;
+-----------+------------------+-------------+-------------+-------------+-----
----------+--------------------------+---------------+-------------+--------
--------+--------------------+----------------------+---------------------
--------------------------------------------------+-------------------+--------
------------+------------------+----------------+-----------------+----------
--------+----------------+------------------+----------------------+
| Host      | User             | Select_priv | Insert_priv | Update_
priv | Delete_priv | Create_priv | Drop_priv | Reload_priv |
.
.
```

25

If we replace the semicolon with \G, the output is formatted vertically, making it easier to read:

```
MariaDB [(none)]> SELECT * FROM mysql.user\G
*************************** 1. row ***************************
                  Host: %
                  User: mrlocal
             Select_priv: N
             Insert_priv: N
             Update_priv: N
             Delete_priv: N
             Create_priv: N
               Drop_priv: N
             Reload_priv: N
           Shutdown_priv: N
            Process_priv: N
               File_priv: N
              Grant_priv: N
         References_priv: N
              Index_priv: N
              Alter_priv: N
.
.
```

5.3 Typing and editing SQL statements

In the previous examples, we have entered SQL statements in uppercase. However, these statements are not case-sensitive when used in the MariaDB client. The following statements, for example, are interpreted identically:

```
show databases;
Show Databases;
SHOW DATABASES;
```

Quoted parameters and the names of databases and tables are case-sensitive. For example, if an account name was created with a capital letter (e.g., Ashley), it must be referenced with the same capitalization in SQL statements:

```
SELECT * FROM mysql.user WHERE user='Ashley';
```

The MariaDB client offers command-line editing and history features. Table 5-2 outlines several keyboard editing options, with support varying by platform:

Key Sequence	Function
Up Arrow	Navigate up through the command history.
Down Arrow	Navigate down through the command history.
Left Arrow	Move left one character in the current line.
Right Arrow	Move right one character in the current line.
Backspace	Delete the character to the left of the cursor position.
Delete	Delete the character to the right of the cursor position.
Ctrl-A	Move to the start of the current line.
Ctrl-U	Delete entire line.
Ctrl-W	Delete the word before the cursor position.

Table 5-2

5.4 Exiting from the MariaDB client

To exit from the MariaDB client, type *quit* or *exit* at the command-prompt:

```
MariaDB [(none)]> exit
Bye
```

5.5 Reference points

The main points covered in this chapter are as follows:

- **Overview**

  - The MariaDB client is a command-line tool for managing MariaDB servers and executing SQL statements.

  - Connects to local and remote MariaDB Server instances.

  - Alternative tools include MySQL Workbench and phpMyAdmin.

- **Connecting** to MariaDB

  - Use: `mariadb -u <username> -p` (prompted for password).

  - For remote servers: `mariadb -h <hostname> -u <username> -p`

  - Default communication port is 3306; specify a different port with `-P <port>`.

- **Executing Commands**

  - Enter commands interactively at the command-prompt.

  - Commands must end with a semicolon (;) or \G for vertical output formatting.

  - Example: `SHOW DATABASES;` or `SELECT * FROM table\G`

- **SQL Statements**

  - SQL is case-insensitive for commands but case-sensitive for quoted parameters.

  - Example: 'User' and 'user' are treated differently.

- **Editing Commands**

  - Supports command-line history and editing.

  - Use up/down arrow keys to navigate through history.

  - Ctrl-A moves to the start of a line, Ctrl-U deletes the current line.

- **Viewing Help**

  - Use help or \h in the client to view available commands.

  - Command-line options can be listed with `mariadb --help`.

- **Exiting the Client**

  - Exit by typing `quit` or `exit` at the MariaDB [(none)]> prompt.

6. MariaDB Users, Privileges, and Security

Security is crucial in any IT environment, particularly concerning databases. When hackers gain access to a system, their primary objective is often to steal sensitive data that can be exploited for financial gain. This sensitive information may include customers' credit card details, personally identifiable information (PII), or intellectual property. Therefore, taking steps to secure your MariaDB databases is essential.

Typically, a database server is protected by multiple layers of defense, including firewalls, encrypted access, and intrusion detection systems. However, frequent news reports about data breaches remind us that these security measures can be circumvented by external threats or employees within the organization.

In the event of a system breach or data exploitation, the database management system acts as the final line of defense against data theft. This chapter provides an overview of securing user access to MariaDB databases and strengthening this critical layer of security.

6.1 MariaDB security

MariaDB security is focused on limiting access to databases and controlling users' actions once they have access. This involves careful consideration of various factors, such as determining which users are allowed to read from or write to specific database tables, and identifying those who have the authority to delete tables or use other MariaDB features.

6.2 The root user

When MariaDB is first installed, the only accessible user account is the root user which has unrestricted power over the MariaDB server instance and the databases it contains. On Linux, we log into MariaDB as root by running the client with superuser permissions, typically using the sudo command:

```
sudo mariadb
```

On Windows systems, the MariaDB root account is accessed either by running the MariaDB Client shortcut, or by referencing the root user when launching the client from a command-prompt and entering the password that was assigned during the installation:

```
mariadb -u root -p
```

If the -u option is not specified when starting the MariaDB client on Windows or Linux, the client assumes that the MariaDB username matches the user's name on the host system. For example, if you are logged into a Linux system as user "db_admin", the MariaDB client will attempt to connect to the MariaDB server as "db_admin" unless a user name is specified on the command-line.

6.3 Getting information about users

The first step in securing a database is identifying which users already have access. This information is stored in a MariaDB database called *mysql.global-priv*, which includes several columns, including the user login name, user privileges, password settings, and connection rights.

To obtain a list of user accounts, log into the MariaDB client as the root user and execute the following command:

```
SELECT user FROM mysql.global_priv\G
```

Unless users were added during the installation, a newly installed MariaDB database will typically display only one user, the root user, along with several reserved user accounts used internally by MariaDB.

```
*************************** 1. row ***************************
user: PUBLIC
*************************** 2. row ***************************
user: demo
*************************** 3. row ***************************
user: mariadb.sys
*************************** 4. row ***************************
user: mysql
*************************** 5. row ***************************
user: root
5 rows in set (0.000 sec)
```

In a more established database, you are likely to find additional users. Some of these users will have been created manually, while others may have been generated automatically as a result of installing third-party software that uses MariaDB, for example:

```
SELECT user FROM mysql.global_priv\G
*************************** 1. row ***************************
user: PUBLIC
*************************** 2. row ***************************
user: demo
*************************** 3. row ***************************
user: wikiuser
*************************** 4. row ***************************
user: mariadb.sys
*************************** 5. row ***************************
user: mysql
*************************** 6. row ***************************
user: root
*************************** 7. row ***************************
user: wordpressuser
```

6.4 Deleting anonymous user accounts

On some systems, the MariaDB server configuration will include an anonymous user account that allows any user to connect into the MariaDB server without having an account. Anonymous accounts appear without a name in the list of users. In the following output, for example, row 2 is an anonymous user account:

```
*************************** 1. row ***************************
user: PUBLIC
*************************** 2. row ***************************
user:
*************************** 3. row ***************************
user: mariadb.sys
.
.
```

It is recommended to remove anonymous accounts to prevent unauthorized server access. To do so, use the following statements as the root user:

```
DELETE FROM mysql.global_priv WHERE User='';
FLUSH PRIVILEGES;
```

Also take this opportunity to delete the test database if it was installed:

```
DROP DATABASE test;
```

6.5 Adding a MariaDB user account

When setting up a new user account, you must provide a user login name. While a password is optional, it is not advisable to create an account without one.

The syntax for creating a user account is as follows:

```
CREATE USER 'username'@'hostname' IDENTIFIED BY 'password';
```

For example, to create a new account for a user named "john" with password protection, you would use the following statement:

```
CREATE USER 'john'@'localhost' IDENTIFIED BY 'password here';
```

You can verify that the new user has been added by querying the user table:

```
SELECT host, user FROM mysql.global_priv WHERE user='john';
+-----------+-----------+
| host      | user      |
+-----------+-----------+
| localhost | john      |
+-----------+-----------+
1 row in set (0.00 sec)
```

You may have noticed that we specified John could only connect from localhost, meaning he can only connect from the same system on which the MariaDB server is running. If John attempts to connect to the MariaDB server from a remote client, the connection will fail. To create an account that can connect from a specific host, simply replace localhost with the desired hostname or IP address in the example above:

```
CREATE USER 'john'@'remoteserver' IDENTIFIED BY 'password here';
CREATE USER 'john'@'192.168.87.23' IDENTIFIED BY 'password here';
```

To enable a user to connect to the MariaDB server from any remote host, use the '%' wildcard character instead of a specific host name:

```
CREATE USER 'john'@'%' IDENTIFIED BY 'password here';
```

If a host is not specified when creating a user, MariaDB grants access from all remote hosts. To modify the host for an existing user, you can use the following UPDATE syntax:

```
UPDATE mysql.global_priv SET Host='newhost' WHERE Host='oldhost' AND
User='username';

FLUSH PRIVILEGES;
```

For example, this statement changes the host for the user "john" from "localhost" to allow access from any host:

```
UPDATE mysql.global_priv SET Host='%' WHERE Host='localhost' AND User='john';

FLUSH PRIVILEGES;
```

6.6 Deleting a MariaDB user

An existing user account can be deleted using the DROP USER statement, which has the following syntax:

```
DROP USER 'username'@'hostname';
```

For example:

```
DROP USER 'john'@'%';
```

6.7 Renaming a MariaDB user

The account name of a MariaDB user can be changed using the RENAME USER statement, using the following syntax:

```
RENAME USER 'username'@'hostname' TO 'new_user_name'@'hostname';
```

For example:

```
RENAME USER 'john'@'localhost' TO 'johnbrown'@'localhost';
```

6.8 Changing the password for a MariaDB user

To change the password for a user account, you can use the SET PASSWORD statement. If you want to change your own password, use the following syntax:

```
SET PASSWORD = 'newpassword';
```

To change the password for another user, use the ALTER USER statement. For example, to change the password for the user account john on localhost, you would use:

```
ALTER USER john IDENTIFIED BY 'newpassword';
```

6.9 Granting privileges

When a new user is created in MariaDB, they can log into the server, but by default, they have no privileges to perform any actions once connected. Therefore, the next step after creating a user account is to grant privileges to that account using the GRANT statement.

Before modifying a user's privileges, check what privileges are currently assigned using the SHOW GRANTS statement and the user's account name. For example:

```
SHOW GRANTS FOR 'john'@'localhost'\G
*************************** 1. row ***************************
Grants for john@localhost: GRANT USAGE ON *.* TO 'john'@'localhost' IDENTIFIED
BY PASSWORD...
```

The statement "USAGE ON *.*" indicates that a user has no privileges on any database or table. In simple terms, this means the user cannot perform any actions after logging into the database server.

To grant a privilege, such as the ability to query any table in a database named MySampleDB, you would issue the following command:

```
GRANT SELECT on MySampleDB.* TO 'john'@'localhost';
```

Once this command is executed, the user john will be able to perform SELECT statements on any table within the MySampleDB database.

If you want to enable john to insert rows into a specific table called *product* in the MySampleDB database, you can use the following command:

```
GRANT INSERT on MySampleDB.product TO 'john'@'localhost';
```

It is also possible to specify multiple privileges in a single GRANT statement. For example:

```
GRANT INSERT, UPDATE on MySampleDB.product TO 'john'@'localhost';
```

6.10 Privileges and grantable levels

MariaDB supports a wide range of privileges that apply to one or more categories or *grantable levels*. These levels define the extent to which the privilege can be applied. The following privilege levels are available in MariaDB:

- **Global** - Global privileges apply to all databases on a server and are typically granted to administrator accounts.

- **Database** - Database-level privileges are specific to individual databases on the server. For instance, you might grant a user permission to insert records into all tables within a particular database while denying access to other databases on the server.

- **Table** - Table-level privileges apply to specific tables within a database. For example, if a database contains two tables, you could use a table-level privilege to allow a user access to only one.

- **Column** - Column privileges are specific to certain columns in a table. For instance, you might allow a user to modify the description column in a product table, but restrict access to the price column.

- **Routine** - In MariaDB, a routine refers to a sequence of SQL statements stored on a server that can be executed without re-entering the individual statements. Routine-level privileges control which users have access to specific routines.

- **Proxy User** - MariaDB allows users to act as proxies for one another, which enables a user to perform tasks using another user's identity and privileges. The proxy user privilege determines whether one user can act as a proxy for another.

The privileges supported by MariaDB are listed in Table 6-1. It's important to note that many privileges are available at multiple grantable levels:

Privilege	Meaning and Grantable Levels	Grantable Levels
ALL [PRIVILEGES]	Grant all privileges at specified access level except GRANT OPTION and PROXY.	global, database, table, column, routine
ALTER	Allow use of ALTER TABLE.	global, database, table
ALTER ROUTINE	Allow stored routines to be altered or dropped.	global, database, routine
CREATE	Allow database and table creation.	global, database, table
CREATE ROLE	Allow role creation.	global
CREATE ROUTINE	Allow stored routine creation..	global, database
CREATE TABLESPACE	Allow tablespaces and log file groups to be created, altered, or dropped.	global
CREATE TEMPORARY TABLES	Allow use of CREATE TEMPORARY TABLE.	global, database
CREATE USER	Allow use of CREATE USER, DROP USER, RENAME USER, and REVOKE ALL PRIVILEGES.	global

CREATE VIEW	Allow views to be created or altered.	global, database, table
DELETE	Allow use of DELETE.	global, database, table
DROP	Allow databases, tables, and views to be dropped.	global, database, table
DROP ROLE	Allow roles to be dropped.	global
EVENT	Allow use of events for the Event Scheduler.	global, database
EXECUTE	Allow the user to execute stored routines.	global, database, routine
FILE	Allow the user to cause the server to read or write files.	global
FLUSH_PRIVILEGES	Allow the user to issue FLUSH PRIVILEGES statements.	global
GRANT OPTION	Allow privileges to be granted to or removed from other accounts. (global, database, table, routine, proxy)	global, database, table, routine, proxy
INDEX	Allow indexes to be created or dropped.	global, database, table
INSERT	Allow use of INSERT.	global, database, table, column
LOCK TABLES	Allow use of LOCK TABLES on tables for which you have the SELECT privilege.	global, database
PROCESS	Allow the user to see all processes with SHOW PROCESSLIST.	global
PROXY	Allow user proxies.	global
REFERENCES	Allow foreign key creation.	global, database, table, column
RELOAD	Allow use of FLUSH operations.	global
REPLICATION CLIENT	Allow the user to ask where source or replica servers are.	global
REPLICATION SLAVE	Allow replicas to read binary log events from the source.	global
SELECT	Allow use of SELECT.	global, database, table, column
SHOW DATABASES	Allow SHOW DATABASES to show all databases.	global
SHOW VIEW	Allow use of SHOW CREATE VIEW.	global, database, table
SHUTDOWN	Allow use of mariadb-admin shutdown.	global
SUPER	Allow use of other administrative operations such as CHANGE REPLICATION SOURCE TO, KILL, PURGE BINARY LOGS, SET GLOBAL, and mariadb-admin debug command.	global
TRIGGER	Allow trigger operations.	global, database, table
UPDATE	Allow use of UPDATE.	global, database, table, column

USAGE	No privileges	global, database, table, column, routine

Table 6-1

6.11 Privilege examples

Now that we have covered MariaDB user privileges, the table below lists some examples of SQL GRANT statements:

Description	SQL Statement
Grant global INSERT privileges on all databases and tables.	`GRANT INSERT ON *.* TO 'john'@'localhost';`
Grant global ALL privileges on all databases and tables.	`GRANT ALL ON *.* TO 'john'@'localhost';`
Grant database level INSERT privileges on all tables of a specific database.	`GRANT INSERT ON MySampleDB.* TO 'john'@'localhost';`
Grant table level DELETE privileges on a specific database table.	`GRANT DELETE ON MySampleDB.product TO 'john'@'localhost';`
Grant column level UPDATE privileges on a specific column in a database table.	`GRANT UPDATE (price) ON MySampleDB.product TO 'john'@'localhost';`
Grant SELECT privilege on the *productname* and *description* columns and UPDATE privilege on the *price* column.	`GRANT SELECT (productname, description), UPDATE (price) ON MySampleDB.product TO 'john'@'localhost';`
Allow a user to CREATE stored routines for a specific database.	`GRANT CREATE ROUTINE ON MySampleDB.* TO 'john'@'localhost';`
Allowing a user to EXECUTE a specific routine.	`GRANT EXECUTE ON ON MySampleDB.listsales TO 'john'@'localhost';`
Allowing a user to act as a proxy for another.	`GRANT PROXY ON 'john'@'localhost' TO 'janet'@'otherhost';`

Table 6-2

6.12 Managing password verification

MariaDB offers an optional plugin that enforces the creation of strong passwords for user accounts. When the plugin is installed, MariaDB will reject passwords that do not meet specific complexity requirements. For example:

```
SET PASSWORD FOR 'john'@'localhost' = PASSWORD('123');
ERROR 1819 (HY000): Your password does not satisfy the current policy
requirements (simple_password_check)
```

To install the Simple Password Check component, you can use the following statement:

```
INSTALL SONAME 'simple_password_check';
```

If you decide to uninstall the component later, you can do so with this command:

```
UNINSTALL SONAME 'simple_password_check';
```

The Simple Password Check plugin contains a set of variables that can be changed to configure the password rules. To view the current settings, run the following SELECT statement:

```
SHOW VARIABLES LIKE 'simple_password%';
+-----------------------------------------+-------+
| Variable_name                           | Value |
+-----------------------------------------+-------+
| simple_password_check_digits            | 1     |
| simple_password_check_letters_same_case | 1     |
| simple_password_check_minimal_length    | 8     |
| simple_password_check_other_characters  | 1     |
+-----------------------------------------+-------+
4 rows in set (0.001 sec)
```

The purpose of each variable is as follows:

- **simple_password_check_digits** - Specifies the minimum number of digits the password must contain.

- **simple_password_check_letters_same_case** - Defines the minimum number of lowercase and upper case characters the password must contain.

- **simple_password_check_minimal_length**- The minimum password character length.

- **simple_password_check_other_characters** - The minimum number of special characters the password must contain (i.e. character that are not digit or letters).

The values assigned to these variables can be updated using SET GLOBAL. The following statement, for example, configure the plugin to accept passwords that are at least 10 characters long,and increases the minimum digits character requirement to 2:

```
SET GLOBAL simple_password_check_minimal_length = 10;
SET GLOBAL simple_password_check_digits = 2;
```

6.13 Reference points

The main points covered in this chapter are as follows:

- **Security Importance**

  - Databases are prime hacker targets for sensitive data.

  - Layers of defense can be bypassed; database security is crucial.

- **User Management**

  - Query users: SELECT user FROM mysql.user;

  - Create users: CREATE USER 'username'@'hostname' IDENTIFIED BY 'password';

  - Modify host access: UPDATE mysql.user SET Host='newhost' WHERE User='username';

  - Delete users: DROP USER 'username'@'hostname';

  - Rename users: RENAME USER 'username'@'hostname' TO 'newname'@'hostname';

- **Privileges**

- Assign privileges: `GRANT [privileges] ON [scope] TO 'user'@'host';`

- Levels: Global, Database, Table, Column, Routine, Proxy.

- Revoke privileges: `REVOKE [privileges] ON [scope] FROM 'user'@'host';`

- **Password Security**

  - Change passwords: `SET PASSWORD FOR 'user'@'host' = PASSWORD('newpassword');`

  - Enforce strong passwords with the Simple Password Check plugin.

- **Best Practices**

  - Restrict root access to local connections.

  - Regularly audit users and privileges.

  - Remove remote root access.

7. Creating Databases and Tables

Before you can do much with MariaDB, you must create a database containing at least one table. This chapter will explain how to create new databases and tables using SQL statements in the MariaDB client. We will also explore some of the storage engines that MariaDB supports.

This chapter assumes that the MariaDB client is running and connected to the MariaDB database server. If this is not the case, and you are unsure how to achieve this, refer to the *"The MariaDB Client"* chapter.

7.1 Adding a user

Before we begin working with databases, we will create a new user account and grant it the privileges needed to complete the examples in the remainder of this book. To add this account, use the MariaDB client to connect to the server as the root user and run the following statements, replacing 'password here' with a suitable password:

```
CREATE USER 'demo'@'localhost' IDENTIFIED BY 'password here';
GRANT ALL ON *.* TO 'demo'@'localhost';
FLUSH PRIVILEGES;
```

Exit and restart the client, this time specifying the demo user account and entering your password when prompted:

```
mariadb -u demo -p
Enter password:
```

7.2 Creating a new MariaDB database

A new database can be created using the CREATE DATABASE statement, followed by the desired name for the database. Alternatively, the CREATE SCHEMA statement can also be used for this purpose.

Begin by entering the following statement at the command prompt to create a new database named sampledb:

```
CREATE DATABASE sampledb;
```

If successful, the command will generate output similar to the following:

```
Query OK, 1 row affected (0.00 sec)
```

If a specified database name conflicts with an existing one, MariaDB will display an error message reporting the issue:

```
ERROR 1007 (HY000): Can't create database 'sampledb'; database exists
```

In this case, a different database name must be chosen, or the IF NOT EXISTS option should be utilized. This option will only create the database if it does not already exist:

```
CREATE DATABASE IF NOT EXISTS sampledb;
Query OK, 1 row affected, 1 warning (0.04 sec)
```

In the example above, MariaDB indicates that the statement generated a warning. To view the warning description, execute the SHOW WARNINGS statement:

```
SHOW WARNINGS;
+-------+------+-------------------------------------------------------+
| Level | Code | Message                                               |
+-------+------+-------------------------------------------------------+
| Note  | 1007 | Can't create database 'sampledb'; database exists     |
+-------+------+-------------------------------------------------------+
1 row in set (0.00 sec)
```

To view a list of databases on the server, use the following command:

```
SHOW DATABASES;
+--------------------+
| Database           |
+--------------------+
| information_schema |
| mysql              |
| performance_schema |
| sampledb           |
| sys                |
| test               |
+--------------------+
6 rows in set (0.000 sec)
```

7.3 Creating tables with SQL

New tables are added to an existing database using the CREATE TABLE statement. The CREATE TABLE statement is followed by the name of the table to be created, followed by a comma-separated list of the names and definitions of each table column:

```
CREATE TABLE table_name ( column_name definitions, column_name definitions ...,
PRIMARY KEY=(column_name));
```

The definitions for each column specify important information, such as the data type, whether the column can store NULL values, and if the column will automatically increment every time a new row is added to the table. The CREATE TABLE statement also allows you to designate a column (or a group of columns) as the primary key. For more information on primary keys, refer to the chapter *"The Basics of Databases"*.

Before creating a table, you must select a database so MariaDB knows where to create it. This is done using the USE command (note that USE is a command rather than a SQL statement; therefore, it does not need to be terminated with a semicolon).

```
USE sampledb
```

When a database has been selected, the MariaDB prompt includes the database name:

```
MariaDB [sampledb]>
```

After selecting a database, the following example creates a table with three columns: customer_id, customer_name, and customer_address. The customer_id and customer_name columns must have values (i.e., they cannot be NULL). The customer_id column will hold an integer that automatically increments as new rows are added, while the customer_name and customer_address columns will contain character strings limited to a maximum length of 20 characters. The primary key for the table is defined as the customer_id column:

```
CREATE TABLE customer
(
  customer_id int NOT NULL AUTO_INCREMENT,
```

```
  customer_name char(20) NOT NULL,
  customer_address char(20) NULL,
  PRIMARY KEY (customer_id)
);
```

7.4 Understanding NULL and NOT NULL values

When a column is defined as NULL, it means that a row can be added to a database without a value assigned to that column. On the other hand, if a column is defined as NOT NULL, it must have a value assigned to it before the row can be added to the table.

7.5 Primary keys

A primary key is a column in a table that uniquely identifies individual records. The values in a primary key column must be unique within that table. If a primary key consists of multiple columns, the combination of values across those columns must also be unique for each row.

The primary key is defined using the PRIMARY KEY statement when creating a table. If multiple columns are used as part of the primary key, they should be separated by commas:

```
PRIMARY KEY (column_name, column_name ... )
```

In the following example, a table is created using two columns as the primary key:

```
CREATE TABLE product
(
  prod_code INT NOT NULL AUTO_INCREMENT,
  prod_name char(30) NOT NULL,
  prod_desc char(60) NULL,
  PRIMARY KEY (prod_code, prod_name)
);
```

7.6 Using AUTO_INCREMENT

AUTO_INCREMENT is one of the simplest and most useful column definitions in SQL. When a column is defined with AUTO_INCREMENT, its value automatically increases each time a new row is added to the table. This feature is particularly helpful for columns used as primary keys, as it eliminates the need to write SQL statements to generate a new unique ID for each row. The MariaDB server manages this process when a new row is inserted.

There are two important rules to follow when using AUTO_INCREMENT. First, only one column per table can be assigned AUTO_INCREMENT status. Second, the AUTO_INCREMENT column must be indexed, typically by declaring it as the primary key.

You can override the AUTO_INCREMENT value by specifying your own value in an INSERT statement. As long as the specified value is unique, it will be used for the new row, and subsequent increments will adjust based on the newly inserted value.

To retrieve the most recent AUTO_INCREMENT value, you can use the LAST_INSERT_ID() function as follows:

```
SELECT LAST_INSERT_ID();
+------------------+
| LAST_INSERT_ID() |
+------------------+
|              192 |
+------------------+
```

```
1 row in set (0.00 sec)
```

7.7 Defining default values during table creation

Default values during table creation allow values to be specified for each column to be used when a value is not explicitly defined when rows are inserted into a database.

Default values are specified using the DEFAULT keyword in the CREATE TABLE statement. For example, the following SQL statement specifies a default value for the *sales_quantity* column:

```
CREATE TABLE sales
(
     sales_number int NOT NULL,
     sales_quantity int NOT NULL DEFAULT 1,
     sales_desc char(20) NOT NULL,
     PRIMARY KEY (sales_number)
);
```

If no quantity is defined when a new row is inserted, MariaDB will insert the default value of 1 for the *sales_quantity* column.

7.8 Displaying table schema

The DESCRIBE statement displays the schema of a database table, including column names, data types, primary key details, null and default settings, and auto-increment information:

```
DESCRIBE customer;
+------------------+----------+------+-----+---------+----------------+
| Field            | Type     | Null | Key | Default | Extra          |
+------------------+----------+------+-----+---------+----------------+
| customer_id      | int      | NO   | PRI | NULL    | auto_increment |
| customer_name    | char(20) | NO   |     | NULL    |                |
| customer_address | char(20) | YES  |     | NULL    |                |
+------------------+----------+------+-----+---------+----------------+
3 rows in set (0.00 sec)
```

7.9 Deleting databases and tables

Databases and tables can be deleted from a MariaDB server using the DROP statement. To delete the sales table from the sampledb database, use the following command:

```
DROP TABLE sales;
```

Alternatively, use the TRUNCATE TABLE statement to permanently remove all rows from a table without deleting the table itself:

```
TRUNCATE TABLE sales;
```

Similarly, you can delete the entire sampledb database using the following command:

```
DROP DATABASE sampledb;
```

7.10 MariaDB storage engine types

MariaDB comes with several storage engines, each offering specific advantages. Using the ENGINE= directive, you can choose the storage engine for each table individually. Some of the storage engines currently available in MariaDB include:

- **InnoDB** - The InnoDB storage engine was introduced with MariaDB version 4.0 and is known for being transaction-safe. A transaction-safe storage engine guarantees that all database transactions are fully completed and will roll back any partially completed transactions (for example, as a result of a server or power failure). This ensures that a database is never left with incomplete data updates.

- **MEMORY** - The MEMORY storage engine stores data in memory rather than on disk. This makes the engine extremely fast. However, the transient nature of data in memory means this engine is more suitable for temporary table storage.

- **CSV** - The CSV storage engine saves data in plain text files using a comma-separated values (CSV) format. This engine is particularly useful when the stored data needs to be exchanged with other platforms, such as spreadsheets or accounting software.

- **ARCHIVE** - The ARCHIVE engine utilizes zlib compression to minimize the storage space required for large data volumes.

To generate a list of supported engines, use the following SHOW ENGINES statement:

```
SHOW ENGINES\G
*************************** 1. row ***************************
      Engine: MEMORY
     Support: YES
     Comment: Hash based, stored in memory, useful for temporary tables
Transactions: NO
          XA: NO
  Savepoints: NO
*************************** 2. row ***************************
      Engine: CSV
     Support: YES
     Comment: Stores tables as CSV files
Transactions: NO
          XA: NO
  Savepoints: NO
*************************** 3. row ***************************
      Engine: PERFORMANCE_SCHEMA
     Support: YES
     Comment: Performance Schema
Transactions: NO
          XA: NO
  Savepoints: NO
*************************** 4. row ***************************
      Engine: Aria
     Support: YES
     Comment: Crash-safe tables with MyISAM heritage. Used for internal
temporary tables and privilege tables
Transactions: NO
.
.
```

Different engine types can be used within a database; for example, some tables may utilize the InnoDB engine, while others might use the CSV engine. If an engine type is not specified when creating a table, MariaDB will default to using the InnoDB engine for that table. To identify the default engine, you can use the following statement:

```
SELECT @@default_storage_engine;
```

Creating Databases and Tables

```
+--------------------------+
| @@default_storage_engine |
+--------------------------+
| InnoDB                   |
+--------------------------+
1 row in set (0.01 sec)
```

To specify a particular engine type for a table, add the appropriate ENGINE= definition after defining the table columns. For instance, the following example specifies the MEMORY engine:

```
CREATE TABLE tmp_orders (
    tmp_number INT NOT NULL,
    tmp_quantity INT NOT NULL,
    tmp_desc CHAR(20) NOT NULL,
    PRIMARY KEY (tmp_number)
) ENGINE=MEMORY;
```

7.11 Reference points

The main points covered in this chapter are as follows:

- **Creating Databases**

    - Use CREATE DATABASE dbname; or CREATE SCHEMA dbname;

    - Avoid conflicts with existing databases using IF NOT EXISTS.

    - List databases with SHOW DATABASES;

- **Enabling Table Encryption**

    - Default encryption is off (default_table_encryption = OFF).

    - Enable encryption during database creation: CREATE DATABASE dbname ENCRYPTION = 'Y';

    - Set encryption globally: SET GLOBAL default_table_encryption=ON;

- **Creating Tables**

    - Use CREATE TABLE to define columns, data types, constraints, and primary keys.

    - Specify a database with USE dbname before creating tables.

- **Key Table Features**

    - Primary Keys: Ensure unique identifiers for rows.

    - AUTO_INCREMENT: Automatically generate unique values for a column.

    - NULL/NOT NULL: Define whether columns can accept null values.

    - DEFAULT Values: Provide default values for columns when no input is given.

- **Viewing Table Schema**

    - Use DESCRIBE tablename; to display column definitions and constraints.

- **Deleting Databases and Tables**

    - Remove tables: DROP TABLE tablename;

- Delete databases: `DROP DATABASE dbname;`

- Remove table data: `TRUNCATE TABLE tablename;`

- **Storage engine Types**

  - InnoDB: Transaction-safe, prevents partial updates, lacks full-text search.

  - MyISAM: High performance with full-text search, not transaction-safe.

  - MEMORY: Stores data in memory for fast access, suitable for temporary tables.

  - Specify engine during table creation: `ENGINE=<engine name>`

8. Inserting Data into Database Tables

Up to this point, we have explored the process of installing MariaDB and covered the essential steps for creating and managing databases and tables. This chapter will take the next step by focusing on populating your database tables with data. Specifically, you will learn how to use the SQL INSERT statement to add rows of data to your tables.

8.1 Creating the sample table

Start the MariaDB client, select the *sampledb* database, and delete the tables created in the previous chapter:

```
USE sampledb
DROP TABLE customer, product, tmp_orders;
```

Next, recreate the *product* table using the SQL statement provided below:

```
CREATE TABLE product
(
  id INT NOT NULL AUTO_INCREMENT,
  name VARCHAR(25) NOT NULL,
  description VARCHAR(20) NULL,
  price DECIMAL(6,2),
  quantity INT,
  PRIMARY KEY (id)

);
```

8.2 The basics of data insertion

The SQL INSERT statement is used to add new rows of data to a specified database table. With the INSERT statement, you can insert entire, partial, or multiple rows or rows generated from a database query. In this chapter, we will explore each of these techniques.

8.3 Inserting a row

To add a single row to a table, the INSERT statement requires the name of the table where the row will be added, along with the corresponding column names and their associated values. The INSERT statement syntax consists of a comma-separated list of column names enclosed in parentheses, followed by the VALUES keyword and then a comma-separated list of values matching the order of the column names, as outlined below:

```
INSERT INTO <table_name>(
     <column_name_1>,
     <column_name_2>,
     <column_name_3>,
     .
     .
     .
)
VALUES(
     <value_1>,
     <value_2>,
     <value_3>,
     .
```

```
};
```

Using the following SQL statement, add a row to the product table:

```
INSERT INTO product(
    id,
    name,
    description,
    price,
    quantity)
VALUES(
    NULL,
    'MacBook Pro M4',
    'Apple laptop',
    2499.99,
    10
);
```

Note that the id value is specified as NULL because the id column in the product table is set to AUTO_INCREMENT. This means we do not need to assign a value manually because the MariaDB database engine will automatically generate a new value each time a row is added.

To verify that the row was successfully inserted into the table, we need to execute a query using the SELECT statement. We will discuss database queries in detail in the next chapter, but for now, run the following statement to list the rows in the product table:

```
SELECT * FROM product;
+----+----------------+--------------------+---------+----------+
| id | name           | description        | price   | quantity |
+----+----------------+--------------------+---------+----------+
|  1 | MacBook Pro M4 | Apple laptop       | 2499.99 |       10 |
+----+----------------+--------------------+---------+----------+
1 row in set (0.00 sec)
```

A more concise way to add records to a table is by providing only the values. While this approach can be effective, the values must be specified in the exact order corresponding to the columns, as defined when the table was created. If the order is incorrect, you may encounter an error message (especially if the data types do not align with the columns), or worse, you could insert data into the wrong columns. Additionally, this method may work with the current table structure, but it could lead to issues if the schema is modified in the future. The syntax for this insertion technique is as follows:

```
INSERT INTO <table_name> VALUES(
    <value_1>,
    <value_2>,
    <value_3>,
    .
    .
    .
);
```

With the above warnings in mind, use the following statement to insert a record without the referencing column names:

```
INSERT INTO product VALUES(
 NULL,
```

```
'MacBook Air M3',
'Apple laptop',
1499.99,
5
);
```

Re-run the SELECT statement to confirm the new row has been added:

```
SELECT * FROM product;
+----+---------------+----------------+---------+----------+
| id | name          | description    | price   | quantity |
+----+---------------+----------------+---------+----------+
|  1 | MacBook Pro M4 | Apple laptop   | 2499.99 |       10 |
|  2 | MacBook Air M3 | Apple laptop   | 1499.99 |        5 |
+----+---------------+----------------+---------+----------+
2 rows in set (0.00 sec)
```

8.4 Adding multiple rows to a table

To add multiple rows to a table, you can use several INSERT statements or include all the rows in a single statement. When adding multiple rows to a MariaDB database table using one statement, separate each set of values with a comma, as shown in the example below:

```
INSERT INTO product(
    id,
    name,
    description,
    price,
    quantity)
VALUES(
    NULL,
    'Mac Mini M3',
    'Apple desktop',
    999.99,
    100
),
(
    NULL,
    'Mac Studio',
    'Apple desktop',
    1999.99,
    15
);
```

Use the SELECT statement once again to verify the insertion worked:

```
SELECT * FROM product;
+----+---------------+----------------+---------+----------+
| id | name          | description    | price   | quantity |
+----+---------------+----------------+---------+----------+
|  1 | MacBook Pro M4 | Apple laptop   | 2499.99 |       10 |
|  2 | MacBook Air M3 | Apple laptop   | 1499.99 |        5 |
|  3 | Mac Mini M3   | Apple desktop  |  999.99 |      100 |
|  4 | Mac Studio    | Apple desktop  | 1999.99 |       15 |
+----+---------------+----------------+---------+----------+
4 rows in set (0.01 sec)
```

8.5 Inserting results from a SELECT statement

A useful technique involves combining the INSERT and SELECT statements. In this approach, the SELECT statement retrieves data from a table, and the INSERT statement adds this data to a different table. This method is known as INSERT SELECT, the syntax for which is as follows:

```
INSERT INTO <table_name>(
    <column_name_1>,
    <column_name_2>,
    <column_name_3>,
)
SELECT <column_name_1>, <column_name_2>, <column_name_3> FROM <table_name>);
```

The syntax outlined above assumes that all rows and columns from the source table are inserted into the destination table. In practice, however, you can select which rows and columns to include in the insertion.

As an example, create a new table named cheaper_product that includes only id, name, and price columns:

```
CREATE TABLE cheaper_product
(
  id INT NOT NULL AUTO_INCREMENT,
  name VARCHAR(25) NOT NULL,
  price DECIMAL(6,2),
  PRIMARY KEY (id)
);
```

The goal is to select rows from the product table where the price is less than $1,500.00 and then insert the values of the id, name, and price columns from those rows into the cheaper_product table. This can be accomplished using the following SQL statement:

```
INSERT INTO cheaper_product
(
    id, name, price
)
SELECT id, name, price FROM product WHERE price < 1500;
```

After the insertion executes, the cheaper_product table should contain only rows matching the price criteria:

```
SELECT * FROM cheaper_product;
+----+----------------+---------+
| id | name           | price   |
+----+----------------+---------+
|  2 | MacBook Air M3 | 1499.99 |
|  3 | Mac Mini M3    |  999.99 |
+----+----------------+---------+
2 rows in set (0.00 sec)
```

The examples above assume that the cheaper_product table already exists and that its schema partly matches the source table. If you want to create a new table and populate it with data from another table, you can combine the CREATE TABLE and SELECT statements. You can copy all the rows and columns from the source table or select specific columns and rows that meet certain criteria.

For instance, in the following example, a new table named expensive_product is created and populated with items from the product table that cost more than $1,500.00:

```
CREATE TABLE expensive_product
```

```
SELECT id, name, price FROM product
WHERE price > 1500;
Query OK, 2 rows affected (0.06 sec)
Records: 2  Duplicates: 0  Warnings: 0

SELECT * FROM expensive_product;
+----+----------------+---------+
| id | name           | price   |
+----+----------------+---------+
|  1 | MacBook Pro M4 | 2499.99 |
|  4 | Mac Studio     | 1999.99 |
+----+----------------+---------+
2 rows in set (0.01 sec)
```

To avoid cluttering the sample database, drop the two new tables before continuing:

```
DROP TABLE cheaper_product,expensive_product;
```

8.6 Reducing the INSERT performance load

The INSERT statement can place a considerable load on the database server, especially during high-volume data insertions. This increased load may adversely affect other transactions, such as data reads, by slowing down their performance.

To minimize the impact of insert operations on the server, you can use the LOW_PRIORITY keyword for non-urgent tasks. This approach ensures that critical operations, such as reads, are prioritized over insertions. For example:

```
INSERT LOW_PRIORITY INTO products(
.
.
VALUES(
.
.
};
```

The LOW_PRIORITY option instructs the database engine to delay the execution of the operation until all other clients have finished accessing the table. This ensures that the operation does not interfere with ongoing transactions, allowing higher-priority tasks to complete without disruption.

8.7 Reference points

The main points covered in this chapter are as follows:

- **Data Insertion Basics**

  - Use the INSERT statement to add rows to a database table.

  - Specify column names for clarity and to prevent errors when table structures change.

- **Single Row Insertion**

  - Add individual rows by providing values for each column or by relying on AUTO_INCREMENT for unique identifiers.

- **Multiple Row Insertion**

  - Insert multiple rows in one statement for efficiency.

- Separate each row's values with commas.

- **Using SELECT for Insertion**

  - Combine `INSERT` and `SELECT` to populate one table with data retrieved from another.

  - Useful for transferring or filtering data between tables.

- **Table Creation with SELECT**

  - Create and populate a new table directly from the results of a `SELECT` query.

  - Customize columns and rows in the new table based on criteria.

- **Improving Insert Performance**

  - Use the `LOW_PRIORITY` keyword to minimize server load during high-volume insert operations, prioritizing other transactions.

9. Updating and Managing MariaDB Tables

Modifying a table after it has been created and populated with data is generally not advised. However, changes are necessary in some circumstances, and these can be made using specific SQL statements. Additionally, it is possible to delete an existing table from a database. This chapter will cover both of these topics in detail.

9.1 Opening the sample database

This chapter assumes that you have completed the steps in the previous chapter. If you haven't, you can import the current database snapshot using the sample files provided in the *"Start Here"* chapter.

To import the snapshot, open a terminal or command prompt, navigate to the directory containing the sample files, and run the following commands:

```
mariadb-admin -u demo -p drop sampledb
mariadb-admin -u demo -p create sampledb
mariadb -u demo -p sampledb < mariadb_managing_tables.sql
```

Once the database is ready, open the MariaDB client and select the *sampledb* database:

```
USE sampledb
```

9.2 Altering a database table

A preexisting table in a database can be modified using the SQL ALTER TABLE statement, which allows you to change the structure of a table. Supported modifications include adding or removing columns, changing a column's data type, and renaming the table or its columns.

Behind the scenes, MariaDB's alteration process typically involves creating a temporary table, applying the desired changes to this temporary table, deleting the original table, and then renaming the temporary table to take its place.

The syntax for ALTER TABLE requires the name of the table to be modified, followed by the list of changes to be made:

```
ALTER TABLE <table_name> <alteration_spec1>, <alteration_spec2>, ....
```

9.3 Adding table columns

To add a column to an existing database table, you need to construct an ALTER TABLE statement. This statement includes the table name, the ADD keyword, and the name along with the data type of the new column. For example, the following SQL statement adds a column named on_sale to the product table:

```
ALTER TABLE product ADD on_sale BOOL;
```

After adding the new column, you can use the SHOW COLUMNS FROM statement to view the updated list of columns:

```
SHOW COLUMNS FROM product;
```

```
+-------------+-------------+------+-----+---------+----------------+
| Field       | Type        | Null | Key | Default | Extra          |
+-------------+-------------+------+-----+---------+----------------+
| id          | int         | NO   | PRI | NULL    | auto_increment |
| name        | varchar(25) | NO   |     | NULL    |                |
| description | varchar(20) | YES  |     | NULL    |                |
| price       | decimal(6,2)| YES  |     | NULL    |                |
| quantity    | int         | YES  |     | NULL    |                |
| on_sale     | tinyint(1)  | YES  |     | NULL    |                |
+-------------+-------------+------+-----+---------+----------------+
6 rows in set (0.00 sec)
```

By default, new columns are added to the end of the current list of columns. To add a column at the beginning of the list, use the ALTER TABLE command with the FIRST keyword. Use the following statement to add a date field as the first column in the table:

```
ALTER TABLE product ADD release_date DATE FIRST;
```

```
SHOW COLUMNS FROM product;
+--------------+-------------+------+-----+---------+----------------+
| Field        | Type        | Null | Key | Default | Extra          |
+--------------+-------------+------+-----+---------+----------------+
| release_date | date        | YES  |     | NULL    |                |
| id           | int         | NO   | PRI | NULL    | auto_increment |
| name         | varchar(25) | NO   |     | NULL    |                |
| description  | varchar(20) | YES  |     | NULL    |                |
| price        | decimal(6,2)| YES  |     | NULL    |                |
| quantity     | int         | YES  |     | NULL    |                |
| on_sale      | tinyint(1)  | YES  |     | NULL    |                |
+--------------+-------------+------+-----+---------+----------------+
7 rows in set (0.00 sec)
```

To insert a column after an existing one, use the AFTER option. The following statement adds a discount field after the price column:

```
ALTER TABLE product ADD discount DECIMAL(6,2) AFTER price;
```

```
SHOW COLUMNS FROM product;
+--------------+-------------+------+-----+---------+----------------+
| Field        | Type        | Null | Key | Default | Extra          |
+--------------+-------------+------+-----+---------+----------------+
| release_date | date        | YES  |     | NULL    |                |
| id           | int         | NO   | PRI | NULL    | auto_increment |
| name         | varchar(25) | NO   |     | NULL    |                |
| description  | varchar(20) | YES  |     | NULL    |                |
| price        | decimal(6,2)| YES  |     | NULL    |                |
| discount     | decimal(6,2)| YES  |     | NULL    |                |
| quantity     | int         | YES  |     | NULL    |                |
| on_sale      | tinyint(1)  | YES  |     | NULL    |                |
+--------------+-------------+------+-----+---------+----------------+
8 rows in set (0.00 sec)
```

The decimal declaration for the price column needs clarification. The syntax for the DECIMAL data type is as follows:

```
DECIMAL (M, D)
```

In the syntax above, M indicates the total number of digits the column can store, and D represents the number of decimal places. Therefore, the (6,2) specification for the price column defines a range from -9999.99 to 9999.99.

9.4 Moving table columns

In addition to adding new columns, the ALTER TABLE statement can be used to change the position of an existing column in a table. This is done using the MODIFY COLUMN clause along with either the AFTER or FIRST options. The syntax is as follows:

```
ALTER TABLE <table_name> MODIFY COLUMN <column> <definition> ... AFTER|FIRST
<column>;
```

For example, to place the *release_date* field immediately after the *price* column, you would use the following statement:

```
ALTER TABLE product MODIFY COLUMN release_date DATE AFTER price;
```

```
SHOW COLUMNS FROM product;
+--------------+--------------+------+-----+---------+----------------+
| Field        | Type         | Null | Key | Default | Extra          |
+--------------+--------------+------+-----+---------+----------------+
| id           | int          | NO   | PRI | NULL    | auto_increment |
| name         | varchar(25)  | NO   |     | NULL    |                |
| description  | varchar(20)  | YES  |     | NULL    |                |
| price        | decimal(6,2) | YES  |     | NULL    |                |
| release_date | date         | YES  |     | NULL    |                |
| discount     | decimal(6,2) | YES  |     | NULL    |                |
| quantity     | int          | YES  |     | NULL    |                |
| on_sale      | tinyint(1)   | YES  |     | NULL    |                |
+--------------+--------------+------+-----+---------+----------------+
8 rows in set (0.01 sec)
```

9.5 Renaming tables

Tables are renamed using variations of the RENAME TABLE or ALTER TABLE statements. The syntax to change a database table name using RENAME TABLE is as follows:

```
RENAME TABLE <old_name> TO <new_name>;
```

The following statement, for example, renames the product table to new_product:

```
RENAME TABLE product TO new_product;
```

The same result can be achieved using an ALTER TABLE statement. The following example renames new_product back to product:

```
ALTER TABLE new_product RENAME product;
```

9.6 Renaming table columns

Columns can be renamed using the ALTER TABLE statement and CHANGE keyword, which requires the old and new column names followed by the column's data type. For example, to change the column name from discount to discount_price, you would use the following statement:

```
ALTER TABLE product CHANGE discount discount_price DECIMAL(6,2);
```

```
SHOW COLUMNS FROM product;
```

```
+----------------+--------------+------+-----+---------+----------------+
| Field          | Type         | Null | Key | Default | Extra          |
+----------------+--------------+------+-----+---------+----------------+
| id             | int          | NO   | PRI | NULL    | auto_increment |
| name           | varchar(25)  | NO   |     | NULL    |                |
| description    | varchar(20)  | YES  |     | NULL    |                |
| price          | decimal(6,2) | YES  |     | NULL    |                |
| release_date   | date         | YES  |     | NULL    |                |
| discount_price | decimal(6,2) | YES  |     | NULL    |                |
| quantity       | int          | YES  |     | NULL    |                |
| on_sale        | tinyint(1)   | YES  |     | NULL    |                |
+----------------+--------------+------+-----+---------+----------------+
8 rows in set (0.00 sec)
```

9.7 Deleting table columns

In addition to adding and renaming columns, you can also delete columns from tables using the DROP COLUMN option of the ALTER TABLE statement. Using the following statement, delete the release_date, discount_price, and on_sale columns:

```
ALTER TABLE product DROP COLUMN release_date;
ALTER TABLE product DROP COLUMN discount_price;
ALTER TABLE product DROP COLUMN on_sale;
```

```
SHOW COLUMNS FROM product;
+-------------+--------------+------+-----+---------+----------------+
| Field       | Type         | Null | Key | Default | Extra          |
+-------------+--------------+------+-----+---------+----------------+
| id          | int          | NO   | PRI | NULL    | auto_increment |
| name        | varchar(25)  | NO   |     | NULL    |                |
| description | varchar(20)  | YES  |     | NULL    |                |
| price       | decimal(6,2) | YES  |     | NULL    |                |
| quantity    | int          | YES  |     | NULL    |                |
+-------------+--------------+------+-----+---------+----------------+
5 rows in set (0.02 sec)
```

9.8 Changing the data type of a column

You can change the data type of a column in a table by using the ALTER TABLE statement along with the MODIFY option. For example, you can change the data type of the quantity column from INT to SMALLINT, and increase the character length of the "description" column to 50 characters as follows:

```
ALTER TABLE product MODIFY quantity SMALLINT;
ALTER TABLE product MODIFY description VARCHAR(50);
```

```
SHOW COLUMNS FROM product;
+-------------+--------------+------+-----+---------+----------------+
| Field       | Type         | Null | Key | Default | Extra          |
+-------------+--------------+------+-----+---------+----------------+
| id          | int          | NO   | PRI | NULL    | auto_increment |
| name        | varchar(25)  | NO   |     | NULL    |                |
| description | varchar(50)  | YES  |     | NULL    |                |
| price       | decimal(6,2) | YES  |     | NULL    |                |
| quantity    | smallint(6)  | YES  |     | NULL    |                |
+-------------+--------------+------+-----+---------+----------------+
5 rows in set (0.00 sec)
```

There are no restrictions on changing column data types in empty tables. However, once a table contains rows, attempts to change a column's data type may fail or result in data loss. In the example above, we successfully increased the character length of the *description* column without any issues. If the table contained data, though, trying to make the column shorter than the longest stored description would lead to an error:

```
ALTER TABLE product MODIFY description VARCHAR(5);
ERROR 1265 (01000): Data truncated for column 'description' at row 1
```

9.9 Deleting tables

A table may be deleted from a database using the DROP TABLE statement. All that is required with this statement is the name of the table to be deleted. The deletion is permanent and cannot be undone:

```
DROP TABLE <table_name>;
```

9.10 Duplicating tables

In MariaDB, tables can be duplicated in two ways: either by duplicating just the table's data or by replicating its entire structure, which includes keys, indexes, and auto increment settings along with the data.

To create a new table based solely on the data from another, we combine the CREATE TABLE and SELECT statements as follows:

```
CREATE TABLE <new_table> AS SELECT * FROM <old_table>;
```

For example, use the following statement to copy the product table as a new table called new_product:

```
CREATE TABLE new_product AS SELECT * FROM product;
```

If we examine the rows in the new_product table, they are identical to those in the original product table:

```
SELECT * FROM new_product;
+----+---------------+----------------+---------+----------+
| id | name          | description    | price   | quantity |
+----+---------------+----------------+---------+----------+
|  1 | MacBook Pro M4| Apple laptop   | 2499.99 |       10 |
|  2 | MacBook Air M3| Apple laptop   | 1499.99 |        5 |
|  3 | Mac Mini M3   | Apple desktop  |  999.99 |      100 |
|  4 | Mac Studio    | Apple desktop  | 1999.99 |       15 |
+----+---------------+----------------+---------+----------+
4 rows in set (0.01 sec)
```

If we examine the column structure, however, we discover that the auto increment and primary key definitions were lost during the duplication:

```
SHOW COLUMNS FROM product;
+-------------+-------------+------+-----+---------+----------------+
| Field       | Type        | Null | Key | Default | Extra          |
+-------------+-------------+------+-----+---------+----------------+
| id          | int         | NO   |     | NULL    |                |
| name        | varchar(25) | NO   |     | NULL    |                |
| description | varchar(50) | YES  |     | NULL    |                |
| price       | decimal(6,2)| YES  |     | NULL    |                |
| quantity    | smallint(6) | YES  |     | NULL    |                |
+-------------+-------------+------+-----+---------+----------------+
5 rows in set (0.02 sec)
```

To maintain the original table's structure in the new table, we must first create a duplicate table using the CREATE TABLE statement along with the LIKE keyword:

```
CREATE TABLE <new_table> LIKE <old_table>;
```

After duplicating the table structure, we can use INSERT and SELECT statements to replicate the data:

```
INSERT INTO <new_table> SELECT * FROM <original_table>;
```

Use the following statements to delete the new_product table and create a duplicate that maintains the table structure:

```
DROP TABLE new_product;

CREATE TABLE new_product LIKE product;
```

Before duplicating the data, check that the table structure has been preserved in the new table:

```
SHOW COLUMNS FROM new_product;
+-------------+--------------+------+-----+---------+----------------+
| Field       | Type         | Null | Key | Default | Extra          |
+-------------+--------------+------+-----+---------+----------------+
| id          | int          | NO   | PRI | NULL    | auto_increment |
| name        | varchar(25)  | NO   |     | NULL    |                |
| description | varchar(50)  | YES  |     | NULL    |                |
| price       | decimal(6,2) | YES  |     | NULL    |                |
| quantity    | smallint(6)  | YES  |     | NULL    |                |
+-------------+--------------+------+-----+---------+----------------+
5 rows in set (0.01 sec)
```

With the table structure duplicated, we can now copy the data to the new table:

```
INSERT INTO new_product SELECT * FROM product;
```

Re-run the earlier SELECT * FROM statement to confirm the data duplication before removing the new_product table from the database:

```
DROP TABLE new_product;
```

When duplicating tables, keep in mind that triggers, constraints, and custom properties are not retained, even if the table structure is preserved. Additionally, duplication is a resource-intensive process, especially for large tables.

9.11 Reference points

The main points covered in this chapter are as follows:

- **Altering Tables**

  - Existing tables can be modified to add, remove, or reposition columns.

  - Use ALTER TABLE to modify an existing table's structure.

- **Repositioning Columns**

  - Columns can be reordered using specific keywords to adjust their placement in the table.

  - Use FIRST or AFTER keywords to adjust column order.

- **Renaming**

  - Tables and columns can be renamed.

  - Use `RENAME TABLE` or `ALTER TABLE` to rename tables and columns.

- **Deleting Columns**

  - Unnecessary columns can be permanently removed from tables.

  - Remove unwanted columns with `ALTER TABLE ... DROP COLUMN`

- **Changing Data Types**

  - Column data types can be modified, though changes to populated tables may risk data truncation or loss.

  - Use `ALTER TABLE ... MODIFY` to alter column data types.

- **Deleting Tables**

  - Tables can be permanently removed.

  - Permanently delete tables using `DROP TABLE`

- **Table Duplication**

  - MariaDB allows duplication of a table's data, structure, or both.

  - Data-only duplication does not preserve keys, indexes, or other structural properties.

  - Structure duplication replicates the original table's schema, including primary keys and auto_increment settings.

- **Data-Only Duplication**

  - Use the `CREATE TABLE ... AS SELECT` statement to duplicate table data into a new table.

  - This approach copies all rows but excludes structural definitions like primary keys, indexes, and auto_ increment properties.

- **Structural Duplication**

  - Use the `CREATE TABLE ... LIKE` statement to duplicate the schema of an existing table.

  - This preserves all column definitions, keys, indexes, and table properties.

- **Combining Structure and Data Duplication**

  - First, duplicate the structure using `CREATE TABLE ... LIKE`.

  - Then, populate the new table with data using an `INSERT INTO ... SELECT` statement.

Chapter 10

10. Updating and Deleting Table Data

After data has been added to a MariaDB database table, there will eventually come a time when some or all of that data needs to be modified or removed. This could involve correcting errors, updating information to reflect changes in the real world, or cleaning up outdated records. Managing existing data is a crucial aspect of working with a database. This chapter will explore the fundamental operations for updating and deleting data in table rows.

10.1 Opening the sample database

This chapter assumes that you have completed the steps in the previous chapters. If you haven't, you can import the current database snapshot using the sample files provided in the *"Start Here"* chapter.

To import the snapshot, open a terminal or command prompt, navigate to the directory containing the sample files, and run the following commands:

```
mariadb-admin -u demo -p drop sampledb
mariadb-admin -u demo -p create sampledb
mariadb -u demo -p sampledb < mariadb_updating_tables.sql
```

Once the database is ready, open the MariaDB client and select the *sampledb* database:

```
USE sampledb
```

10.2 Updating database data

When updating data in a table, you can update specific rows or all rows at once. This is done using the SQL UPDATE statement, along with the SET and WHERE keywords.

The UPDATE statement requires several key pieces of information. First, you need to specify the name of the table you want to update. Next, you must indicate which columns will be updated and provide the new values for those columns. It is also essential to specify which specific rows should be updated using the WHERE keyword. The WHERE condition is crucial to remember; if you omit it, the update will affect every row in the table. The syntax for the UPDATE statement is as follows:

```
UPDATE <table_name>
SET <column_name1> = <new_value1>,
    <column_name2> = <new_value2>,
.
.
WHERE <select_criteria>;
```

To illustrate this, we will modify the description of a specific item in the product table. Start by listing the current rows using the following SELECT statement:

```
SELECT * FROM product;
+----+----------------+--------------------+---------+----------+
| id | name           | description        | price   | quantity |
+----+----------------+--------------------+---------+----------+
|  1 | MacBook Pro M4 | Apple laptop       | 2499.99 |       10 |
|  2 | MacBook Air M3 | Apple laptop       | 1499.99 |        5 |
```

```
|   3 | Mac Mini M3     | Apple desktop       |  999.99 |      100 |
|   4 | Mac Studio      | Apple desktop       | 1999.99 |       15 |
+----+-----------------+---------------------+---------+----------+
4 rows in set (0.00 sec)
```

The objective is to update the MacBook Pro M4 record by adding the screen size to both the name and description columns. To perform this modification, enter the following UPDATE statement at the MariaDB> prompt:

```
UPDATE product
  SET name = 'MacBook Pro M4 14-in',
  description = 'Apple 14-in laptop'
  WHERE name = 'MacBook Pro M4';
```

After updating the row, use the following statement to verify that the change was successful:

```
SELECT * from product WHERE name= 'MacBook Pro M4 14-in';
+----+----------------------+----------------------+---------+----------+
| id | name                 | description          | price   | quantity |
+----+----------------------+----------------------+---------+----------+
|  1 | MacBook Pro M4 14-in | Apple 14-in laptop   | 2499.99 |       10 |
+----+----------------------+----------------------+---------+----------+
1 row in set (0.00 sec)
```

Let's assume we have received a delivery of 50 units for each of the MacBook models at our hypothetical warehouse. To update the table with this information, we can use the LIKE keyword and the '%' wildcard to select all MacBook products. We will then add 50 to the existing quantity for each matching item. Use the following statement to perform this update operation:

```
UPDATE product
SET quantity = quantity + 50
WHERE name LIKE 'MacBook%';
```

The statement selects all rows where the product name starts with "MacBook", increments the current quantity by 50, and updates each row. Run the following SELECT statement to verify the results:

```
SELECT * FROM product WHERE name LIKE 'Macbook%';
+----+----------------------+----------------------+---------+----------+
| id | name                 | description          | price   | quantity |
+----+----------------------+----------------------+---------+----------+
|  1 | MacBook Pro M4 14-in | Apple 14-in laptop   | 2499.99 |       60 |
|  2 | MacBook Air M3       | Apple laptop         | 1499.99 |       55 |
+----+----------------------+----------------------+---------+----------+
2 rows in set (0.04 sec)
```

10.3 Ignoring update errors

If an UPDATE statement is intended to update multiple rows, but an error occurs while updating some of those rows, the entire update is canceled. Consequently, any rows that were changed will revert to their original values. However, if you use the IGNORE keyword, the update will proceed, skipping over any rows that cause problems:

```
UPDATE IGNORE <table_name>
  SET ...
  WHERE ...;
```

10.4 Understanding auto-commit

Before we discuss deleting table rows and the associated risks of accidentally removing data, it's essential to understand the concept of commits in MariaDB. By default, a MariaDB Server installation is set to commit changes automatically. This means that once an SQL statement is executed, the change is immediately saved to the database, and no "undo" option is available.

The *autocommit* variable controls auto-commit behavior. You can check the current state of this variable using the following statement:

```
SHOW VARIABLES WHERE Variable_name='autocommit';
+---------------+-------+
| Variable_name | Value |
+---------------+-------+
| autocommit    | ON    |
+---------------+-------+
1 row in set (0.01 sec)
```

The benefit of auto-commit is that you don't have to remember to execute a COMMIT after making changes. To understand the significance of committing changes, first turn off auto-commit as follows:

```
SET autocommit = 0;
```

Changes to the autocommit variable only take effect in the current session. The next time you start the client, auto-commit will be enabled again.

Next, add a new row to the product table:

```
INSERT INTO product(
    id,
    name,
    description,
    price,
    quantity)
VALUES(
    NULL,
    'iPhone 17 Pro',
    'Apple iPhone',
    999.99,
    30
);
```

After adding the row, verify that it appears in the table before exiting the MariaDB client:

```
SELECT * FROM product WHERE name LIKE 'iPhone%';
+----+---------------+--------------+--------+----------+
| id | name          | description  | price  | quantity |
+----+---------------+--------------+--------+----------+
|  5 | iPhone 17 Pro | Apple iPhone | 999.99 |       30 |
+----+---------------+--------------+--------+----------+
1 row in set (0.00 sec)
```

```
exit
Bye
```

Restart the MariaDB client and check for the new row again:

```
USE sampledb
SELECT * FROM product WHERE name LIKE 'iPhone%';
Empty set (0.00 sec)
```

The iPhone product entry is no longer listed because the INSERT operation was not committed before the client session ended. If auto-commit is disabled, always enter the COMMIT statement before ending the session to avoid losing changes:

```
INSERT ....
COMMIT;
```

Re-insert the iPhone record and execute the COMMIT statement. Then, exit and restart the client to verify that the iPhone record has been preserved.

Since it prevents data loss from forgotten commits, auto-commit is ideal for adding rows and columns to a table. However, it does have some drawbacks. A particular risk is that destructive operations are also committed automatically, such as executing a DELETE operation that removes all records from a table. To avoid this risk, consider using transactions and rollbacks when performing operations that could lead to data loss.

Re-enable autocommit before proceeding:

```
SET autocommit = 1;
```

10.5 Transactions and rollbacks

A MariaDB *transaction* is a series of SQL statements executed sequentially. You can use the START TRANSACTION or BEGIN statements to initiate a transaction. It's important to note that even if the autocommit setting is enabled, the operations performed within a transaction must be committed manually. For example:

```
BEGIN;
INSERT ....;
DELETE ....;
ALTER ...;
COMMIT;
```

Transactions are advantageous when used in conjunction with the ROLLBACK statement. You can think of ROLLBACK as the opposite of the COMMIT statement. While a COMMIT operation finalizes the changes made since the transaction began, a ROLLBACK discards those changes and restores the database to its state before the transaction started. Instead of turning off auto-commit before executing potentially risky operations, it is better to perform those operations within a transaction. After reviewing the changes, you can commit or roll back the transaction.

10.6 Deleting table rows

You can delete all rows or specific rows from a table using the SQL DELETE statement. Using this statement in combination with the WHERE clause is highly recommended. If you omit the WHERE clause, all rows in the table will be deleted. To ensure that your criteria work as intended, it's advisable to test them first using a SELECT statement. Additionally, consider performing the deletion within a transaction for added safety.

To remove rows from our product table where the name field is equal to 'Mac Studio', you can run the following transaction:

```
BEGIN;
DELETE FROM product WHERE name = 'Mac Studio';
```

The Mac Studio row should no longer appear in the table:

```
SELECT * FROM product;
+----+----------------------+------------------------+---------+----------+
| id | name                 | description            | price   | quantity |
+----+----------------------+------------------------+---------+----------+
|  1 | MacBook Pro M4 14-in | Apple 14-in laptop     | 2499.99 |       60 |
|  2 | MacBook Air M3       | Apple laptop           | 1499.99 |       55 |
|  3 | Mac Mini M3          | Apple desktop          |  999.99 |      100 |
|  6 | iPhone 17 Pro        | Apple iPhone           |  999.99 |       30 |
+----+----------------------+------------------------+---------+----------+
4 rows in set (0.00 sec)
```

Next, use ROLLBACK to reverse the deletion:

```
ROLLBACK;
```

```
SELECT * FROM product;
+----+----------------------+------------------------+---------+----------+
| id | name                 | description            | price   | quantity |
+----+----------------------+------------------------+---------+----------+
|  1 | MacBook Pro M4 14-in | Apple 14-in laptop     | 2499.99 |       60 |
|  2 | MacBook Air M3       | Apple laptop           | 1499.99 |       55 |
|  3 | Mac Mini M3          | Apple desktop          |  999.99 |      100 |
|  4 | Mac Studio           | Apple desktop          | 1999.99 |       15 |
|  6 | iPhone 17 Pro        | Apple iPhone           |  999.99 |       30 |
+----+----------------------+------------------------+---------+----------+
5 rows in set (0.00 sec)
```

Note that the row has been restored to its original position in the table.

When using the DELETE statement to remove all rows from a table, be aware that it only deletes the rows themselves while leaving the table intact. To permanently delete the table and all of its contents, use the DROP TABLE statement:

```
DROP TABLE <table_name>;
```

10.7 Reference points

The main points covered in this chapter are as follows:

- **Updating Data**

  - Use the UPDATE statement with SET to modify specific columns in a table.

  - Include a WHERE clause to target specific rows; omitting it updates all rows in the table.

  - Use wildcards (e.g., %) with LIKE to update rows matching a pattern.

- **Ignoring Update Errors**

  - Use the IGNORE keyword to skip problematic rows during updates while processing others.

- **Understanding Auto-Commit**

  - MariaDB commits changes immediately by default.

  - Disable auto-commit temporarily to review changes before committing them.

  - Use COMMIT to save changes or ROLLBACK to discard them when auto-commit is off.

Updating and Deleting Table Data

- **Transactions and Rollbacks**

  - Transactions group multiple operations, providing the ability to commit or roll back as a unit.

  - Use `BEGIN` or `START TRANSACTION` to initiate, and `COMMIT` or `ROLLBACK` to finalize.

- **Deleting Data**

  - Use the `DELETE` statement to remove specific rows, and always include a `WHERE` clause to avoid deleting all rows.

  - Test criteria with a `SELECT` statement before performing deletions.

- **Reversing Deletions**

  - Use transactions to allow rollbacks if a deletion operation needs to be undone.

- **Removing All Rows vs. Dropping Tables**

  - `DELETE` removes rows but retains the table structure.

  - `DROP TABLE` deletes the table and its contents permanently.

Chapter 11

11. Retrieving Data from MariaDB Databases

A database system is only as valuable as its ability to retrieve the data it stores. Among the most widely used SQL commands is the SELECT statement, which is specifically designed to extract data from database tables according to defined criteria. This chapter will explore using the SELECT statement to perform basic database queries.

11.1 Opening the sample database

This chapter assumes that you have completed the steps in the previous chapters. If you haven't, you can import the current database snapshot using the sample files provided in the *"Start Here"* chapter.

To import the snapshot, open a terminal or command prompt, navigate to the directory containing the sample files, and run the following commands:

```
mariadb-admin -u demo -p drop sampledb
mariadb-admin -u demo -p create sampledb
mariadb -u demo -p sampledb < mariadb_retrieving_data.sql
```

Once the database is ready, open the MariaDB client and select the *sampledb* database:

```
USE sampledb
```

Next, insert two more rows into the product table:

```
INSERT INTO product
VALUES(
     NULL,
     'iPhone 17',
     'Apple iPhone',
     799.99,
     30
),
(
     NULL,
     'iMac',
     'Apple desktop',
     1299.99,
     30
);
```

11.2 Retrieving a single column

The most straightforward SELECT statement retrieves a single column from a table's rows. The following SQL statement, for example, extracts all entries from the description column in the product table:

```
SELECT description FROM product;
```

Once executed, this command will display a list of every product description contained in the product table:

```
+------------------------+
| description            |
+------------------------+
| Apple 14-in laptop     |
| Apple laptop           |
| Apple desktop          |
| Apple desktop          |
| Apple iPhone           |
| Apple iPhone           |
| Apple desktop          |
+------------------------+
7 rows in set (0.00 sec)
```

11.3 Using SELECT to retrieve multiple columns

So far, we've explored how simple it is to extract a single column from each table row. In reality, it's more common to need information from multiple columns. Fortunately, the SELECT statement allows us to do this easily. To retrieve data from multiple columns, you can list the column names after the SELECT statement, separating each name with a comma. For example, use the following statement to extract data from three columns in our database table:

```
SELECT name, description, quantity FROM product;
+---------------------+------------------------+----------+
| name                | description            | quantity |
+---------------------+------------------------+----------+
| MacBook Pro M4 14-in | Apple 14-in laptop     |       60 |
| MacBook Air M3      | Apple laptop           |       55 |
| Mac Mini M3         | Apple desktop          |      100 |
| Mac Studio          | Apple desktop          |       15 |
| iPhone 17 Pro       | Apple iPhone           |       30 |
| iPhone 17           | Apple iPhone           |       30 |
| iMac                | Apple desktop          |       30 |
+---------------------+------------------------+----------+
7 rows in set (0.00 sec)
```

While this approach works well if you want to display only some columns in a table, it can become cumbersome if the table has many columns and you want to retrieve all of them. A simpler solution is to use the wildcard symbol (*) instead of listing each column name individually. For example:

```
SELECT * FROM product;
+----+---------------------+------------------------+---------+----------+
| id | name                | description            | price   | quantity |
+----+---------------------+------------------------+---------+----------+
|  1 | MacBook Pro M4 14-in | Apple 14-in laptop    | 2499.99 |       60 |
|  2 | MacBook Air M3      | Apple laptop           | 1499.99 |       55 |
|  3 | Mac Mini M3         | Apple desktop          |  999.99 |      100 |
|  4 | Mac Studio          | Apple desktop          | 1999.99 |       15 |
|  6 | iPhone 17 Pro       | Apple iPhone           |  999.99 |       30 |
|  7 | iPhone 17           | Apple iPhone           |  799.99 |       30 |
|  8 | iMac                | Apple desktop          | 1299.99 |       30 |
+----+---------------------+------------------------+---------+----------+
7 rows in set (0.00 sec)
```

11.4 Restricting the number of results

To limit the number of rows returned by a SELECT statement when retrieving data from a table, you can use the LIMIT keyword, followed by the number of rows to be retrieved. The following example retrieves the first two rows from the product table:

```
SELECT * FROM product LIMIT 2;
+----+----------------------+-------------------------+---------+----------+
| id | name                 | description             | price   | quantity |
+----+----------------------+-------------------------+---------+----------+
|  1 | MacBook Pro M4 14-in | Apple 14-in laptop      | 2499.99 |       60 |
|  2 | MacBook Air M3       | Apple laptop            | 1499.99 |       55 |
+----+----------------------+-------------------------+---------+----------+
2 rows in set (0.00 sec)
```

Using the LIMIT clause alongside the OFFSET keyword allows you to set a specific starting point for data retrieval within the table. The following example retrieves three rows, starting after the second row:

```
SELECT * FROM product LIMIT 3 OFFSET 2;
+----+---------------+--------------+---------+----------+
| id | name          | description  | price   | quantity |
+----+---------------+--------------+---------+----------+
|  3 | Mac Mini M3   | Apple desktop|  999.99 |      100 |
|  4 | Mac Studio    | Apple desktop| 1999.99 |       15 |
|  6 | iPhone 17 Pro | Apple iPhone |  999.99 |       30 |
+----+---------------+--------------+---------+----------+
3 rows in set (0.00 sec)
```

The same results can be achieved by omitting the OFFSET keyword and specifying the offset and limit values as a comma-separated list, as follows:

```
SELECT * FROM product LIMIT <offset>, <row_count>;
```

The following statement, for example, retrieves three rows starting after the first row:

```
SELECT * FROM product LIMIT 1, 3;
+----+----------------+-------------------+---------+----------+
| id | name           | description       | price   | quantity |
+----+----------------+-------------------+---------+----------+
|  2 | MacBook Air M3 | Apple laptop      | 1499.99 |       55 |
|  3 | Mac Mini M3    | Apple desktop     |  999.99 |      100 |
|  4 | Mac Studio     | Apple desktop     | 1999.99 |       15 |
+----+----------------+-------------------+---------+----------+
3 rows in set (0.00 sec)
```

11.5 Eliminating duplicate values

It is common for a combination of column values to be duplicated across multiple rows in a database. As a result, when retrieving data—especially when focusing on a single column in a table—you may encounter repeated values in the results. In our product table, some rows have matching description text, resulting in duplicate items in the result set:

```
SELECT description FROM product;
+-------------------------+
| description             |
+-------------------------+
```

```
| Apple 14-in laptop       |
| Apple laptop             |
| Apple desktop            |
| Apple desktop            |
| Apple iPhone             |
| Apple iPhone             |
| Apple desktop            |
+--------------------------+
7 rows in set (0.00 sec)
```

The output above indicates that our fictional online store offers multiple types of Mac desktops and Apple iPhones. While the product IDs and names are unique, the descriptions contain duplications. To create a list of product descriptions without any duplicates, we can use the SELECT DISTINCT statement:

```
SELECT DISTINCT description FROM product;
+--------------------------+
| description              |
+--------------------------+
| Apple 14-in laptop       |
| Apple laptop             |
| Apple desktop            |
| Apple iPhone             |
+--------------------------+
4 rows in set (0.00 sec)
```

11.6 Sorting result sets

A SELECT statement typically retrieves data from a table in the order in which it was added. However, this order can change if the database table has undergone updates or deletions, making it difficult to predict the exact order of the data retrieval. To address this issue, SQL offers the ORDER BY clause, which allows us to sort the data as the SELECT statement retrieves it.

Let's begin by performing a retrieval on the product table:

```
SELECT description FROM product;
+--------------------------+
| description              |
+--------------------------+
| Apple 14-in laptop       |
| Apple laptop             |
| Apple desktop            |
| Apple desktop            |
| Apple iPhone             |
| Apple iPhone             |
| Apple desktop            |
+--------------------------+
7 rows in set (0.00 sec)
```

When this command is executed and the data is extracted, the rows may seem to have been retrieved in no particular order. When we retrieve all the columns from the table instead of just the description column, we observe that the results are listed in the order of the id column. This is not surprising, as the id is an auto-increment value that reflects the order in which the data was added.

While these results might be acceptable in certain situations, there may be cases where you want the results set to be sorted. This is where the ORDER BY clause comes into play. Using ORDER BY, you can control the order in which the query results are displayed, ensuring they are sorted according to your specific requirements. The syntax for incorporating ORDER BY in a SELECT statement is as follows:

```
SELECT <column_1>, <column_2> ... FROM <table_name> ORDER By <column_name>;
```

To continue with our example, we could, therefore, sort the product descriptions as follows:

```
SELECT description FROM product ORDER BY description;
+-------------------------+
| description             |
+-------------------------+
| Apple iPhone 17 Pro     |
| Apple desktop           |
| Apple desktop           |
| Apple laptop            |
| Apple 14-in laptop      |
+-------------------------+
5 rows in set (0.04 sec)
```

In this case, the result set has been ordered alphabetically according to the description column.

The column used to order the result set does not have to be included in the retrieved columns. It is possible to sort by any column in a table, even if it is not referenced in the SELECT statement. The statement below retrieves the name column based on the quantity field, sorted from lowest to highest:

```
SELECT name FROM product ORDER BY quantity;
+---------------------+
| name                |
+---------------------+
| Mac Studio          |
| iPhone 17           |
| iMac                |
| iPhone 17 Pro       |
| MacBook Air M3      |
| MacBook Pro M4 14-in |
| Mac Mini M3         |
+---------------------+
7 rows in set (0.000 sec)
```

11.7 Sorting on multiple columns

In the previous examples, we used a single column from a table as the criterion for sorting result sets. However, the ORDER BY clause allows us to sort based on multiple columns. The columns to be used for sorting should be specified after the ORDER BY clause and separated by commas. For instance, to sort by both the product description and price in our table, we would execute the following SQL statement:

```
SELECT * FROM product ORDER BY description, price;
```

11.8 Sorting data in descending order

In this chapter, we have primarily focused on sorting our MariaDB database queries in ascending order. However, there may be instances when, for example, a visitor to your website wants to view prices for a list of items, starting with the most expensive. The standard ORDER BY clause won't fulfill this requirement. Fortunately, SQL provides the DESC keyword, which allows you to specify that the results of a SELECT statement should be sorted in descending order. For example, to sort the products by price in descending order, you would use the following statement:

```
SELECT name, price FROM product ORDER BY price DESC;
+----------------------+----------+
| name                 | price    |
+----------------------+----------+
| MacBook Pro M4 14-in | 2499.99  |
| Mac Studio           | 1999.99  |
| MacBook Air M3       | 1499.99  |
| iMac                 | 1299.99  |
| Mac Mini M3          |  999.99  |
| iPhone 17 Pro        |  999.99  |
| iPhone 17            |  799.99  |
+----------------------+----------+
7 rows in set (0.00 sec)
```

11.9 Expressions and aggregate functions

Many SQL statements, such as SELECT and INSERT, support a variety of expressions. We can even use SELECT to perform arithmetic:

```
SELECT SUM(2 * 10 / 6);
+------------+
| 2 * 10 / 6 |
+------------+
|     3.3333 |
+------------+
1 row in set (0.00 sec)
```

The previous example used the SUM() aggregate function to return the calculation result. MariaDB offers a wide range of aggregate functions for various operations on data sets. Some of the most commonly used functions are summarized in Table 11-1:

Function	Description
AVG()	Returns the average of the values in the selected column
BIT_AND()	Return bitwise AND
BIT_OR()	Return bitwise OR
BIT_XOR()	Return bitwise XOR
COUNT()	Returns the number of rows returned for a selection
GROUP_CONCAT()	Return a concatenated string
MAX()	Returns the maximum value for a column
MIN()	Returns the minimum value of a column
SUM()	Returns the sum of the values in a specified column

Table 11-1

The syntax for using aggregate functions in SELECT statements is as follows:

```
SELECT <column_name>, <aggregate_func>(<column_name>)
FROM <table_name> GROUP BY <column_name>;
```

Aggregate functions operate on rows that share matching column values. For example, consider the product table, which shows three Mac desktops, two Apple iPhones, and two MacBook models categorized by the description column. To calculate the average price for each category, we would use the AVG() function. When applying aggregate functions, we must specify the column used to group the results using the GROUP BY clause. In this case, we group the results based on the description column. With this information, we can determine the average price for each product category:

```
SELECT description, AVG(price) FROM product GROUP BY description;
+------------------------+-------------+
| description            | AVG(price)  |
+------------------------+-------------+
| Apple 14-in laptop     | 2499.990000 |
| Apple laptop           | 1499.990000 |
| Apple desktop          | 1433.323333 |
| Apple iPhone           |  899.990000 |
+------------------------+-------------+
4 rows in set (0.00 sec)
```

We can also use the COUNT() function to determine the number of device types in each category:

```
SELECT description, COUNT(*) FROM product GROUP BY description;
+------------------------+----------+
| description            | COUNT(*) |
+------------------------+----------+
| Apple 14-in laptop     |        1 |
| Apple laptop           |        1 |
| Apple desktop          |        3 |
| Apple iPhone           |        2 |
+------------------------+----------+
4 rows in set (0.01 sec)
```

Similarly, we can restrict our criteria to count the number of products priced above a specific threshold:

```
SELECT COUNT(price) FROM product WHERE price > 1000;
+--------------+
| COUNT(price) |
+--------------+
|            4 |
+--------------+
1 row in set (0.00 sec)
```

When using aggregation, we create temporary columns that hold the results returned by the aggregate function. Often, you may need to reference these aggregate columns later in the statement. For example, consider the case where the SUM() function is used to multiply the price and quantity columns to calculate the total inventory value grouped by name:

```
SELECT name, SUM(price*quantity) FROM product GROUP BY name;
+--------------------+---------------------+
| name               | SUM(price*quantity) |
+--------------------+---------------------+
| iMac               |            38999.70 |
| iPhone 17          |            23999.70 |
| iPhone 17 Pro      |            29999.70 |
| Mac Mini M3        |            99999.00 |
| Mac Studio         |            29999.85 |
| MacBook Air M3     |            82499.45 |
| MacBook Pro M4 14-in |         149999.40 |
+--------------------+---------------------+
7 rows in set (0.00 sec)
```

However, suppose you need to sort the results based on the total value ranked from the lowest to the highest. We know the ORDER BY option will do this for us, but we need a way to reference the unnamed total column. The solution is to assign an alias to the aggregate column and reference it when using ORDER BY. In the statement below, the aggregate column is assigned an alias (total), which is used to order the result set:

```
SELECT name, SUM(price*quantity) AS total FROM product GROUP BY name ORDER BY
total;
+----------------------+-----------+
| name                 | total     |
+----------------------+-----------+
| iPhone 17            |  23999.70 |
| iPhone 17 Pro        |  29999.70 |
| Mac Studio           |  29999.85 |
| iMac                 |  38999.70 |
| MacBook Air M3       |  82499.45 |
| Mac Mini M3          |  99999.00 |
| MacBook Pro M4 14-in | 149999.40 |
+----------------------+-----------+
7 rows in set (0.000 sec)
```

SELECT statements are not restricted to a single aggregate function. It is perfectly valid to include calls to multiple functions, for example:

```
SELECT MIN(price) AS min_price, MAX(price) AS max_price FROM product;
+-----------+-----------+
| min_price | max_price |
+-----------+-----------+
|    799.99 |   2499.99 |
+-----------+-----------+
1 row in set (0.00 sec)
```

11.10 Reference points

The main points covered in this chapter are as follows:

- **Single-Column Retrieval**

  - Use `SELECT <column_name> FROM <table_name>` to extract data from a single column in a table.

- **Multi-Column Retrieval**

  - List multiple column names after `SELECT` to retrieve data from several columns.

  - Use `SELECT *` to retrieve all columns from a table.

- **Limiting Results**

  - Use `LIMIT` to restrict the number of rows returned.

  - Combine `LIMIT` with `OFFSET` to skip a specific number of rows before retrieving data.

- **Eliminating Duplicates**

  - Use `SELECT DISTINCT` to return unique values from a column, removing duplicates.

- **Sorting Results**

- Use `ORDER BY` to sort data in ascending (default) or descending (`DESC`) order.

- Sort by multiple columns by separating them with commas.

- **Descending Order Sorting**

  - Use the `DESC` keyword to sort results in descending order, such as prices from highest to lowest.

- **Combining Multiple Criteria for Sorting**

  - Use `ORDER BY` with multiple columns to create more complex sorting patterns (e.g., by description and then price).

- **Expressions in SQL**

  - SQL supports expressions for arithmetic operations in statements like `SELECT`.

  - Example functions include basic math and aggregate calculations.

- **Aggregate Functions**

  - Common functions include `SUM()`, `AVG()`, `MIN()`, `MAX()`, and `COUNT()`.

  - Aggregate functions process rows grouped by shared values, often paired with `GROUP BY`.

- **Using GROUP BY**

  - Groups result sets based on matching column values.

  - Example: Calculate average prices by product category or count items per category.

- **Column Aliases**

  - Aggregations generate temporary columns that can be referenced using aliases.

Chapter 12

12. Filtering Result Sets with the WHERE Clause

In the previous chapters, we explored various methods for retrieving data using the SELECT statement and examined how to sort the results. A key requirement when retrieving data is the ability to filter it, ensuring that only rows meeting specific search criteria are returned. This chapter will focus on filtering query results using the WHERE clause and the SELECT statement.

12.1 Opening the sample database

This chapter assumes that you have completed the steps in the previous chapters. If you haven't, you can import the current database snapshot using the sample files provided in the *"Start Here"* chapter.

To import the snapshot, open a terminal or command prompt, navigate to the directory containing the sample files, and run the following commands:

```
mariadb-admin -u demo -p drop sampledb
mariadb-admin -u demo -p create sampledb
mariadb -u demo -p sampledb < mariadb_where_filtering.sql
```

Once the database is ready, open the MariaDB client and select the *sampledb* database:

```
USE sampledb
```

12.2 The basics of the WHERE clause

The WHERE clause is used with SELECT, INSERT, UPDATE, and DELETE statements to filter results based on specified criteria. The syntax for a SELECT WHERE statement is as follows:

```
SELECT column(s) FROM table WHERE column = value
```

The first part of the statement resembles a typical SELECT query. The WHERE clause changes things, however. After the WHERE keyword, you need to specify the column on which the filtering will be based, followed by an operator that defines the type of comparison to perform (in this case, we are looking for equality), and finally, the value that the column must match.

Using our product table as an example, a standard, unfiltered SELECT statement will return the following result set:

```
SELECT * FROM product;
+----+--------------------+-------------------------+---------+----------+
| id | name               | description             | price   | quantity |
+----+--------------------+-------------------------+---------+----------+
|  1 | MacBook Pro M4 14-in | Apple14-in laptop     | 2499.99 |       60 |
|  2 | MacBook Air M3     | Apple laptop            | 1499.99 |       55 |
|  3 | Mac Mini M3        | Apple desktop           |  999.99 |      100 |
|  4 | Mac Studio         | Apple desktop           | 1999.99 |       15 |
|  6 | iPhone 17 Pro      | Apple iPhone            |  999.99 |       30 |
|  7 | iPhone 17          | Apple iPhone            |  799.99 |       30 |
```

77

```
|  8 | iMac               | Apple desktop          | 1299.99 |        30 |
+----+--------------------+------------------------+---------+----------+
7 rows in set (0.01 sec)
```

This result set is helpful if we want to view every row in our table. However, needing only a subset of the data is more common. For instance, if we want to select rows where the price column equals a specific value, we can construct an SQL statement like this:

```
SELECT * FROM product WHERE price = 999.99;
```

Such a statement will result in the following output when executed on our product table:

```
+----+--------------+--------------+--------+----------+
| id | name         | description  | price  | quantity |
+----+--------------+--------------+--------+----------+
|  3 | Mac Mini M3  | Apple desktop| 999.99 |      100 |
|  6 | iPhone 17 Pro| Apple iPhone | 999.99 |       30 |
+----+--------------+--------------+--------+----------+
2 rows in set (0.00 sec)
```

Now that we have looked at the equality operator (=), we can explore other WHERE clause operators.

12.3 Comparison Operators

So far, we have only reviewed the WHERE clause equality operator (=). Equality is just one of several comparison operators that can be used to refine data retrieval results. Table 12-1 lists the comparison operators that are supported by the WHERE clause:

Operator	Description
=	Equal to
!=	Not equal to
<>	Not equal to
>	Greater than
<	Less than
<=	Less than or equal to
>=	Greater than or equal to
BETWEEN x AND y	Falls between the two values x and y

Table 12-1

We have already used the equality (=) operator to check for numerical equality. This operator can also evaluate other data types, including comparing string values. For instance, if we want to find the price and product description of an iPhone 17 Pro, we would use the following SQL statement:

```
SELECT description, price FROM product WHERE name = "iPhone 17 Pro";
+--------------+--------+
| description  | price  |
+--------------+--------+
| Apple iPhone | 999.99 |
+--------------+--------+
1 row in set (0.00 sec)
```

Additionally, we can list all products priced at or below a specified threshold using the less than (<=) operator:

```
SELECT name, price FROM product WHERE price <= 1299.99;
+---------------+---------+
| name          | price   |
+---------------+---------+
| Mac Mini M3   |  999.99 |
| iPhone 17 Pro |  999.99 |
| iPhone 17     |  799.99 |
| iMac          | 1299.99 |
+---------------+---------+
4 rows in set (0.01 sec)
```

We can also retrieve data rows where a value does not match specific criteria. The following example retrieves all rows where the price is not equal to $999.99:

```
SELECT * FROM product WHERE price != 999.99;
+----+--------------------+--------------------+---------+----------+
| id | name               | description        | price   | quantity |
+----+--------------------+--------------------+---------+----------+
|  1 | MacBook Pro M4 14-in | Apple 14-in laptop | 2499.99 |       60 |
|  2 | MacBook Air M3     | Apple laptop       | 1499.99 |       55 |
|  4 | Mac Studio         | Apple desktop      | 1999.99 |       15 |
|  7 | iPhone 17          | Apple iPhone       |  799.99 |       30 |
|  8 | iMac               | Apple desktop      | 1299.99 |       30 |
+----+--------------------+--------------------+---------+----------+
5 rows in set (0.00 sec)
```

12.4 Checking for NULL values

In addition to checking the values of a column, it's also possible to identify columns that contain no value. Columns with no value are referred to as containing NULL values. Consequently, we can check for these empty columns by looking for equality with NULL. However, it's important to note that when checking for NULL values, we must use the IS keyword instead of the equals sign (=):

```
SELECT * FROM product WHERE name IS NULL;
```

The above SELECT statement will retrieve any rows which do not contain a product name.

12.5 Searching within value ranges

Table 12-1 above included the BETWEEN...AND operator. This operator selects rows that fall within specified upper and lower limits. For example, we can list all products in our table priced between $500 and $1,400:

```
SELECT * FROM product WHERE price BETWEEN 500 AND 1400;
+----+---------------+---------------+---------+----------+
| id | name          | description   | price   | quantity |
+----+---------------+---------------+---------+----------+
|  3 | Mac Mini M3   | Apple desktop |  999.99 |      100 |
|  6 | iPhone 17 Pro | Apple iPhone  |  999.99 |       30 |
|  7 | iPhone 17     | Apple iPhone  |  799.99 |       30 |
|  8 | iMac          | Apple desktop | 1299.99 |       30 |
+----+---------------+---------------+---------+----------+
4 rows in set (0.00 sec)
```

12.6 Reference points

The main points covered in this chapter are as follows:

Filtering Result Sets with the WHERE Clause

- **Purpose of the WHERE Clause**

  - Filters rows in a result set based on specific criteria.

  - Ensures only relevant data is retrieved from a table.

  - `WHERE` clauses can be used with `SELECT`, `UPDATE`, `INSERT`, and `DELETE` statements.

- **Basic Syntax**

  - `SELECT <columns> FROM <table> WHERE <column> = value` filters rows matching the given condition.

- **Comparison Operators**

  - = Equal to

  - != or <> Not equal to

  - > and < Greater than or less than

  - >= and <= Greater than or equal to, less than or equal to

  - BETWEEN x AND y Within a specified range.

- **Filtering Examples**

  - Filter by exact matches, value ranges, or specific criteria (e.g., products priced below a certain amount).

  - Use != to exclude rows with specific values.

- **Handling NULL Values**

Use IS NULL or IS NOT NULL to filter rows based on the presence or absence of values in a column.

- **Range Searches**

Use `BETWEEN...AND` to retrieve rows with values falling within an upper and lower limit.

- **Practical Use Cases**

  - Combine multiple operators for complex filters.

  - Validate criteria with `SELECT` queries before applying further actions.

13. Filtering Results with Logical Operators

The previous chapter covered the basics of filtering retrieved data using comparison operators and the WHERE clause. While those fundamentals addressed simple filtering techniques, more advanced methods are often required. This chapter will explain using logical operators with the WHERE clause to define multiple conditions.

Although most examples in this chapter use the SELECT statement to demonstrate logical operators, these same techniques can also be applied to other statements, including INSERT, DELETE, and UPDATE.

13.1 Opening the sample database

This chapter assumes that you have completed the steps in the previous chapters. If you haven't, you can import the current database snapshot using the sample files provided in the *"Start Here"* chapter.

To import the snapshot, open a terminal or command prompt, navigate to the directory containing the sample files, and run the following commands:

```
mariadb-admin -u demo -p drop sampledb
mariadb-admin -u demo -p create sampledb
mariadb -u demo -p sampledb < mariadb_logical_operators.sql
```

Once the database is ready, open the MariaDB client and select the *sampledb* database:

```
USE sampledb
```

13.2 Filtering results with the OR operator

In the previous chapter, we examined how to filter data retrieved using WHERE based on a single criterion. For instance, we retrieved all products in a table with prices below a specified threshold. Imagine you want to retrieve all rows from a table where the product meets either of two conditions. This can be accomplished using the WHERE clause with the OR logical operator.

For example, if we want to list all products in our sample database that cost less than $1000 or more than $2000, the SQL statement would read as follows:

```
SELECT name, price FROM product WHERE price < 1000 OR price > 2000;
+-----------------------+---------+
| name                  | price   |
+-----------------------+---------+
| MacBook Pro M4 14-in  | 2499.99 |
| Mac Mini M3           |  999.99 |
| iPhone 17 Pro         |  999.99 |
| iPhone 17             |  799.99 |
+-----------------------+---------+
4 rows in set (0.00 sec)
```

The result set from the above SQL statement contains all products except those priced between $1000 and $2000.

13.3 Filtering results with the AND operator

The AND operator combines multiple filtering criteria in a WHERE clause. Unlike the OR operator, which allows for either condition to be true, the AND operator requires both to be true. Suppose, for example, we need to find an Apple iPhone that costs less than $500. To do so, we can run the following SELECT statement:

```
SELECT name, price FROM product
 WHERE description = 'Apple iPhone' AND price < 500;
Empty set (0.00 sec)
```

In this case, no matches are returned because no products in the table satisfy both criteria. If the customer is willing to spend more, we can adjust our search to find a suitable item:

```
SELECT name, price FROM product
WHERE description = "Apple iPhone" AND price < 800;
+-----------+--------+
| name      | price  |
+-----------+--------+
| iPhone 17 | 799.99 |
+-----------+--------+
1 row in set (0.00 sec)
```

This time, the query returns a result that meets both the product description and price criteria.

13.4 Combining AND and OR operators

The WHERE clause can combine multiple AND and OR operators to create complex filtering requirements. For example, we can combine operators to find a Mac Desktop or iPhone that costs $999.99 using the following statement:

```
SELECT name, price FROM product WHERE price = 999.99
AND (description = 'Apple desktop' OR description = 'Apple iPhone');
+---------------+--------+
| name          | price  |
+---------------+--------+
| Mac Mini M3   | 999.99 |
| iPhone 17 Pro | 999.99 |
+---------------+--------+
2 rows in set (0.01 sec)
```

13.5 Understanding operator precedence

When combining operators, it is essential to understand *operator precedence,* which dictates the order in which operators within the same statement are evaluated. You might have noticed the parentheses surrounding the OR expression in the previous example. To grasp the significance of these parentheses, try running the statement without them:

```
SELECT name, price FROM product WHERE price = 999.99
AND description = 'Apple desktop' OR description = 'Apple iPhone';
+---------------+--------+
| name          | price  |
+---------------+--------+
| Mac Mini M3   | 999.99 |
| iPhone 17 Pro | 999.99 |
| iPhone 17     | 799.99 |
+---------------+--------+
3 rows in set (0.05 sec)
```

You may notice that the results now include a product that doesn't match the $999.99 price point. This inconsistency occurs because MariaDB evaluates AND expressions before OR expressions, regardless of the order in which they appear when reading the statement from left to right. As a result, the query retrieves all Mac Desktop devices priced at $999.99, along with all Apple iPhone products, regardless of their price.

To adjust the operator precedence and ensure the OR expression was evaluated before the AND expression in the original statement, we used parentheses around the OR condition:

```
SELECT name, price FROM product WHERE price = 999.99
AND (description = 'Apple desktop' OR description = 'Apple iPhone');
```

13.6 Specifying condition ranges using the IN operator

The IN operator allows us to specify multiple filter criteria within a WHERE clause by listing them in parentheses, separated by commas. The syntax for using IN with the WHERE clause is as follows:

```
SELECT <columns> FROM <table> WHERE <column>
IN (<criteria_1>, <criteria_2>, ...);
```

For instance, suppose we want to retrieve all products from our database priced at $799.99, $999.99, or $1999.99. While it is possible to achieve this using a series of OR expressions, such an approach can be lengthy and cumbersome. A more concise option is to use the IN clause as shown below:

```
SELECT name, price FROM product
WHERE price IN (799.99, 999.99, 1999.99);
+----------------+---------+
| name           | price   |
+----------------+---------+
| Mac Mini M3    |  999.99 |
| Mac Studio     | 1999.99 |
| iPhone 17 Pro  |  999.99 |
| iPhone 17      |  799.99 |
+----------------+---------+
4 rows in set (0.04 sec)
```

13.7 Using the NOT Operator

The next operator to look at in this chapter is the NOT operator. The NOT operator is used to negate the result of an expression and is of particular use when using the IN operator. For example, we could very easily change our previous IN example so that it lists all the products in our table that do NOT cost $799.99, $999.99, or $1999.99 using the following NOT IN operator combination:

```
SELECT name, price FROM product
WHERE price NOT IN (799.99, 999.99, 1999.99);
+----------------------+---------+
| name                 | price   |
+----------------------+---------+
| MacBook Pro M4 14-in | 2499.99 |
| MacBook Air M3       | 1499.99 |
| iMac                 | 1299.99 |
+----------------------+---------+
3 rows in set (0.00 sec)
```

13.8 Using subqueries with WHERE IN clauses

In the example above, we manually entered a list of pricing criteria. A valuable feature of the IN keyword is that the criteria can be generated using a SELECT statement with the following syntax:

```
SELECT <columns> FROM <table> WHERE <column>
IN (SELECT <column> FROM <table> WHERE ....);
```

To illustrate this technique, we will create a new table to track discontinued products. Use the following statement to create this new table:

```
CREATE TABLE availability
(
  id INT NOT NULL AUTO_INCREMENT,
  name char(30) NOT NULL,
  discontinued BOOL NOT NULL,
  PRIMARY KEY (id)
);
```

Next, populate the table with several rows, including a mix of available and discontinued products:

```
INSERT INTO availability
VALUES
    (NULL, 'Mac Mini M3', true),
    (NULL, 'Mac Studio', false),
    (NULL, 'iMac', true),
    (NULL, 'iPhone 17', true),
    (NULL, 'MacBook Air M3', false),
    (NULL, 'iPhone 17 Pro', true);
```

Run the following SELECT statement to check that the rows were inserted correctly:

```
SELECT * FROM availability;
+----+----------------+--------------+
| id | name           | discontinued |
+----+----------------+--------------+
|  1 | Mac Mini M3    |            1 |
|  2 | Mac Studio     |            0 |
|  3 | iMac           |            1 |
|  4 | iPhone 17      |            1 |
|  5 | MacBook Air M3 |            0 |
|  6 | iPhone 17 Pro  |            1 |
+----+----------------+--------------+
6 rows in set (0.00 sec)
```

Now that we have a table containing product availability information, we can use this data to retrieve discontinued items from the product table as follows:

```
SELECT name, description FROM product
WHERE name IN (SELECT name FROM availability WHERE discontinued = true);
+---------------+--------------+
| name          | description  |
+---------------+--------------+
| Mac Mini M3   | Apple desktop|
| iPhone 17 Pro | Apple iPhone |
| iPhone 17     | Apple iPhone |
```

```
| iMac          | Apple desktop|
+---------------+--------------+
4 rows in set (0.01 sec)
```

As previously discussed, WHERE clauses can be used not only with the SELECT statement. For instance, we will use the WHERE IN construct to delete discontinued items from the product table. However, since we will need these rows in later chapters, we will perform the deletion within a transaction, allowing us to roll it back afterward:

```
BEGIN;
DELETE FROM product WHERE name IN
(SELECT name FROM availability WHERE discontinued);
```

Execute a SELECT statement to verify that discontinued items have been removed from the product table:

```
SELECT name, description FROM product;
+----------------------+-------------------------+
| name                 | description             |
+----------------------+-------------------------+
| MacBook Pro M4 14-in | Apple 14-in laptop      |
| MacBook Air M3       | Apple laptop            |
| Mac Studio           | Apple desktop           |
+----------------------+-------------------------+
3 rows in set (0.01 sec)
```

Finally, roll back the deletions to restore the table to its original state.

```
ROLLBACK;
```

Before proceeding, execute the following statement to delete the availability table:

```
DROP TABLE availability;
```

13.9 Reference points

The main points covered in this chapter are as follows:

- **Logical Operators for Filtering**

  - OR: Retrieves rows that match at least one of the specified conditions.

  - AND: Retrieves rows that meet all specified conditions.

  - Combine AND and OR to create complex filters, using parentheses to define precedence.

  - WHERE clauses can be used with SELECT, UPDATE, INSERT, and DELETE statements.

- **Operator Precedence**

  - AND takes precedence over OR in queries.

  - Use parentheses to explicitly control the evaluation order for desired results.

- **IN Operator**

  - Simplifies filtering with multiple criteria by listing them in parentheses.

  - Can use subqueries within IN to generate dynamic filtering criteria.

Filtering Results with Logical Operators

- **Purpose of the NOT Operator**
  - Negates the result of an expression, filtering rows that do not meet the specified condition.
  - Useful for exclusion-based filtering.

- **Combining NOT with IN**
  - `NOT IN` excludes rows with values matching the list in the `IN` clause.
  - Example: Retrieve products with prices not in a specified range.

- **Subqueries in WHERE Clauses**
  - Subqueries can be used with IN to filter results based on criteria from another table.
  - Example: Identifying discontinued products using availability data from a related table.

- **Deleting with Filters**
  - `WHERE` clauses can filter rows to delete, ensuring only the intended records are removed.
  - Perform deletions within transactions to allow rollbacks if needed.

Chapter 14

14. Wildcard and Regular Expression Matching

In the previous chapters, we discussed how to retrieve data from MariaDB database tables based on specific criteria, such as matching exact strings or comparing values. While this method is effective in many situations, there are times when more flexible criteria are needed. In this chapter, we will explore how to retrieve data using patterns by employing wildcards, regular expressions, and the LIKE and REGEXP operators. These operators enable more dynamic searches, making finding data that partially matches your criteria easier.

14.1 What are wildcards?

Wildcards are used when matching string values. A typical comparison requires using specific strings where each character in the two strings must exactly match before they are considered equal. Wildcards, however, provide more flexibility by allowing any character or group of characters in a string to be acceptable as a match for another string. As with most concepts, this is best demonstrated through examples.

14.2 Opening the sample database

This chapter assumes that you have completed the steps in the previous chapters. If you haven't, you can import the current database snapshot using the sample files provided in the *"Start Here"* chapter.

To import the snapshot, open a terminal or command prompt, navigate to the directory containing the sample files, and run the following commands:

```
mariadb-admin -u demo -p drop sampledb
mariadb-admin -u demo -p create sampledb
mariadb -u demo -p sampledb < mariadb_regex.sql
```

Once the database is ready, open the MariaDB client and select the *sampledb* database:

```
USE sampledb
```

Next, execute the following statement to add two rows to the product table:

```
INSERT INTO product
VALUES(
    NULL,
    'NZXT Mid Tower',
    'NZXT PC case (grey)',
    129.99,
    100
),
(
    NULL,
    'Corsair Full Tower',
    'Corsair PC case (gray)',
    179.99,
    15
),
```

```
(
     NULL,
     'Dell XPS Model 4823',
     'Dell Desktop PC',
     299.99,
     35
),
(
     NULL,
     'Dell XPS Model 7823',
     'Dell Desktop PC',
     749.99,
     16
);
```

14.3 Single character wildcards

Suppose our product table is part of an online commerce site selling electronic items to customers worldwide. One problem, even between English-speaking nations, is a difference in spelling. For example, a particular color would be spelled "gray" in the United States, while the same color is spelled "grey" in the United Kingdom. If we have items in our product database that contain both spellings, we would, under normal circumstances, need to perform a search for each spelling to retrieve the required data. For example, we might choose to use the IN clause:

```
SELECT name, description FROM product WHERE description
IN ('NZXT PC case (grey)', 'Corsair PC case (gray)');
+-------------------+--------------------------+
| name              | description              |
+-------------------+--------------------------+
| NZXT Mid Tower    | NZXT PC case (grey)      |
| Corsair Full Tower| Corsair PC case (gray)   |
+-------------------+--------------------------+
2 rows in set (0.01 sec)
```

A more straightforward and flexible approach is to use a *character wildcard* instead of the 'e' and 'a' characters in the comparison value. This can be done using the underscore wildcard (_) and the LIKE operator. To use this wildcard, insert an underscore in character positions where multiple matches are acceptable.

For example, in the following SELECT statement, any character that falls between the 'Gr' and 'y' will be considered a match. Try the following statement:

```
SELECT name, description FROM product
WHERE description LIKE 'gr_y';
Empty set (0.00 sec)
```

The empty result set occurs because, although the statement uses a character wildcard, the LIKE clause requires a complete match. While we can successfully search for "NZXT PC case (gr_y)" or "Corsair PC case (gr_y)," we need to employ multiple character wildcards to find descriptions that include "gray" or "grey" in addition to other text.

14.4 Multiple character wildcards

The single-character wildcard (_) is often useful, but the multiple-character percent sign (%) wildcard is even more powerful. The percent sign can represent any number of characters in a value match. When you use wildcards, not only do the characters not have to match, but the number of characters can also vary.

You can place wildcards in any number of positions within a string value. For example, you can place a wildcard at the beginning of the comparison value to find all rows where the product name ends with "Tower," as follows:

```
SELECT name, description FROM product WHERE name LIKE '%Tower';
+-------------------+------------------------+
| name              | description            |
+-------------------+------------------------+
| NZXT Mid Tower    | NZXT PC case (grey)    |
| Corsair Full Tower | Corsair PC case (gray) |
+-------------------+------------------------+
2 rows in set (0.00 sec)
```

Alternatively, the wildcard could be placed at the end of a value, for example, to retrieve all Mac devices:

```
SELECT name, description FROM product WHERE name LIKE 'Mac%';
+---------------------+------------------------+
| name                | description            |
+---------------------+------------------------+
| MacBook Pro M4 14-in | Apple 14-in laptop    |
| MacBook Air M3      | Apple laptop           |
| Mac Mini M3         | Apple desktop          |
| Mac Studio          | Apple desktop          |
+---------------------+------------------------+
4 rows in set (0.00 sec)
```

Multiple wildcards can be used to retrieve all the rows in our product table where the name contains 'Book' and 'Air' (in that order):

```
SELECT name, description FROM product WHERE name LIKE '%Book%Air%';
+----------------+-------------------+
| name           | description       |
+----------------+-------------------+
| MacBook Air M3 | Apple laptop      |
+----------------+-------------------+
1 row in set (0.00 sec)
```

Finally, the following statement combines single and multiple-character wildcards to retrieve product descriptions that contain either "gray" or "grey":

```
SELECT name, description FROM product WHERE description LIKE '%gr_y%';
+-------------------+------------------------+
| name              | description            |
+-------------------+------------------------+
| NZXT Mid Tower    | NZXT PC case (grey)    |
| Corsair Full Tower | Corsair PC case (gray) |
+-------------------+------------------------+
2 rows in set (0.00 sec)
```

14.5 What are regular expressions?

The term "regular expressions" can be confusing, as it doesn't clearly convey their purpose. Regular expressions, often referred to as *regex*, are a feature found in many programming languages, and entire books have been dedicated to the topic. Luckily, MariaDB offers more limited support for regular expressions compared to other languages, which can simplify the learning process. However, this may also be frustrating for those familiar with the more complex regular expressions in other programming languages.

Regular expressions are instructions written in a predefined syntax, allowing flexible text matching. For instance, they enable us to extract all occurrences of a specific word or phrase from a text block. Additionally, you can search for a particular piece of text and replace it with an alternate version.

14.6 Regular expression character matching

To introduce the REGEXP operator, we will begin by exploring regular expressions that are similar to those used with the LIKE operator. As mentioned in a previous example, we need to retrieve rows from a table while considering the different spellings of the color "gray" (and "grey").

To perform this query, we will use the regex dot character (.) for matching. This character functions similarly to the LIKE underscore wildcard, indicating that any character in that position within the text will be considered a match. For example:

```
SELECT name, description FROM product WHERE description REGEXP 'gr.y';
+-------------------+--------------------------+
| name              | description              |
+-------------------+--------------------------+
| NZXT Mid Tower    | NZXT PC case (grey)      |
| Corsair Full Tower| Corsair PC case (gray)   |
+-------------------+--------------------------+
2 rows in set (0.00 sec)
```

So far, we haven't done anything that couldn't be accomplished using wildcards. However, regular expressions offer capabilities that extend beyond this basic functionality.

14.7 Matching with a group of characters

One limitation of the previous approach is that any letter between 'gr' and 'y' would be considered a match. In reality, we are only interested in words that contain either an 'a' or an 'e' in that position. Regular expressions provide a way to specify a group of acceptable characters for any given position in the match. This is done using square brackets around the permissible characters. For example:

```
SELECT name, description FROM product WHERE description REGEXP 'gr[ae]y';
```

This syntax ensures that only the words 'grey' and 'gray' match the search criteria. There is no limit to the number of characters included within the brackets. For instance:

```
SELECT * FROM product WHERE description REGEXP 'gr[aeiou]y';
```

14.8 Matching character ranges

The syntax for character group matching can be extended to include a range of characters. For instance, instead of specifying a regular expression that covers the letters A through F as [ABCDEF], we can use a hyphen (-) to indicate a range, writing it as [A-F]. Similarly, we can use the range syntax to list products based on model numbers that begin with digits from 1 to 6, for example:

```
SELECT name, description FROM product
WHERE name REGEXP 'Model [1-6]823';
+------------------------+------------------+
| name                   | description      |
+------------------------+------------------+
| Dell XPS Model 4823    | Dell Desktop PC  |
+------------------------+------------------+
1 row in set (0.00 sec)
```

14.9 Handling special characters

Regular expressions give special significance to certain characters. For instance, the dot (.) and square brackets ([]) each have specific meanings. You might be wondering how to handle character sequences that include one or more special characters in your search. Obviously, if you are looking for text that looks like a regular expression, the text you are searching for is, itself, going to be viewed as regular expression syntax.

To address this issue, a concept known as *escaping* is used. In SQL, escaping involves preceding any characters that would be misinterpreted as a regular expression special character with double backslashes (\\).

Let's start by adding a row to our product table and including square brackets in the name field:

```
INSERT INTO product
VALUES(
    NULL,
    'Dell Dock Model [4807]',
    'Dell docking station',
    299.99,
    35
);
```

If we search for this row without regard to the fact that the name value contains special characters, we don't get the results we expect:

```
SELECT name, description FROM product
WHERE name REGEXP 'Model [4807]';
+-----------------------+-----------------+
| name                  | description     |
+-----------------------+-----------------+
| Dell XPS Model 4823   | Dell Desktop PC |
| Dell XPS Model 7823   | Dell Desktop PC |
+-----------------------+-----------------+
2 rows in set (0.00 sec)
```

The issue arises because the regular expression is incorrectly interpreted as a search for entries containing "Model' followed by either the numbers 4, 8, 0, or 7. What we actually intended to find was the text "[4807]." To achieve the desired result, we need to escape the brackets using the \\ escape sequence, as follows:

```
SELECT name, description FROM product
WHERE name REGEXP 'Model \\[4807\\]';
+-----------------------+----------------------+
| name                  | description          |
+-----------------------+----------------------+
| Dell Dock Model [4807] | Dell docking station |
+-----------------------+----------------------+
1 row in set (0.00 sec)
```

14.10 Whitespace metacharacters

Regular expression syntax includes a way to reference whitespace characters such as tabs, carriage returns, and line feeds. These characters are represented in regular expressions using specific *metacharacters*. Table 14-1 outlines the whitespace metacharacters supported by MariaDB:

Metacharacter	Description
\\n	New line (line feed)
\\f	Form feed
\\t	Tab
\\r	Carriage return
\\v	Vertical tab

Table 14-1

For instance, if we want to search for text that contains a tab character using a regular expression, we would do so as follows:

```
SELECT * from product where name REGEXP 'Microsoft Mouse\\tWireless';
```

14.11 Matching by character type

Another valuable technique in regular expressions is matching characters by their type or class. For instance, you may need to specify that a character must be a letter, a number, or an alphanumeric character. This can be achieved using the special class definitions outlined in the table below:

Class Keyword	Description of Matches
[[:alnum:]]	Alphanumeric - any number or letter. Equivalent to [a-z], [A-Z] and [0-9]
[[:alpha:]]	Alpha - any letter. Equivalent to [a-z] and [A-Z]
[[:blank:]]	Space or Tab. Equivalent to [\\t] and [ ]
[[:cntrl:]]	ASCII Control Character
[[:digit:]]	Numeric. Equivalent to [0-9]
[[:graph:]]	Any character with the exception of space
[[:lower:]]	Lower case letters. Equivalent to [a-z]
[[:print:]]	Any printable character
[[:punct:]]	Characters that are neither control characters, nor alphanumeric (i.e., punctuation characters)
[[:space:]]	Any whitespace character (tab, new line, form feed, space etc)
[[:upper:]]	Upper case letters. Equivalent to [A-Z]
[[:xdigit:]]	Any hexadecimal digit. Equivalent to [A-F], [a-f] and [0-9]

Table 14-2

Before we try some type-matching examples, we need to add a few more rows to our product table using the following INSERT statement:

```
INSERT INTO product
VALUES(
    NULL,
    'One2One USB-C Hub',
    '2-port USB hub',
    29.99,
    60
),
(
```

```
        NULL,
        'One4One USB-C Hub',
        'Two 2-port USB hubs',
        29.99,
        60
),
(
        NULL,
        'One&One Touch 200',
        'Touch sensitive touchpad',
        29.99,
        60
);
```

Suppose we want to retrieve a list of USB hub devices from the product table. At first glance, it looks like this might be possible using a single-character match expression:

```
SELECT name, description FROM product
WHERE name REGEXP 'One.One';
+-------------------+---------------------------+
| name              | description               |
+-------------------+---------------------------+
| One2One USB-C Hub | 2-port USB hub            |
| One4One USB-C Hub | Two 2-port USB hubs       |
| One&One Touch 200 | Touch sensitive touchpad  |
+-------------------+---------------------------+
3 rows in set (0.00 sec)
```

As we can see from the results, the search also returned the One&One touchpad. To limit the search to numerical characters in the specified position, we can use the [[:digit:]] character class as follows:

```
SELECT name, description FROM product
WHERE name REGEXP 'One[[:digit:]]One';
+-------------------+---------------------+
| name              | description         |
+-------------------+---------------------+
| One2One USB-C Hub | 2-port USB hub      |
| One4One USB-C Hub | Two 2-port USB hubs |
+-------------------+---------------------+
2 rows in set (0.00 sec)
```

Similarly, we can use the [[:punct:]] class to restrict the results to punctuation characters (which includes the ampersand character):

```
SELECT name, description FROM product
WHERE name REGEXP 'One[[:punct:]]One';
+-------------------+---------------------------+
| name              | description               |
+-------------------+---------------------------+
| One&One Touch 200 | Touch sensitive touchpad  |
+-------------------+---------------------------+
1 row in set (0.00 sec)
```

14.12 Repetition metacharacters

In addition to enabling searches on individual instances, regular expressions can also be written to identify repetition in text using the repetition metacharacters listed in Table 14-3:

Metacharacter	Description
*	Any number of matches
+	One or more matches
{n}	n number of matches
{n,}	Not less than n number of matches
{n1,n2}	A range of matches between n1 and n2
?	Optional single character match (character may be present or not to qualify as match)

Table 14-3

Examples illustrate concepts more effectively than tabular lists. Let's begin by searching for all 3-digit sequences in the name column:

```
SELECT name, description FROM product
WHERE name REGEXP '[[:digit:]]{3}';
+-----------------------+--------------------------+
| name                  | description              |
+-----------------------+--------------------------+
| Dell XPS Model 4823   | Dell Desktop PC          |
| Dell XPS Model 7823   | Dell Desktop PC          |
| Dell Dock Model [4807]| Dell docking station     |
| One&One Touch 200     | Touch sensitive touch pad|
+-----------------------+--------------------------+
4 rows in set (0.00 sec)
```

In the above example, we have indicated that we are looking for any sequence of 3 digits by using the [[:digit:]] {3} regular expression. In this case, we picked up entries with three and four-digit sequences. If we want to limit the result set to four digits, we can use {4,} to exclude sequences with less than four digits:

```
SELECT name, description FROM product
WHERE name REGEXP '[[:digit:]]{4,}';
+-----------------------+----------------------+
| name                  | description          |
+-----------------------+----------------------+
| Dell XPS Model 4823   | Dell Desktop PC      |
| Dell XPS Model 7823   | Dell Desktop PC      |
| Dell Dock Model [4807]| Dell docking station |
+-----------------------+----------------------+
3 rows in set (0.00 sec)
```

Our One&One Touch 200 is no longer listed because it only contains a three-digit sequence.

The '?' metacharacter is particularly useful when we need to allow for plural words. For example, we may want to list product descriptions where the word "hub" or "hubs" is used. To achieve this, we follow the 's' with a '?', thereby making the trailing 's' optional for a match:

```
SELECT name, description FROM product WHERE name REGEXP 'hubs?';
+--------------------+--------------------+
| name               | description        |
```

```
+-------------------+---------------------+
| One2One USB-C Hub | Two port USB hub    |
| One4One USB-C Hub | Two 2-port USB hubs |
+-------------------+---------------------+
2 rows in set (0.01 sec)
```

14.13 Matching by text position

The next area of regular expressions to cover in this chapter involves matching based on the location of text in a string. For example, we may want to find a match that requires a word to appear at the beginning or end of a text string. Once again, this requires the use of some special metacharacters:

Metacharacter	Description
^	Beginning of text
$	End of text
\\b	Word boundary

Table 14-4

For instance, we can look for strings that start with a digit:

```
SELECT name, description FROM product
WHERE description REGEXP '^[[:digit:]]';
+-------------------+----------------+
| name              | description    |
+-------------------+----------------+
| One2One USB-C Hub | 2-port USB hub |
+-------------------+----------------+
1 row in set (0.00 sec)
```

We can also stipulate that character sequences are separate words within a string. For example, if we search for product names containing "air" we get the following result set:

```
SELECT name FROM product WHERE name REGEXP 'air';
+-------------------+
| name              |
+-------------------+
| MacBook Air M3    |
| Corsair Full Tower |
+-------------------+
2 rows in set (0.01 sec)
```

As we can see from the above example, because the word "Corsair" contains "air," we have retrieved more rows than we anticipated. To focus specifically on instances where "air" appears as a standalone word, we can use the word boundary metacharacter (\\b):

```
SELECT name FROM product WHERE name REGEXP '\\bair\\b';
+----------------+
| name           |
+----------------+
| MacBook Air M3 |
+----------------+
1 row in set (0.01 sec)
```

We can also use the end of text character to select names ending with a specific sequence of characters:

```
SELECT name FROM product WHERE name REGEXP 'hub$';
+-------------------+
| name              |
+-------------------+
| One2One USB-C Hub |
| One4One USB-C Hub |
+-------------------+
2 rows in set (0.00 sec)
```

14.14 Replacing text with regular expressions

So far, in this chapter, we have focused on using regular expressions to refine search criteria using the REGEXP operator. Regular expressions can also replace occurrences of text patterns within string values. Replacements are performed using the REGEXP_REPLACE operator, the basic syntax for which is as follows:

```
REGEXP_REPLACE(string, pattern, replacement);
```

The parameters accepted by REGEXP_REPLACE are as follows:

- **string** - The input string where the replacement will occur. This can be a string, or a table column that contains a string value.

- **pattern**: The regular expression pattern to search for.

- **replacement**: The replacement string.

In addition to directly manipulating strings, we can use regular expression replacement to update values in table columns. The following statement, for example, changes all occurrences of "USB-C" to "USB-A" in the product name column:

```
UPDATE product SET name = REGEXP_REPLACE(name ,'USB-C', 'USB-A');
Query OK, 2 rows affected (0.00 sec)
Rows matched: 15  Changed: 2  Warnings: 0
```

After executing the statement, check that "USB-C" has been changed to "USB-A":

```
SELECT name FROM product WHERE name LIKE '%USB%';
+-------------------+
| name              |
+-------------------+
| One2One USB-A Hub |
| One4One USB-A Hub |
+-------------------+
2 rows in set (0.00 sec)
```

14.15 Reference points

The main points covered in this chapter are as follows:

- **Introduction to Wildcards**

    - Wildcards enable flexible string matching in SQL queries.

    - Useful for finding patterns rather than exact matches.

- **Single-Character Wildcard (_)**

    - Matches any single character at a specific position.

- **Multiple-Character Wildcard (%)**
  - Matches any sequence of characters, including none.

- **Regular Expressions (REGEXP)**
  - REGEXP allows for advanced pattern matching beyond wildcards.
  - Offers greater flexibility for text searches and transformations.

- **Character Matching in REGEXP**
  - Regex dot (.) character similar to underscore (_) in `LIKE`.
  - Use [aefg...] to match specific characters, e.g., "gr̲ay" or "gr̲ey."

- **Character Ranges in REGEXP**
  - Use [a-z] or [1-6] to define ranges for matches.

- **Escaping Special Characters**
  - Use \\ to escape special characters like '[' and ']' in text searches.

- **Whitespace Matching with Metacharacters**
  - Match whitespace characters like tabs (\\t) or newlines (\\n).

- **Class-Based Matching in REGEXP**
  - Use character classes like `[[:digit:]]` or `[[:alpha:]]` to match types of characters.

- **Repetition Matching**
  - Use repetition metacharacters like *, +, or {n} for matches.

- **Position-Based Matching**
  - Use ^ to match text at the beginning, $ for the end, and \\b for word boundaries.

- **Combining Wildcards and REGEXP**
  - Wildcards are simpler for basic matches; `REGEXP` is better for complex patterns.

- **String Replacement (REGEXP_REPLACE)**
  - Enables dynamic text replacement in strings or table columns based on regular expression pattern.
  - Provides flexibility in pattern matching and replacements.

- **Basic Syntax of REGEXP_REPLACE**
  - `REGEXP_REPLACE(string, pattern, repl, position, occurrence, type);`
  - Defaults: Position starts at 1, occurrence is 0 (all matches), and match type is case-sensitive unless modified.

15. Understanding Joins and Unions

Up to this point, we have focused on creating a table that contains information about a single category—specifically, the products sold by an online electronics store. However, we would also need to store information about each product's supplier in a real-world scenario. Supplier data might include the supplier's name, address, and telephone number. We would also need to link these suppliers to the products they provide.

In this scenario, we have two options for storing contact information about the supplier. One option is to include the supplier's contact details in each row of the product table for every product sourced from that supplier. While this approach would be functional, it is highly inefficient, as it requires duplicating the supplier's contact information for every product they sell to us. Additionally, if the supplier relocates, we would have to update every row in the product table related to that supplier.

A more effective approach would be to create a separate supplier table that includes the contact information for each supplier. We can then reference this table when we want to retrieve supplier information for a specific product in the product table or list products by supplier. These connections between tables are known as a *joins* and are the foundation of relational databases.

15.1 How joins work

A join operates by leveraging the relationships between keys in different tables. For instance, in the above example, the supplier table includes a column called id, configured as the primary key, and the company name and address, as illustrated in Figure 15-1. (For more details on primary keys, see the chapter on *"The Basics of Databases"*).

	Suppliers
PK	<u>**id int NOT NULL**</u>
	company varchar(25) NOT NULL
	address varchar(40) NOT NULL

Figure 15-1

The product table, however, stores information about our products, such as product ID, name, and description. Additionally, it contains a supplier_id column, which specifies the supplier from which each product is sourced. Since this supplier_id corresponds to a key in another table (the id key in the supplier table), it is known as a *foreign key*:

Products	
PK	**id int NOT NULL**
	name varchar(25)
	description varchar(50)
	price decimal(6,2)
	quantity int
FK	**supplier_id int**

Figure 15-2

When writing a SELECT statement to retrieve data from the product table, we can use this foreign key to link it to the supplier table, extracting supplier information for each product. This approach allows us to combine data from both tables seamlessly, making it easier to analyze the relationships between products and their suppliers:

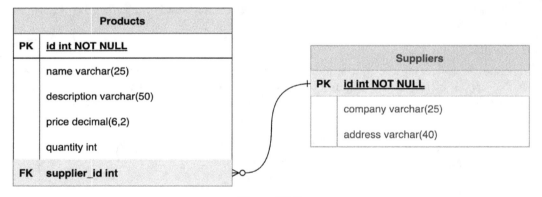

Figure 15-3

15.2 Opening the sample database

This chapter assumes that you have completed the steps in the previous chapters. If you haven't, you can import the current database snapshot using the sample files provided in the *"Start Here"* chapter.

To import the snapshot, open a terminal or command prompt, navigate to the directory containing the sample files, and run the following commands:

```
mariadb-admin -u demo -p drop sampledb
mariadb-admin -u demo -p create sampledb
mariadb -u demo -p sampledb < mariadb_joins.sql
```

Once the database is ready, open the MariaDB client and select the *sampledb* database:

```
USE sampledb
```

15.3 Creating the supplier table

Before exploring table joins in MariaDB, we need to add a table to the *sampledb* database to contain supplier information. Using the MariaDB client, execute the following statement to create the supplier table:

```
CREATE TABLE supplier
(
  id int NOT NULL AUTO_INCREMENT,
  company Varchar(25) NOT NULL,
  address VARCHAR(40) NULL,
  PRIMARY KEY (id)
);
```

After the supplier table has been created, use the following INSERT statement to add some supplier records:

```
INSERT INTO supplier VALUES (
    NULL, 'Apple', 'Cupertino, CA'
),
(
    NULL, 'Dell', 'Round Rock, TX'
),
(
    NULL, 'NZXT', 'City of Industry, CA'
),
(
    NULL, 'Corsair', 'Milpitas, CA'
);
```

15.4 Adding the foreign key to the product table

Our product table currently lacks a column to store the supplier ID reference, so use the following ALTER TABLE statement to add a column named supplier_id:

```
ALTER TABLE product ADD supplier_id INT;
```

Though we have added the supplier_id column, we still need to let MariaDB know that it contains foreign keys. We do this using the FOREIGN KEY and REFERENCES keywords. These keywords enable us to define the new column as a foreign key and specify the corresponding table and column it refers to, thereby establishing a relationship between the product and supplier tables:

```
ALTER TABLE product
ADD FOREIGN KEY(supplier_id)
REFERENCES supplier(id);
```

15.5 Adding key values to supplier_id

The next step is to populate the supplier_id field of each product table row with the corresponding ID from the supplier table. Although the product row count is low enough that we could do this manually, the process would need to be automated for larger datasets. In this case, we use an UPDATE SET statement with the WHERE and LIKE operators to compare the first word of the product.description field (which consistently contains the manufacturer name) with the supplier.company column as follows:

```
UPDATE product
SET supplier_id = (SELECT id FROM supplier
WHERE product.description LIKE CONCAT(supplier.company, '%'));
```

In the statement above, we used the CONCAT() function to combine multiple strings into one string. In this case, the current company name is followed by the '%' wildcard. After the update, check that products with matching suppliers have been assigned the correct supplier id:

```
SELECT description, supplier_id FROM product;
+-----------------------+-------------+
| description           | supplier_id |
+-----------------------+-------------+
| Apple laptop          |           1 |
| Apple laptop          |           1 |
| Apple desktop         |           1 |
| Apple desktop         |           1 |
| Apple iPhone          |           1 |
| Apple iPhone          |           1 |
| Apple desktop         |           1 |
| NZXT PC case (gray)   |           3 |
| Corsair PC case (grey)|           4 |
| Dell desktop          |           2 |
| Dell desktop          |           2 |
| Dell docking station  |           2 |
| One2One touchpad      |        NULL |
| One2One 2-port USB hub|        NULL |
| One2One 4 port USB hub|        NULL |
+-----------------------+-------------+
15 rows in set (0.00 sec)
```

With the table updates completed, we can begin exploring table joins.

15.6 Performing a cross join

When you join two tables using the CROSS JOIN clause, the result set will consist of all possible combinations of rows from both tables. Each row from the first table is paired with every row from the second table. The diagram in Figure 15-4 illustrates this concept:

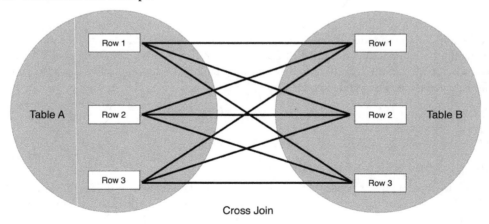

Figure 15-4

The SQL syntax for cross joins is as follows:

```
SELECT <column_names> FROM <table_1> CROSS JOIN <table_2>;
```

A cross join between our product and supplier tables will generate the following output (abbreviated for conciseness):

```
SELECT name, supplier.id from product CROSS JOIN supplier;
+------------------------+----+
| name                   | id |
+------------------------+----+
| MacBook Pro M4 14-in   |  4 |
| MacBook Pro M4 14-in   |  3 |
| MacBook Pro M4 14-in   |  2 |
| MacBook Pro M4 14-in   |  1 |
| MacBook Air M3         |  4 |
| MacBook Air M3         |  3 |
| MacBook Air M3         |  2 |
| MacBook Air M3         |  1 |
| Mac Mini M3            |  4 |
.
.
.
| One2One USB-A Hub      |  2 |
| One2One USB-A Hub      |  1 |
| One4One USB-A Hub      |  4 |
| One4One USB-A Hub      |  3 |
| One4One USB-A Hub      |  2 |
| One4One USB-A Hub      |  1 |
+------------------------+----+
60 rows in set (0.01 sec)
```

Cross joins include all row combinations, including those for which tables are not matched. For example, the USB hub rows are listed in the above result set, even though no corresponding supplier exists for those products.

Note that we have to use what is known as the *fully qualified name* for the supplier id column since both tables contain an id column. A fully qualified column name is defined by specifying the table name followed by a dot (.) and then the column name (i.e., supplier.id).

15.7 Performing an inner join

The inner join combines rows from two or more tables based on comparisons between a specific column in each table, as illustrated in Figure 15-5:

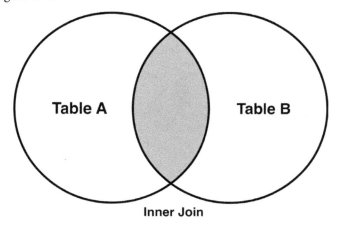

Figure 15-5

We could, for example, use an inner join to select rows from one or more tables that share a common customer phone number. Alternatively, a join could be established to retrieve rows where one table's price column value is less than another's. Inner joins use the following syntax:

```
SELECT <column_names>
 FROM <table_1>
  INNER JOIN <table_2>
   ON <column_1> <comparison_operator> <column_2>
  INNER JOIN <table_3>
   ON <column_3> <comparison_operator> <column_4> .. ;
```

The following statement, for example, retrieves the product name and supplier company from rows where the product.supplier_id and supplier.id columns match:

```
SELECT product.name, supplier.company
FROM product
INNER JOIN supplier
ON product.supplier_id = supplier.id;
+-----------------------+---------+
| name                  | company |
+-----------------------+---------+
| MacBook Pro M4 14-in  | Apple   |
| MacBook Air M3        | Apple   |
| Mac Mini M3           | Apple   |
| Mac Studio            | Apple   |
| iPhone 17 Pro         | Apple   |
| iPhone 17             | Apple   |
| iMac                  | Apple   |
| Dell XPS Model 4823   | Dell    |
| Dell XPS Model 7823   | Dell    |
| Dell Dock Model [4807]| Dell    |
| NZXT Mid Tower        | NZXT    |
| Corsair Full Tower    | Corsair |
+-----------------------+---------+
12 rows in set (0.00 sec)
```

15.8 Performing left joins

A left join retrieves all records from the left table and the matching records from the right table. If no match is found in the right table, the corresponding columns in the result set will contain NULL values, guaranteeing that all rows from the left table are included, regardless of whether a match exists in the right table:

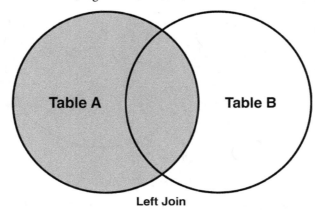

Figure 15-6

Left joins are created using the following syntax:

```
SELECT <column_names>
 FROM <table_1>
  LEFT JOIN <table_2>
   ON <column_1> <comparison_operator> <column_2>;
```

One key difference with LEFT JOIN is that it will include rows from the left table for which there is no match in the right table. For example, suppose we have rows in our product table for which there is no matching supplier in the supplier table. For example, when we run the following SELECT statement, the rows will still be displayed, but with NULL values for the supplier columns where no supplier exists:

```
SELECT product.name, supplier.company
FROM product
LEFT JOIN supplier
ON product.supplier_id = supplier.id;
+------------------------+---------+
| name                   | company |
+------------------------+---------+
| MacBook Pro M4 14-in   | Apple   |
| MacBook Air M3         | Apple   |
| Mac Mini M3            | Apple   |
| Mac Studio             | Apple   |
.
.
.
| Dell Dock Model [4807] | Dell    |
| One&One Touch 200      | NULL    |
| One2One USB-A Hub      | NULL    |
| One4One USB-A Hub      | NULL    |
+------------------------+---------+
15 rows in set (0.00 sec)
```

15.9 Performing right joins

As the name suggests, a right join achieves the opposite result of a left join. With a right join, all the rows from the second table (in this case, the supplier table) are included in the result set, regardless of any matching entries in the product table. If a supplier does not have any associated products in the product table, the corresponding columns from the product table will contain NULL values:

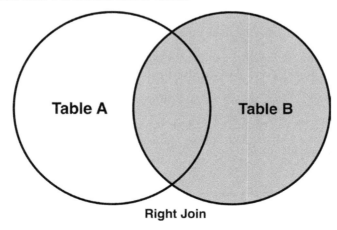

Right Join

Figure 15-7

Right joins are formed using the following syntax:

```
SELECT <column_names>
  FROM <table_1>
   RIGHT JOIN <table_2>
    ON <column_1> <comparison_operator> <column_2>;
```

15.10 Understanding WHERE in join statements

The WHERE keyword allows us to narrow the results of table joins based on specific filtering criteria. Say, for example, that we want to list only products supplied by Dell. To do so, we would create a right join using the following statement:

```
SELECT product.name, supplier.company
FROM product
RIGHT JOIN supplier
ON product.supplier_id = supplier.id
WHERE company = 'Dell';
+------------------------+---------+
| name                   | company |
+------------------------+---------+
| Dell XPS Model 4823    | Dell    |
| Dell XPS Model 7823    | Dell    |
| Dell Dock Model [4807] | Dell    |
+------------------------+---------+
3 rows in set (0.00 sec)
```

15.11 Working with unions

Although it is not considered a join, the UNION operator is a valuable tool for combining the results of multiple tables. As we will see later, it can also merge join statements. A UNION combines the result sets from two or more SELECT queries and follows this syntax:

```
SELECT <column_names> FROM <table_1>
  UNION
   SELECT <column_names> FROM <table_2>;
UNION
  SELECT ... ;
```

When using the UNION operator, there are several rules to follow:

- Each SELECT statement must return the same number of columns.

- The data types of the columns in the corresponding positions of each SELECT statement must be compatible. For example, you cannot mix INT and VARCHAR types in the same column position.

- The column names in each SELECT statement must be presented in the same order.

By default, the UNION operator will eliminate duplicate rows from the combined result set. If you want to keep duplicate rows, you can use the UNION ALL operator instead:

```
SELECT <column_names> FROM <table_1>
  UNION ALL
   SELECT <column_names> FROM <table_2> ... ;
```

To demonstrate unions, we will add a second supplier table to our sample database containing information about European suppliers. We will then create a union to retrieve the supplier addresses from both tables. This scenario is illustrated in Figure 15-8:

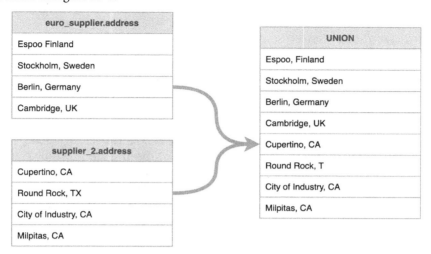

Figure 15-8

Start by adding the European supplier table to the sampledb database:

```
CREATE TABLE euro_supplier
(
   id int NOT NULL AUTO_INCREMENT,
   company Varchar(25) NOT NULL,
   address VARCHAR(40) NULL,
   PRIMARY KEY (id)
);
```

Next, insert four supplier rows into the euro_supplier table:

```
INSERT INTO euro_supplier VALUES (
   NULL, 'Nokia', 'Espoo, Finland'
),
(
   NULL, 'Ericsson', 'Stockholm, Sweden'
),
(
   NULL, 'Siemens', 'Berlin, Germany'
),
(
   NULL, 'ARM', 'Cambridge, UK'
);
```

Now that we have two supplier tables, we can use the SELECT statement and the UNION operator to retrieve supplier addresses from both tables:

```
SELECT address FROM euro_supplier
UNION SELECT address FROM supplier;
+----------------------+
| address              |
+----------------------+
| Espoo, Finland       |
| Stockholm, Sweden    |
```

```
| Berlin, Germany      |
| Cambridge, UK        |
| Cupertino, CA        |
| Round Rock, TX       |
| City of Industry, CA |
| Milpitas, CA         |
+----------------------+
8 rows in set (0.08 sec)
```

15.12 Full outer joins in MariaDB

A full outer join, also known as a full join, combines the results of both left and right joins. It returns all rows from both tables being joined, even if there are no matching rows. The diagram below illustrates this concept:

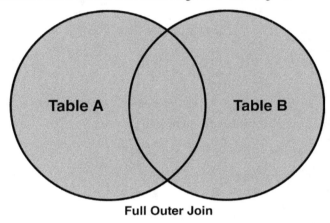

Full Outer Join

Figure 15-9

Unlike some other SQL implementations, MariaDB does not support FULL OUTER JOIN or FULL JOIN clauses. However, we can achieve the same results by creating a union of a left join and a right join using the following syntax:

```
SELECT <column_names> FROM <table_1>
LEFT JOIN <table_2> ON <column_1> <comparison_operator> <column_2>
UNION
SELECT <column_names> FROM <table_1>
 RIGHT JOIN <table_2> ON <column_1> <comparison_operator> <column_2>;
```

In previous examples, we have observed that some items in the product table do not have corresponding suppliers. To illustrate the impact of missing matches in both tables, we will also add a company to the supplier table for which there are no entries in the product table:

```
INSERT INTO supplier VALUES (NULL, 'Nvidia', 'Santa Clara, CA');
Query OK, 1 row affected (0.03 sec)
```

We can now use a full outer join to list products and corresponding supplier names using the following statement:

```
SELECT product.name, supplier.company FROM product
LEFT JOIN supplier
ON product.supplier_id = supplier.id
UNION
SELECT product.name, supplier.company FROM product
RIGHT JOIN supplier
```

```
ON product.supplier_id = supplier.id;
+------------------------+---------+
| name                   | company |
+------------------------+---------+
| MacBook Pro M4 14-in   | Apple   |
| MacBook Air M3         | Apple   |
| Mac Mini M3            | Apple   |
| Mac Studio             | Apple   |
| iPhone 17 Pro          | Apple   |
| iPhone 17              | Apple   |
| iMac                   | Apple   |
| NZXT Mid Tower         | NZXT    |
| Corsair Full Tower     | Corsair |
| Dell Model 4823        | Dell    |
| Dell XPS Model 7823    | Dell    |
| Dell Dock Model [4807] | Dell    |
| One&One Touch 200      | NULL    |
| One2One USB-A Hub      | NULL    |
| One4One USB-A Hub      | NULL    |
| NULL                   | Nvidia  |
+------------------------+---------+
16 rows in set (0.04 sec)
```

The result set above displays all products and suppliers, substituting a NULL value when there is no match between the two tables. To replace NULL with a more descriptive value, we can use the COALESCE() function. This function returns the first non-NULL value from a provided list of values. For example, the following call to the function will return the supplier's company name if it is not NULL; if it is NULL, it will return the word 'Unknown':

```
COALESCE(supplier.company, 'Unknown')
```

Modify the original statement to handle NULL values for product and company names and provide an alias for the product name column:

```
SELECT product.name, COALESCE(supplier.company, 'Unknown')
AS company
FROM product
LEFT JOIN supplier ON product.supplier_id = supplier.id
UNION
SELECT COALESCE(product.name, 'No product'), supplier.company
FROM product
RIGHT JOIN supplier ON product.supplier_id = supplier.id;
+------------------------+---------+
| name                   | company |
+------------------------+---------+
| MacBook Pro M4 14-in   | Apple   |
| MacBook Air M3         | Apple   |
| Mac Mini M3            | Apple   |
| Mac Studio             | Apple   |
| iPhone 17 Pro          | Apple   |
| iPhone 17              | Apple   |
| iMac                   | Apple   |
| NZXT Mid Tower         | NZXT    |
| Corsair Full Tower     | Corsair |
| Dell Model 4823        | Dell    |
```

```
| Dell XPS Model 7823    | Dell     |
| Dell Dock Model [4807] | Dell     |
| One&One Touch 200      | Unknown  |
| One2One USB-A Hub      | Unknown  |
| One4One USB-A Hub      | Unknown  |
| No product             | Nvidia   |
+------------------------+----------+
16 rows in set (0.01 sec)
```

15.13 Reference points

The main points covered in this chapter are as follows:

- **Introduction to Joins**

  - Joins enable relationships between tables.

  - Foreign keys connect rows in different tables, linking a primary key in one table to a column in another.

  - The FOREIGN KEY constraint establishes relationships between tables.

- **Cross Join**

  - Produces all possible combinations of rows from two tables.

  - Useful for exploratory analysis but inefficient for practical queries.

- **Inner Join**

  - Combines rows from two tables based on matching values in specified columns.

  - Returns only rows with matches in both tables.

- **Left Join**

  - Returns all rows from the left table and matching rows from the right table.

  - Unmatched rows in the right table are filled with NULL.

- **Right Join**

  - Returns all rows from the right table and matching rows from the left table.

  - Unmatched rows in the left table are filled with NULL.

- **Union Operator**

  - Combines result sets from multiple SELECT queries into a single set.

  - The number and order of columns must match in all queries.

  - Data types must be compatible.

  - UNION ALL retains duplicate rows, whereas UNION eliminates them.

- **Full Outer Join Simulation**

  - MariaDB does not natively support FULL OUTER JOIN.

  - Achieved by combining LEFT JOIN and RIGHT JOIN with UNION.

- Includes all rows from both tables, with unmatched rows filled with NULL.

- Use the COALESCE() function to replace NULL values with default or descriptive placeholders.

- **Populating Foreign Keys**

  - Use UPDATE with subqueries and string functions like CONCAT() to link rows across tables.

16. An Introduction to MariaDB Views

When we execute a SELECT query, the MariaDB server returns a result set that meets the specified search criteria. These results can be used in various ways, such as displaying them to users within an application or as input for further operations like updates or insertions.

In this chapter, we will explore views in MariaDB, which provide another way to interact with the results of SELECT queries.

16.1 An introduction to MariaDB views

MariaDB views allow us to create reusable virtual tables from SELECT queries. Once created, we can search, update, and modify result sets by referencing the view, just as we would with any other table, rather than repeating the associated SELECT statement.

For example, consider two tables named *customer* and *order*, as illustrated in Figure 16-1 below:

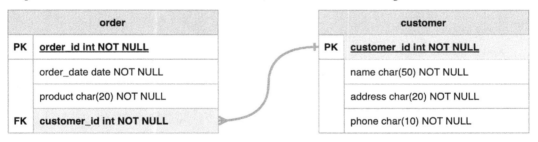

Figure 16-1

To retrieve a result set matching customers with their orders, we can use the following SELECT statement:

```
SELECT order.date, order.product, customer.name
FROM order
INNER JOIN customer
ON order.customer_id = customer.id;
```

The result set from the above query will include order dates, products, and the corresponding customer names. Typically, we would need to execute this statement each time we want to obtain the same results. Instead, we can create a view that includes these three columns, allowing us to reference the result set as if it were a database table.

To create a view in MariaDB, we use the CREATE VIEW statement. The syntax for this is as follows:

```
CREATE VIEW <table_name> AS SELECT <conditions>;
```

To create a view called *customer_orders* from the previous customer order query, we would use the following CREATE VIEW statement:

```
CREATE VIEW customer_orders
```

```
AS SELECT order.date, order.product, customer.name
FROM order
INNER JOIN customer
ON order.customer_id = customer.id;
```

The diagram in Figure 16-2 illustrates the relationship between the two tables and the view:

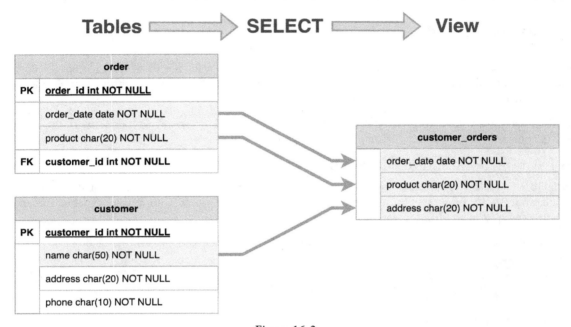

Figure 16-2

Once created, the view's result set updates automatically whenever accessed and can, with a few exceptions, be treated like an ordinary database table.

16.2 Opening the sample database

This chapter assumes that you have completed the steps in the previous chapters. If you haven't, you can import the current database snapshot using the sample files provided in the *"Start Here"* chapter.

To import the snapshot, open a terminal or command prompt, navigate to the directory containing the sample files, and run the following commands:

```
mariadb-admin -u demo -p drop sampledb
mariadb-admin -u demo -p create sampledb
mariadb -u demo -p sampledb < mariadb_views.sql
```

Once the database is ready, open the MariaDB client and select the *sampledb* database:

```
USE sampledb
```

16.3 Creating a basic view

The simplest type of view pulls data from a single table. For instance, you may have a standard SELECT statement that formats data from a table in a specific way. The following SELECT statement, for example, retrieves supplier data with some additional formatting:

```
SELECT CONCAT(UPPER(company), ' - ', address) FROM supplier;
+---------------------------------------+
| CONCAT(UPPER(company), ' - ', address) |
+---------------------------------------+
| APPLE - Cupertino, CA                 |
| DELL - Round Rock, TX                 |
| NZXT - City of Industry, CA           |
| CORSAIR - Milpitas, CA                |
| NVIDIA - Santa Clara, CA              |
+---------------------------------------+
5 rows in set (0.00 sec)
```

If we want to repeat this selection, we could re-enter the same SELECT statement each time. However, a more efficient approach would be to create a virtual table based on this SELECT statement. This would allow us to reference it by name, just like any other table, without needing to retype the lengthy query. We can accomplish this by using views.

For instance, we can create a view called *supplier_summary* using the SELECT statement from before:

```
CREATE VIEW supplier_summary
AS SELECT CONCAT(UPPER(company), ' - ', address) FROM supplier;
```

We have now created a virtual table from our SELECT statement, which we can reference in other SELECT statements:

```
SELECT * FROM supplier_summary;
+---------------------------------------+
| CONCAT(UPPER(company), ' - ', address) |
+---------------------------------------+
| APPLE - Cupertino, CA                 |
| DELL - Round Rock, TX                 |
| NZXT - City of Industry, CA           |
| CORSAIR - Milpitas, CA                |
| NVIDIA - Santa Clara, CA              |
+---------------------------------------+
5 rows in set (0.01 sec)
```

Similarly, we could create a view comprising all the desktop computers in the *product* table listed alphabetically:

```
CREATE VIEW desktop_computers
AS SELECT name FROM product
WHERE description LIKE '%desktop%' ORDER BY name;
```

A query of the *desktop_computers* view will generate the following result set:

```
SELECT * FROM desktop_computers;
+-------------------+
| name              |
+-------------------+
| Dell Model 4823   |
| Dell XPS Model 7823 |
| iMac              |
| Mac Mini M3       |
| Mac Studio        |
+-------------------+
5 rows in set (0.00 sec)
```

Views offer similar querying capabilities to those of tables. For instance, we can use SELECT to display only Mac-based desktop computers, as demonstrated below:

```
SELECT * FROM desktop_computers WHERE name LIKE '%Mac%';
+-------------+
| name        |
+-------------+
| iMac        |
| Mac Mini M3 |
| Mac Studio  |
+-------------+
3 rows in set (0.01 sec)
```

16.4 Joins and views

In the *"Understanding Joins and Unions"* chapter, we learned how to create a join between two tables to extract data from both. By crafting a SELECT statement that joined the tables, we matched the supplier ID column in each table to identify corresponding rows. This join allowed us to display product details from the product table alongside the related supplier information from the supplier table. The statement below utilizes an inner join to list the product names and supplier companies for products manufactured by Apple:

```
SELECT product.name, supplier.company
FROM product
INNER JOIN supplier
ON product.supplier_id = supplier.id
WHERE supplier.company = 'Apple';
+----------------------+---------+
| name                 | company |
+----------------------+---------+
| MacBook Pro M4 14-in | Apple   |
| MacBook Air M3       | Apple   |
| Mac Mini M3          | Apple   |
| Mac Studio           | Apple   |
| iPhone 17 Pro        | Apple   |
| iPhone 17            | Apple   |
| iMac                 | Apple   |
+----------------------+---------+
7 rows in set (0.00 sec)
```

We can create a virtual table using the CREATE VIEW statement based on a join operation, similar to how we created a view from a single SELECT statement:

```
CREATE VIEW join_demo
AS SELECT product.name, supplier.company
FROM product
INNER JOIN supplier
ON product.supplier_id = supplier.id
WHERE supplier.company = 'Apple';

SELECT * FROM join_demo;
+----------------------+---------+
| name                 | company |
+----------------------+---------+
| MacBook Pro M4 14-in | Apple   |
| MacBook Air M3       | Apple   |
| Mac Mini M3          | Apple   |
```

```
| Mac Studio           | Apple   |
| iPhone 17 Pro        | Apple   |
| iPhone 17            | Apple   |
| iMac                 | Apple   |
+----------------------+---------+
7 rows in set (0.00 sec)
```

16.5 Updating view-based tables

In some cases, a view can be used to update the tables it references, allowing operations such as INSERT, UPDATE, and DELETE to be performed. To demonstrate this, use the following SQL statement to create a view named simpleview that lists companies based in California from the supplier table:

```
CREATE VIEW simpleview
AS SELECT company, address FROM supplier
WHERE address LIKE '%CA';
```

```
SELECT * FROM simpleview;
+---------+----------------------+
| company | address              |
+---------+----------------------+
| Apple   | Cupertino, CA        |
| NZXT    | City of Industry, CA |
| Corsair | Milpitas, CA         |
| Nvidia  | Santa Clara, CA      |
+---------+----------------------+
5 rows in set (0.01 sec)
```

The simplicity of simpleview allows us to update the underlying supplier table without restrictions. For instance, we can use the following INSERT statement to add a supplier:

```
INSERT INTO simpleview VALUES ('Intel', 'Palo Alto, CA');
```

If we check the product table, we can see that the new supplier was added via the view:

```
SELECT * FROM simpleview;
+---------+----------------------+
| company | address              |
+---------+----------------------+
| Apple   | Cupertino, CA        |
| NZXT    | City of Industry, CA |
| Corsair | Milpitas, CA         |
| Nvidia  | Santa Clara, CA      |
| Intel   | Palo Alto, CA        |
+---------+----------------------+
5 rows in set (0.00 sec)
```

Update operations can also be performed using simpleview, for example:

```
UPDATE simpleview
SET address='Santa Clara, CA'
WHERE company='Intel';
```

We can also refer to the view when deleting rows from the underlying table:

```
DELETE FROM simpleview WHERE company='Intel';
```

An Introduction to MariaDB Views

The results can sometimes be confusing when using a view to update an underlying table. For example, use the following INSERT statement to add another supplier row:

```
INSERT INTO simpleview VALUES ('Silicon Labs', 'Austin, TX');
```

Next, confirm that the 'Silicon Labs' row appears in the supplier table:

```
SELECT * FROM supplier;
+----+--------------+----------------------+
| id | company      | address              |
+----+--------------+----------------------+
|  1 | Apple        | Cupertino, CA        |
|  2 | Dell         | Round Rock, TX       |
|  3 | NZXT         | City of Industry, CA |
|  4 | Corsair      | Milpitas, CA         |
|  5 | Nvidia       | Santa Clara, CA      |
|  7 | Silicon Labs | Austin, TX           |
+----+--------------+----------------------+
6 rows in set (0.00 sec)
```

The unexpected behavior occurs when we try to remove Silicon Labs from the supplier table using the DELETE statement on simpleview:

```
DELETE FROM simpleview WHERE company='Silicon Labs';
```

In theory, Silicon Labs should no longer exist in the supplier table. When we look, however, we find that not to be the case:

```
SELECT * FROM supplier;
+----+--------------+----------------------+
| id | company      | address              |
+----+--------------+----------------------+
|  1 | Apple        | Cupertino, CA        |
|  2 | Dell         | Round Rock, TX       |
|  3 | NZXT         | City of Industry, CA |
|  4 | Corsair      | Milpitas, CA         |
|  5 | Nvidia       | Santa Clara, CA      |
|  7 | Silicon Labs | Austin, TX           |
+----+--------------+----------------------+
6 rows in set (0.00 sec)
```

The issue is that Silicon Labs is located in Texas, while the records from simpleview only include companies based in California. When we try to delete the Silicon Labs row, the DELETE operation searches the company column of the simpleview result set, finds no matching rows, and concludes there is nothing to delete. This leaves the Silicon Labs row intact in the supplier table.

Essentially, inserting rows into a view does not guarantee they will appear in the result set. Instead, we must execute the deletion directly on the supplier table to remove Silicon Labs:

```
DELETE FROM supplier WHERE company='Silicon Labs';
```

One limitation of view-based table updates is that we can only reference columns that exist within the context of the view. For example, consider our desktop_computers view, which only includes the product.name column. When we attempt to add a new row, we can only provide a value for the product name. We will encounter an error if we try to reference other columns, such as the description field:

```
INSERT INTO desktop_computers (name, description)
VALUES ('Mac Mini M4', 'Apple desktop');
ERROR 1054 (42S22): Unknown column 'description' in 'field list'
```

We can, however, add the row if we only provide the name value:

```
INSERT INTO desktop_computers VALUES ('Mac Mini M4');
```

If we inspect the new row, we see that the other fields, except the auto-incremented id have been set to NULL:

```
SELECT * FROM product WHERE name='Mac Mini M4';
+----+-------------+-------------+-------+----------+-------------+
| id | name        | description | price | quantity | supplier_id |
+----+-------------+-------------+-------+----------+-------------+
| 22 | Mac Mini M4 | NULL        | NULL  | NULL     | NULL        |
+----+-------------+-------------+-------+----------+-------------+
1 row in set (0.00 sec)
```

This type of update is only possible if the table columns outside the view have been assigned a default value or can store null values. To demonstrate this requirement, delete the 'Mac Mini M4' row and modify the product table to disallow null values in the description column:

```
DELETE from product WHERE name='Mac Mini M4';
```

```
ALTER TABLE product MODIFY description varchar(50) NOT NULL;
```

Next, attempt to re-insert the 'Mac Mini M4' product row:

```
INSERT INTO desktop_computers VALUES ('Mac Mini M4');
ERROR 1423 (HY000): Field of view 'sampledb.desktop_computers' underlying table
doesn't have a default value
```

Inserting the row is no longer possible because the description field cannot store null, and no default value has been configured.

MariaDB also does not support view-based updates for columns derived from aggregate functions. We cannot, therefore, update our supplier table using the supplier_summary view because the CONCAT() function was used within the original CREATE VIEW statement:

```
INSERT INTO supplier_summary VALUES ('HP', 'Palo Alto, CA');
ERROR 1471 (HY000): The target table supplier_summary of the INSERT is not
insertable-into
```

Before continuing, revert the description column to a nullable state:

```
ALTER TABLE product MODIFY description varchar(50) NULL;
```

16.6 Updating join-based views

Views based on joins can also be updated, though only inner joins are supported by MariaDB. For example, we can change the product name field for the iMac row via the join_demo view as follows:

```
UPDATE join_demo SET name='iMac M2' WHERE name='iMac';
```

Rows can also be inserted into views based on joins, but the same restrictions that apply to other view updates must be followed. Specifically, only the columns in the view can be referenced, and all other columns must either have default values or be nullable. Additionally, only one underlying table can be updated at a time when working with a join view. For instance, if we want to insert rows into the product and supplier tables using the join_demo view, we need to use separate INSERT statements for each table:

```
UPDATE join_demo SET name='iMac' WHERE name='iMac M2';

INSERT INTO join_demo (name) VALUES ('iMac Classic');

INSERT INTO join_demo (company) VALUES ('Cisco');
```

Note that we must specify the column names when inserting values. For this reason, a view cannot contain duplicate column names.

Execute the following statements to revert the product and supplier tables to their original state:

```
DELETE FROM product WHERE name = 'iMac Classic';

DELETE FROM supplier WHERE company = 'Cisco';
```

16.7 Altering existing views

The structure of an existing view can be changed by providing a new SELECT query to the ALTER TABLE statement. For example, the statement below expands the scope of our desktop_computers view to include the product description column:

```
ALTER VIEW desktop_computers
AS SELECT name, description FROM product
WHERE description LIKE '%desktop%' ORDER BY name;

SELECT * FROM desktop_computers;
+---------------------+---------------+
| name                | description   |
+---------------------+---------------+
| Dell Model 4823     | Dell desktop  |
| Dell XPS Model 7823 | Dell desktop  |
| iMac                | Apple desktop |
| Mac Mini M3         | Apple desktop |
| Mac Studio          | Apple desktop |
+---------------------+---------------+
5 rows in set (0.00 sec)
```

16.8 Deleting and replacing views

To remove an existing view from a database, use the DROP VIEW statement. Execute the following statements to delete the views created in this chapter:

```
DROP VIEW simpleview;
DROP VIEW supplier_summary;
DROP VIEW desktop_computers;
```

Alternatively, a view may be replaced using either the CREATE OR REPLACE VIEW statement combined with a SELECT query:

```
CREATE OR REPLACE VIEW <view_name> AS SELECT <conditions>;
```

The above statement will either replace or create the specified view depending on whether the view already exists.

16.9 Reference points

The main points covered in this chapter are as follows:

- **Definition of Views**

  - A view is a virtual table created by encapsulating a `SELECT` query.

  - Views enable reusable queries, making it easier to reference complex queries as if they were tables.

- **Creating Views**

  - Use the `CREATE VIEW` statement with a `SELECT` query.

  - Views can be created to represent a specific subset or transformation of data from one or more tables.

  - Views can include operations such as filtering, joining, and formatting data.

- **Querying Views**

  - Treat views like regular tables in `SELECT` statements.

  - Views behave like regular tables and can be queried to retrieve data.

  - Views update dynamically, reflecting changes in the underlying tables.

- **Using Views with Joins**

  - Views can be created based on join operations to combine data from multiple tables.

- **Updating Tables via Views**

  - Updates (`INSERT`, `UPDATE`, `DELETE`) can be performed on views under certain conditions:

  - The view must reference updatable columns.

  - Columns outside the view must have default values or allow NULLs.

  - Aggregate or derived columns are not updatable.

- **Limitations of Updates via Views**

  - Cannot modify aggregate or computed columns.

  - Updates on views with restrictive filters may behave unexpectedly.

  - Views based on joins can only update one table at a time.

- **Altering Views**

  - Modify an existing view using `ALTER VIEW`.

  - Views can be modified to change their structure or logic without altering the underlying tables

  - If a view already exists, it can be replaced with a new definition.

- **Replacing Views**

  - Use `CREATE OR REPLACE VIEW` to update an existing view or create a new one if it doesn't exist:

- **Deleting Views**

- Remove a view using the `DROP VIEW` statement:

Chapter 17

17. Understanding MariaDB Indexes

A lot happens behind the scenes of the MariaDB server to ensure that data retrieval requests are handled quickly and efficiently. Maintaining this high-performance level becomes increasingly critical as databases grow in size and complexity. Simply put, the more data that needs to be searched, the longer it can take MariaDB to find what it is looking for. In this chapter, we will introduce MariaDB indexes and explain how they are used to maintain and improve database performance. We will also look at the limitations of indexes and explain why indexes can sometimes be too much of a good thing.

17.1 Understanding MariaDB indexes

Much like a book index helps you find specific content without reading every page, database indexes allow MariaDB to quickly fulfill retrieval requests without searching an entire table for matching rows. In addition to improving database performance, indexes control whether a column can contain duplicate values.

Indexes can be declared when a table is created or added to existing tables, and each index entry comprises the values of one or more columns within the indexed table.

MariaDB supports several index types, each of which will be explained before we look at some examples.

17.2 Primary index

We have already been using primary indexes in many of the book examples so far. Primary indexes are automatically created when a PRIMARY KEY constraint is declared and ensure that indexed column values are unique and non-null. As discussed in the *"Creating Databases and Tables"* chapter, a primary key can be based on a single column or a combination of table columns, for example:

```
CREATE TABLE customer
(
  id INT NOT NULL AUTO_INCREMENT,
  name char(30) NOT NULL,
  address VARCHAR(60) NULL,
  email VARCHAR(25) NOT NULL,
  PRIMARY KEY (id, name)
);
```

17.3 Unique index

Like primary indexes, unique indexes ensure that the values in indexed columns are unique. Unique indexes differ, however, in that the indexed columns can store null values. The syntax to declare a unique index when creating a table is as follows:

```
CREATE TABLE <table_name>
(
    <column_1> <type>,
    <column_2> <type>,
  .
  .

    UNIQUE INDEX <index_name> (<column_name>),
  .
```

123

```
    .
  );
```

Use the CREATE UNIQUE INDEX statement with the following syntax to add a unique index to a table:

```
CREATE UNIQUE INDEX <index_name> ON <table_name>(<column_name>);
```

The following statement, for example, adds a unique index to the address column of the customer table:

```
CREATE UNIQUE INDEX idx_address ON customer(address);
```

Once the index has been created, only rows with unique or null address values can be added to the table.

17.4 Regular index

A regular index (also known as a secondary or non-unique index) improves the performance of queries involving the indexed column but does not enforce the uniqueness of the column's values. The syntax for adding a regular index during table creation is as follows:

```
CREATE TABLE <table_name>
(
    <column_1> <type>,
    <column_2> <type>,
    .
    .


    INDEX <index_name> (<column_name>),
    .
    .
);
```

Regular indexes are added to existing tables using the CREATE INDEX statement as follows:

```
CREATE INDEX <index_name> ON <table_name>(<column_name>);
```

17.5 Full-text indexes

A full-text index is used for improved text searching performance and can be included at table creation using the following syntax:

```
CREATE FULLTEXT INDEX <index_name> ON <table_name>(<column_name>);
```

Full-text indexes are optimized for operations like searching for words or phrases in text-heavy fields using the MATCH and AGAINST keywords, for example:

```
SELECT <column_1>, <column_2>
FROM <table_name>
WHERE MATCH(<column_name>[, ...]) AGAINST ('<search_string>' [<search_mode>]);
```

The AGAINST keyword is used exclusively for searching in columns with a full-text index and can search for words, phrases, or patterns in natural language or boolean mode. Searches performed using AGAINST return a relevance score for each row ranked on how well the content matches the search text and the frequency with which matches occurred. The following is an example of a natural language search using the AGAINST keyword:

```
SELECT *
FROM manuscript
WHERE MATCH(subtitle, body_text) AGAINST ('quantum coherence');
```

Boolean mode searches can include logical operators such as +, -, <, and > to fine-tune the search criteria, such as excluding matches that contain certain words. The following search uses AGAINST in boolean mode to include the rows containing the term "Linux" in the results but excludes those containing "macOS":

```
SELECT *
FROM manuscript
WHERE MATCH(subtitle, body_text) AGAINST ('+Linux -macOS' IN BOOLEAN MODE);
```

Queries can also be extended to include terms related to the search pattern using the WITH QUERY EXPANSION clause, for example:

```
SELECT *
FROM manuscript
WHERE MATCH(subtitle, body_text)
AGAINST ('quantum computing' WITH QUERY EXPANSION);
```

Full-text indexes are intended for text-heavy fields and should be avoided for short or repetitive text-based data.

17.6 Composite index

Composite indexes comprise two or more columns and improve performance for queries involving multiple columns. All index types covered so far in this chapter support composite columns. The following syntax is used when creating a composite index during table creation:

```
CREATE TABLE <table_name>
(
    <column_1> <type>,
    <column_2> <type>,
.
.

    <index_type> <index_name> (<column_1>, <column_2>, ...),
.
.
);
```

Composite indexes can also be applied to existing tables using the syntax below:

```
CREATE <index_type> <index_name> ON <table_name>(<column_1>, <column_2> ... );
```

Use the following statement to create a composite regular index for the customer table based on the name and email columns:

```
CREATE INDEX idx_composite ON customer(name, email);
```

A composite unique index ensures that the combination of values across multiple columns is unique. In other words, while individual columns in the composite index can have duplicate values, the combination of values across all the indexed columns must be unique.

When creating composite indexes, the order in which the indexed columns are declared can impact query performance. As a general rule, the column names should be ordered from high to low based on the frequency with which they are included in query requests. For instance, if searches are more likely to be performed based on the customer's email address than their name, the above index should be created as follows:

```
CREATE INDEX idx_composite ON customer(email, name);
```

17.7 Spatial index

A spatial index is used to index spatial data types, such as geographic information, and is supported only on tables using the InnoDB or MyISAM storage engines. Spatial indexes are typically used for specialized data such as map coordinates, positions of polygon vertices, or line start and end points using the POLYGON() and LINESTRING() functions, respectively.

Spatial indexes are declared using a syntax similar to previous indexes:

```
CREATE TABLE <table_name>
(
    <column_1> <type>,
    <column_2> <type>,
.
.

    SPATIAL INDEX <index_name> (<column_name>),
.
.
.
);
```

The example below generates a spacial index while creating a table:

```
CREATE TABLE poly (
    id INT AUTO_INCREMENT PRIMARY KEY,
    zone_name VARCHAR(100),
    area POLYGON NOT NULL,
    SPATIAL INDEX (area)
);
```

Alternatively, use the syntax below to add a spatial index to an existing table:

```
CREATE SPATIAL INDEX <index_name> ON <table_name>(<column_name>);
```

Unlike the other index types, it is not possible to create composite spacial indexes.

17.8 Getting index details

Information about the indexes associated with a table is accessed using the SHOW INDEX statement and referencing the table name. Run the following statement to generate a list of indexes associated with the customer table:

```
SHOW INDEX FROM customer\G
```

The output from the SHOW INDEX statement will include a row for each index similar to the one below:

```
*************************** 3. row ***************************
        Table: customer
   Non_unique: 0
     Key_name: idx_address
 Seq_in_index: 1
  Column_name: address
    Collation: A
  Cardinality: 0
     Sub_part: NULL
       Packed: NULL
         Null: YES
```

```
    Index_type: BTREE
       Comment:
 Index_comment:
       Visible: YES
    Expression: NULL
```

Table 17-1 describes the columns contained within the SHOW INDEX output:

Column	Description
Non_unique	Indicates whether the index allows duplicate values (0 for unique indexes, 1 for non-unique indexes).
Key_name	The name of the index.
Seq_in_index	The sequence number of the column in the index (used in composite indexes).
Column_name	The name of the column included in the index.
Collation	How the column is sorted in the index (A for ascending, NULL for no sorting).
Cardinality	An estimate of the number of unique values in the index.
Sub_part	If the index is on a prefix of the column, this indicates the number of indexed characters. NULL if the entire column is indexed.
Packed	Indicates whether the index is compressed. NULL if not.
Null	Specifies whether the indexed column can contain NULL values.
Index_type	The type of index (e.g., BTREE, FULLTEXT, or HASH).
Comment	Additional information about the index.

Table 17-1

17.9 Deleting indexes

To remove an index, use the DROP INDEX statement:

```
DROP INDEX idx_address ON customer;
```

17.10 Limitations of indexes

The old saying that nothing in life is free also applies to database indexes. While indexes can improve database query performance when used correctly, some drawbacks must be considered.

Like most server data, indexes take up disk space. As the number and size of the indexes in a database grow, they will consume increasing amounts of disk space. In a world where most servers are hosted in the cloud and storage is charged by the Gigabyte, consideration needs to be given to the potential costs of indexing large tables.

Additionally, while indexes can improve the performance of database queries, they can have the opposite effect on INSERT, UPDATE, or DELETE operations. Each time a table is updated, those changes must be reflected in the corresponding indexes. For example, adding or modifying a row in a table with multiple indexes requires MariaDB to update each index, reducing overall database performance.

Although indexes are useful tools for improving database performance, they require planning, management, and monitoring to ensure optimal results.

17.11 Reference points

The main points covered in this chapter are as follows:

Understanding MariaDB Indexes

- **Overview**
  - Indexes enhance MariaDB query performance by allowing faster data retrieval.
  - They function similarly to a book index, allowing quick searches without scanning entire tables.
  - MariaDB supports different types of indexes, each serving a specific purpose.
  - Indexes can be added when creating a table or later applied to existing tables.

- **Types of Indexes**
  - **Primary Index**
    - Automatically created with a `PRIMARY KEY`, ensures uniqueness and non-null values.
  - **Unique Index**
    - Guarantees unique values in a column but allows `NULL` values.
  - **Regular (Non-Unique) Index**
    - Improves query performance but does not enforce unique values.
  - **Full-Text Index**
    - Optimized for text searching with support for natural language and Boolean mode.
  - **Composite Index**
    - Indexes multiple columns together to improve multi-column queries.
  - **Spatial Index**
    - Used for indexing geographic or spatial data types, supported in InnoDB and MyISAM.

- **Managing Indexes**
  - Indexes can be created during table creation or added later.
  - The `SHOW INDEX` command provides details about indexes in a table.
  - Indexes can be removed using the `DROP INDEX` statement.

- **Limitations**
  - Indexes consume disk space, increasing storage costs.
  - They can slow down `INSERT`, `UPDATE`, and `DELETE` operations due to required updates.
  - Overuse of indexes can lead to performance degradation instead of improvements.
  - Requires proper planning and monitoring to ensure effective optimization.

Chapter 18

18. MariaDB Stored Routines

By now, it should be clear that SQL statements can often become lengthy and complex. While we have been typing these statements directly into the MariaDB client, a significant part of your role as a database administrator will involve writing and maintaining sequences of SQL statements that are executed repeatedly. These statements might be run manually using a MariaDB client, automatically through server or client-side scripts, or in response to a front-end client such as a website or software application. The key objective in such scenarios is reusability, the cornerstone of which, and this chapter's topic, is *stored routines*. While exploring stored routines, we will also look at variables and Common Table Expressions.

18.1 An overview of stored routines

Stored routines are database objects that encapsulate SQL code for repeated execution. They come in two forms: *stored procedures* and *stored functions*. Stored procedures perform actions without necessarily returning a value, whereas stored functions are designed to return a value, much like functions in programming languages such as C#, Python, or Java. These routines efficiently centralize logic within the database, providing reusability and consistency in database operations.

18.2 The benefits of stored routines

To perform database operations, a client will send SQL statements to the server and await the results. Based on the results, further instructions may be sent by the client, followed by yet more based on subsequent return values, and so on. If the client is remote from the server, each transaction will introduce a delay due to network latency. Stored routines eliminate much of this communication by storing the SQL logic on the server. Instead of a repetitive back and forth between the client and server, the client can call the routine and await the final result.

When working with distributed systems like client-server databases, it is important to minimize the number of places where changes to code logic need to be made. Consider, for example, a set of SQL statements common to various clients of a specific database. If this code is stored within the clients instead of the server, any bug fixes or code updates must be applied to every client. If the code is instead stored centrally on the database server, however, the code updates only need to be made in one location, resulting in easier code maintenance.

Stored routines also provide an extra layer of database security. Instead of providing a user with access privileges to a table containing sensitive data, the user can be allowed to run a stored routine that performs only the necessary actions to complete a task.

18.3 Creating stored procedures

Stored procedures are created in MariaDB using the CREATE PROCEDURE statement, defining the procedure's name, specifying its parameters (if any), and encapsulating the SQL logic within a BEGIN...END block. The syntax for declaring stored procedures is as follows:

```
DELIMITER //
CREATE PROCEDURE
    <procedure_name>(IN/OUT/INOUT <param> <type>, <param> <type> .. )
BEGIN
     <SQL statements>
END //
DELIMITER ;
```

The DELIMITER statements in the syntax above require some clarification. Throughout this book, we have used the semi-colon (;) to indicate the end of a statement and to initiate execution. However, when writing a procedure, we still need to use the semi-colon, but we want to prevent the code from executing until we call the procedure later. To address this issue, we temporarily change the delimiter to something else (typically '//' or '$$') while we write the procedure and then switch it back to the semi-colon once we have finished.

Stored routines support three parameter types: IN, OUT, and INOUT. The IN parameter allows a value to be passed into the routine, while an OUT parameter enables the routine to return a value to the caller. The INOUT parameter serves as both an input and an output, allowing the caller to pass in a value and receive an updated value in return.

18.4 Opening the sample database

This chapter assumes that you have completed the steps in the previous chapters. If you haven't, you can import the current database snapshot using the sample files provided in the *"Start Here"* chapter.

To import the snapshot, open a terminal or command prompt, navigate to the directory containing the sample files, and run the following commands:

```
mariadb-admin -u demo -p drop sampledb
mariadb-admin -u demo -p create sampledb
mariadb -u demo -p sampledb < mariadb_routines.sql
```

Once the database is ready, open the MariaDB client and select the *sampledb* database:

```
USE sampledb
```

18.5 Working with MariaDB variables

Before we look at some stored routine examples, we need to briefly discuss MariaDB variables, which form the basis of output parameters.

MariaDB variables store temporary values that can be referenced and manipulated during a session or within a query. MariaDB supports both user-defined and system variables.

User-defined variable names are prefixed with the '@' character and created using the SET statement:

```
SET @myVar = 150;
```

User-defined variables can also be set from query results using the SELECT INTO statement, the syntax for which is as follows:

```
SELECT <column_1>, <column_2> ...
  INTO <variable_1>, <variable_2>, ...
    FROM <table>;
```

These variables are session-specific, persist until the session ends and can be inspected using the SELECT statement:

```
SELECT @myVar;
```

System variables, on the other hand, control the configuration and behavior of the MariaDB server and can be either global or session-specific. They are predefined by MariaDB and can be viewed or modified using the SHOW VARIABLES and SET commands, respectively.

18.6 Stored procedure examples

The following code creates a procedure named *ProductsBySupplier()* that takes a company name as an input parameter and retrieves a list of associated products:

```
DELIMITER //

CREATE PROCEDURE ProductsBySupplier(IN company_name varchar(25))
BEGIN
  SELECT product.name
    FROM product
    RIGHT JOIN supplier
    ON product.supplier_id = supplier.id
    WHERE company = company_name;
END //

DELIMITER ;
```

To execute this procedure, we use the CALL statement, as shown below:

```
CALL ProductsBySupplier('Apple');
+-----------------------+
| name                  |
+-----------------------+
| MacBook Pro M4 14-in  |
| MacBook Air M3        |
| Mac Mini M3           |
| Mac Studio            |
| iPhone 17 Pro         |
| iPhone 17             |
| iMac                  |
+-----------------------+
7 rows in set (0.00 sec)
```

The procedure below demonstrates the use of IN and OUT parameters in the same routine. The input parameter is the supplier name, while the output parameters will contain the lowest and highest prices of the supplier's products:

```
DELIMITER //

CREATE PROCEDURE SupplierMinMax(
  IN company_name varchar(25),
  OUT min_price DECIMAL(6,2),
  OUT max_price DECIMAL(6,2))
  BEGIN
    SELECT MIN(price), MAX(price)
    INTO min_price, max_price
    FROM product
    RIGHT JOIN supplier
    ON product.supplier_id = supplier.id
    WHERE company = company_name;
  END //

DELIMITER ;
```

When we call the procedure, we will pass references to variables for the OUT parameters. After the procedure finishes, these variables will hold the minimum and maximum product prices. We assign these values to the variables within the procedure using the following SELECT INTO statement:

```
SELECT MIN(price), MAX(price) INTO min_price, max_price ...
```

Use the following CALL statement to execute the procedure:

```
CALL SupplierMinMax('Apple', @min_price, @max_price);
```

After calling the procedure, run the following SELECT statement to inspect the two result variables:

```
SELECT @min_price, @max_price;
+------------+------------+
| @min_price | @max_price |
+------------+------------+
|     799.99 |    2499.99 |
+------------+------------+
1 row in set (0.00 sec)
```

We could also, for example, use these variables in a SELECT statement to identify products with minimum and maximum prices:

```
SELECT name, price
FROM product
WHERE price = @min_price OR price = @max_price;
+----------------------+---------+
| name                 | price   |
+----------------------+---------+
| MacBook Pro M4 14-in | 2499.99 |
| iPhone 17            |  799.99 |
+----------------------+---------+
2 rows in set (0.00 sec)
```

18.7 Creating stored functions

MariaDB stored functions are blocks of SQL code that perform a task and return a result. A set of keywords are used when writing functions, including RETURNS, RETURN, and DETERMINISTIC, as well as *interaction clauses* like NO SQL, CONTAINS SQL, MODIFIES SQL DATA, and READS SQL DATA. These keywords and clauses define how the function interacts with the database and how MariaDB optimizes its execution. We will start by outlining the syntax for declaring a function:

```
DELIMITER //

CREATE FUNCTION <function_name>(<param> <type>, <param> <type> ..)
RETURNS <return_type>
NO SQL | READS SQL DATA | MODIFIES SQL DATA | CONTAINS SQL
DETERMINISTIC | NOT DETERMINISTIC
BEGIN
    RETURN <expression>;
END //

DELIMITER ;
```

Before we try out some example functions, we need to explain each of the clauses included in the above syntax:

18.7.1 RETURNS

The RETURNS keyword declares the data type of the function's return value, which is mandatory for all stored functions. Declaring the incorrect return type may result in unpredictable behavior.

18.7.2 RETURN

The RETURN keyword is used within a function's body to indicate the value that will be returned to the caller. Each function can have only one RETURN statement for every possible execution path, and the value returned must be consistent with the data type defined in the RETURNS clause. For instance, if the RETURNS clause specifies a DECIMAL type, attempting to return a CHAR or any other incompatible type will result in an error.

18.7.3 DETERMINISTIC

When you write functions, you must declare them as either deterministic or non-deterministic. If a function is declared as deterministic, it must return the same result each time it is called when passed the same input parameters. This predictability allows MariaDB to cache return values and return the results from previous matching calls without executing the overhead of rerunning the function.

Do not declare a non-deterministic function as deterministic. Doing so often results in inaccurate return values.

18.7.4 NON DETERMINISTIC

The return results of non-deterministic functions vary, even when passed the same input parameters. This variability is usually the result of a dependency on dynamic values within the function's logic, such as the current date or random number generation.

18.7.5 NO SQL

The NOSQL interaction clause indicates to MariaDB that the function body does not execute SQL statements. In other words, the function relies entirely on its input parameters and internal logic to perform calculations or operations without interacting with the database.

18.7.6 READS SQL DATA

A function declared with READS SQL DATA can execute SQL queries that retrieve data from the database but cannot modify any data. This clause is used for functions that depend on database queries to calculate their results.

18.7.7 MODIFIES SQL DATA

The MODIFIES SQL DATA clause tells MariaDB that the function will perform database updates such as inserting, updating, or deleting data. Stored functions are generally intended to return results without altering data, so this clause is not frequently used.

18.7.8 CONTAINS SQL

The CONTAINS SQL clause tells MariaDB that the function uses SQL statements that neither read from tables nor modify the database. While the function may perform operations such as declaring variables or calling other stored routines, it does not directly interact with table data.

Table 18-1 provides a summary of the interaction clauses that are supported by the CREATE FUNCTION statement:

Clause	Description	Example Use Case
NO SQL	The function does not execute any SQL statements and relies entirely on input parameters.	Mathematical calculations.

READS SQL DATA	The function retrieves data from the database but does not modify it.	Table queries.
CONTAINS SQL	The function contains SQL statements but does not read or modify table data.	Internal processing or reading and manipulating variables.
MODIFIES SQL DATA	The function modifies table data by inserting, updating, or deleting records.	Data updates, deletions, and insertions.

Table 18-1

18.8 Stored function examples

With the basics of stored functions covered in the previous section, the next step is to try out some examples, starting with the following example:

```
DELIMITER //

CREATE FUNCTION
CalculateTax(price DECIMAL(10, 2), tax_rate DECIMAL(10, 2))
  RETURNS DECIMAL(10, 2)
  NO SQL
  DETERMINISTIC
  BEGIN
    RETURN price * (tax_rate / 100);
  END //

DELIMITER ;
```

The CalculateTax() function accepts two values representing the product price and the tax rate percentage. The function body converts the tax rate to the decimal equivalent and then multiplies the price by the result. The function does not use SQL statements and will return the same value when provided the same input values, so it is declared using the NO SQL and DETERMINISTIC clauses. After adding the function to the database, execute it as follows:

```
SELECT CalculateTax(220, 5.25);
+------------------------+
| CalculateTax(220, 5.25) |
+------------------------+
|                  11.55 |
+------------------------+
1 row in set (0.00 sec)
```

The following example declares a function called FormatName(), which uses the customer's first and last names as parameters. The returned result is a concatenation of the first and last names, separated by a space character:

```
DELIMITER //

CREATE FUNCTION FormatName(first_name VARCHAR(20), last_name VARCHAR(20))
  RETURNS VARCHAR(40)
  CONTAINS SQL
  DETERMINISTIC
  BEGIN
      DECLARE full_name VARCHAR(40);
      SET full_name = CONCAT(first_name, ' ', last_name);
      RETURN full_name;
  END //
```

```
DELIMITER ;
```

In the above example, the FormatName() function is deterministic and uses the SQL CONCAT function. Since the function does not access the database, it was declared using the CONTAINS SQL clause. Use the following SELECT statement to test the function:

```
SELECT FormatName('Davy', 'Crockett');
+------------------------------+
| FormatName('Davy', 'Crockett') |
+------------------------------+
| Davy Crockett                |
+------------------------------+
1 row in set (0.00 sec)
```

The final example is a function designed to return a random item from the product table to be awarded as a customer prize:

```
DELIMITER //

CREATE FUNCTION GetRandomPrize()
 RETURNS VARCHAR(25)
 READS SQL DATA
 NOT DETERMINISTIC
BEGIN
    DECLARE prize VARCHAR(25);
    SELECT name INTO prize FROM product ORDER BY RAND() LIMIT 1;
    RETURN prize;
END //

DELIMITER ;
```

The random behavior of GetRandomPrize() requires that we declare it a non-deterministic function. Since the function body queries but does not update the product table, we have included the READS SQL DATA interaction clause. The function then declares a local variable named prize to store the name of the selected product and executes the following SELECT statement:

```
SELECT name INTO prize FROM product ORDER BY RAND() LIMIT 1;
```

The above statement uses the RAND() function to generate a random number and uses it to shuffle the result set randomly. The LIMIT 1 operator narrows the result set to a single row, which is stored in the prize variable using the INTO operator and returned to the caller. Test the function using the following statement:

```
SELECT GetRandomPrize();
+------------------+
| GetRandomPrize() |
+------------------+
| One2One USB-A Hub |
+------------------+
1 row in set (0.00 sec)
```

We can also assign the result to a variable and use it in subsequent statements, for example:

```
SET @random_prize = GetRandomPrize();

SELECT name, price FROM product WHERE name = @random_prize;
```

135

```
+--------------------+--------+
| name               | price  |
+--------------------+--------+
| Corsair Full Tower | 179.99 |
+--------------------+--------+
1 row in set (0.00 sec)
```

18.9 Using stored functions as subqueries

Stored functions may also be used within subqueries, though doing so can sometimes result in inconsistent results, mainly when using non-deterministic functions. To experience this first-hand, run the following SELECT statement repeatedly, which invokes GetRandomPrize() as a subquery and note the results:

```
SELECT name FROM product WHERE name = (SELECT GetRandomPrize());
```

Occasionally, the queries will return a single, random product name as intended, but you will also see empty result sets and even results containing multiple products like the following:

```
SELECT name FROM product WHERE name = (SELECT GetRandomPrize());
+--------------------+
| name               |
+--------------------+
| iPhone 17          |
| Dell XPS Model 7823 |
| One2One USB-A Hub  |
+--------------------+
3 rows in set (0.04 sec)
```

There are several potential causes for the above behavior:

- MariaDB uses a query optimizer when it executes queries. Depending on the query, the optimizer may evaluate a subquery more than once during a single query operation.

- When used within a WHERE clause, MariaDB may treat some functions as dynamic expressions that need to be evaluated for each row. While this isn't an issue for deterministic functions, it can cause problems with non-deterministic functions that produce different results each time they are called.

- MariaDB does not generally cache or optimize the results of non-deterministic expressions. Functions like RAND() inherently produce different values with each call, which leads MariaDB to treat them as dynamic. As a result, the server re-executes these functions whenever they are referenced. This means that even within a single query execution, the subquery may generate unpredictable results.

There are several ways to avoid unpredictable behavior when using stored functions in subqueries. One option, as we have already seen, is to assign the function result to a variable, which is then used within the subsequent query:

```
SET @random_prize = GetRandomPrize();
SELECT name, price FROM product WHERE name = @random_prize;
```

Another way to do this is by wrapping the subquery in another query to store its result temporarily. For example, we can use a subquery to compute the result of GetRandomPrize() and then reference that result in the main query:

```
SELECT name FROM product
 WHERE name = (SELECT random_prize FROM (SELECT GetRandomPrize()
  AS random_prize) AS temp_prize);
```

```
+-----------+
| name      |
+-----------+
| iPhone 17 |
+-----------+
1 row in set (0.00 sec)
```

A third alternative is to use a Common Table Expression (CTE) to pre-compute the random value and reuse it without multiple evaluations.

18.10 Introducing Common Table Expressions

Common Table Expressions (CTE) allow you to collect results from a query in a temporary result set and reference that set by name elsewhere in the same query expression. CTEs are defined using the WITH keyword with the following syntax:

```
WITH <cte_name> AS (
    SELECT ...
)
SELECT ...
FROM <table_name>;
```

CTEs are useful for simplifying complex queries and for reusing the result of a subquery multiple times within the same query. They exist only for the duration of the query in which they are used.

The following statement, for example, uses a CTE to produce consistent results from the GetRandomPrize() function:

```
WITH prize_cte AS (
    SELECT GetRandomPrize() AS random_prize
)
SELECT name
FROM product
WHERE name = (SELECT random_prize FROM prize_cte);
+---------------------+
| name                |
+---------------------+
| Dell XPS Model 7823 |
+---------------------+
1 row in set (0.00 sec)
```

18.11 Viewing procedures and functions

Information about routines is stored in the *routines* and *functions* tables of the built-in MariaDB information_schema database and is accessed using the following syntax:

```
SELECT <column names>
FROM information_schema.routines
WHERE routine_type = '[PROCDECURE | FUNCTION]'
AND routine_schema = '<database name>'\G
```

The following statement, for example, displays all the fields for each function declared within the sampledb database:

```
SELECT * FROM information_schema.routines
WHERE routine_type = 'FUNCTION'
AND routine_schema = 'sampledb'\G
```

```
*************************** 1. row ***************************
            SPECIFIC_NAME: CalculateTax
          ROUTINE_CATALOG: def
           ROUTINE_SCHEMA: sampledb
             ROUTINE_NAME: CalculateTax
             ROUTINE_TYPE: FUNCTION
                DATA_TYPE: decimal
CHARACTER_MAXIMUM_LENGTH: NULL
  CHARACTER_OCTET_LENGTH: NULL
        NUMERIC_PRECISION: 10
  .
  .
  .
*************************** 2. row ***************************
            SPECIFIC_NAME: FormatName
          ROUTINE_CATALOG: def
           ROUTINE_SCHEMA: sampledb
             ROUTINE_NAME: FormatName
             ROUTINE_TYPE: FUNCTION
                DATA_TYPE: varchar
CHARACTER_MAXIMUM_LENGTH: 40
  CHARACTER_OCTET_LENGTH: 160
        NUMERIC_PRECISION: NULL
  .
  .
```

Similarly, the following statement displays the name and definition of all functions within the database:

```
SELECT ROUTINE_NAME, ROUTINE_DEFINITION FROM information_schema.routines
WHERE routine_type = 'PROCEDURE'
AND routine_schema = 'sampledb'\G
*************************** 1. row ***************************
      ROUTINE_NAME: ProductsBySupplier
ROUTINE_DEFINITION: BEGIN
 SELECT product.name
  FROM product
   RIGHT JOIN supplier
   ON product.supplier_id = supplier.id
   WHERE company = company_name;
END
*************************** 2. row ***************************
      ROUTINE_NAME: SupplierMinMax
ROUTINE_DEFINITION: BEGIN
   SELECT MIN(price), MAX(price)
    INTO min_price, max_price
    FROM product
    RIGHT JOIN supplier
    ON product.supplier_id = supplier.id
    WHERE company = company_name;
  END
2 rows in set (0.00 sec)
```

18.12 Deleting stored procedures and functions

Stored routines are deleted using the DROP FUNCTION and DROP PROCEDURE statement. Before continuing, execute the following statements to delete the example routines:

```
DROP PROCEDURE SupplierMinMax;
DROP PROCEDURE ProductsBySupplier;
DROP FUNCTION CalculateTax;
DROP FUNCTION FormatName;
DROP FUNCTION GetRandomPrize;
```

18.13 Reference points

The main points covered in this chapter are as follows:

- **Overview**

  - Stored routines encapsulate reusable SQL logic in the database.

- **Routine Types**

  - **Stored Procedure**s: Execute SQL statements without necessarily returning a value.

  - **Stored Functions:** Return a value based on SQL logic, similar to programming functions.

- **Benefits**

  - **Reduced Client-Server Communication:** Minimize network latency by centralizing logic on the database server.

  - **Simplified Maintenance:** Updates to logic are applied once on the server instead of across multiple clients.

  - **Enhanced Security**: Restrict user access to sensitive data by granting permission to execute routines rather than direct table access.

- **MariaDB Variables**

  - **User-defined variables:** Session-specific and prefixed with @ (e.g., @myVar).

  - **System variables:** Predefined by MariaDB for configuration and operational control.

  - Variables can store query results using SELECT INTO and are used extensively in stored procedures.

- **Stored Procedures**

  - Created using the CREATE PROCEDURE statement and structured with a BEGIN...END block.

  - Support IN, OUT, and INOUT parameters for passing and returning values.

  - Useful for handling complex operations, such as filtering and aggregations.

- **Stored Functions**

  - Created with CREATE FUNCTION, they must return a value.

  - Use clauses like RETURNS, RETURN, DETERMINISTIC, and interaction clauses (NO SQL, READS SQL DATA, etc.).

  - Examples include mathematical operations, formatting, and retrieving specific data.

  - Deterministic functions return consistent results for the same input.

- **Interaction Clauses**

- `NO SQL`: Function does not interact with database tables.

- `READS SQL DATA`: Function reads from the database but does not modify data.

- `MODIFIES SQL DATA`: Function updates, deletes, or inserts data.

- `CONTAINS SQL`: Function uses SQL but does not interact with tables directly.

- **Common Table Expressions (CTEs)**

  - Simplify complex queries by creating temporary named result sets.

  - Defined using the `WITH` clause and used within the same query.

  - Useful for ensuring consistent results, especially when working with non-deterministic functions.

  - Avoid multiple evaluations of non-deterministic expressions.

- **Viewing Stored Procedures and Functions**

  - MariaDB stores information about stored routines in the information_schema.routines table.

  - Routine details can be retrieved using SQL queries, filtering by `ROUTINE_TYPE` (`PROCEDURE` or `FUNCTION`) and `ROUTINE_SCHEMA` (database name).

  - The `ROUTINE_NAME` and `ROUTINE_DEFINITION` fields provide the name and logic of stored procedures and functions.

- **Deleting Stored Procedures and Functions**

  - The `DROP FUNCTION` and `DROP PROCEDURE` statements permanently remove stored routines from a database.

19. Working with Control Flow

Control flow allows us to build logic into our code and move beyond executing linear sequences of SQL statements. MariaDB includes a set of statements that we can use to control the execution path of our code, including conditional statements for decision-making and iteration loops. This chapter will explore MariaDB's various control flow constructs and demonstrate how to use them in your code.

19.1 Opening the sample database

This chapter assumes that you have completed the steps in the previous chapters. If you haven't, you can import the current database snapshot using the sample files provided in the *"Start Here"* chapter.

To import the snapshot, open a terminal or command prompt, navigate to the directory containing the sample files, and run the following commands:

```
mariadb-admin -u demo -p drop sampledb
mariadb-admin -u demo -p create sampledb
mariadb -u demo -p sampledb < mariadb_control_flow.sql
```

Once the database is ready, open the MariaDB client and select the *sampledb* database:

```
USE sampledb
```

19.2 Looping in MariaDB

We will begin by looking at loop-based control flow. Loops are sequences of SQL statements to be executed repeatedly until a specified condition is met. The first looping statement we will explore is the WHILE loop.

19.2.1 The WHILE loop

The WHILE loop executes a block of SQL statements repeatedly until a specified condition is no longer true. For example, a loop might iterate through table records until a counter variable exceeds a maximum value. A key characteristic of WHILE loops is that the condition is evaluated before executing the code block. Consequently, if the condition is initially evaluated as false, the loop body will not run, as illustrated in Figure 19-1:

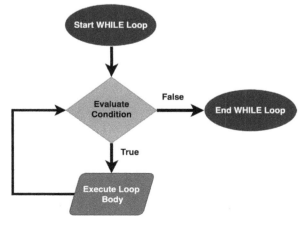

Figure 19-1

Working with Control Flow

WHILE loops are declared in MariaDB using the following syntax:

```
WHILE <condition> DO
    <sql statements>
END WHILE;
```

Enter the following into the MariaDB client to declare a procedure called SquareNumbers() that uses a WHILE loop to output the square of the numbers within a range defined by the start and end parameters:

```
DELIMITER //

CREATE PROCEDURE SquareNumbers(IN start INT, IN end INT)
BEGIN
    DECLARE result INT;

    WHILE start <= end DO
        SET result = start * start;
        SELECT result;
        SET start = start + 1;
    END WHILE;
END //

DELIMITER ;
```

The procedure begins by creating a variable to store the calculation result before declaring a WHILE loop to be performed until the start variable is greater than the end value. The loop's body calculates the square of the current start value, displays the result, and increments the start value.

Use the statement below to test the loop:

```
CALL SquareNumbers(5, 8);
+--------+
| result |
+--------+
|     25 |
+--------+
1 row in set (0.01 sec)

+--------+
| result |
+--------+
|     36 |
+--------+
1 row in set (0.01 sec)
.
.
.
1 row in set (0.01 sec)
```

The above output shows that the loop was executed for each number in the specified range. If, instead, we provide a start value that is already greater than the end value, we will see that the condition initially evaluates to false and the loop is not executed:

```
CALL SquareNumbers(8, 5);
Query OK, 0 rows affected (0.00 sec)
```

19.2.2 The REPEAT loop

You can think of the REPEAT loop as an inverted WHILE loop. As previously discussed, a WHILE loop evaluates a condition before executing the code in the loop code block. The code is not executed if the condition is evaluated as false on the first check. On the other hand, the REPEAT loop is provided for situations where you know that the code contained in the code block of the loop will always need to be executed at least once. For example, you may want to keep updating the rows in a table until a specific match is found. You know that you have to check the first row at least to have any hope of finding the record you need. The diagram in Figure 19-2 illustrates the REPEAT loop execution path:

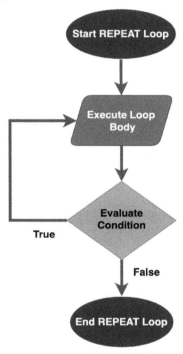

Figure 19-2

The syntax for the REPEAT loop is as follows:

```
REPEAT
    <sql statements>
UNTIL <condition>
END REPEAT;
```

To demonstrate the REPEAT loop, we will write a procedure to calculate the factorial of a number. Enter the following statements to declare a procedure called Factorial():

```
DELIMITER //

CREATE PROCEDURE Factorial(IN num INT)
BEGIN
    DECLARE result INT DEFAULT 1;

    REPEAT
        SET result = result * num;
        SET num = num - 1;
```

```
      UNTIL num = 0
      END REPEAT;

      SELECT result;
END //

DELIMITER ;
```

Test that the procedure works using the following CALL statement:

```
CALL Factorial(10);
+---------+
| result  |
+---------+
| 3628800 |
+---------+
1 row in set (0.01 sec)
```

19.3 The LOOP construct

The LOOP statement provides a way to execute a block of code repeatedly, but unlike the WHILE and REPEAT loops, it does not include a built-in condition to control when the loop must exit. Instead, the LEAVE clause is used within the LOOP code block to indicate points where the loop must terminate. This moves the condition logic into the loop code block, allowing for greater flexibility and multiple exit conditions:

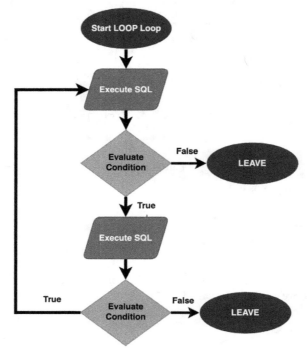

Figure 19-3

Each LOOP construct must be assigned a label, which, in turn, is referenced in the LEAVE statement. The LOOP construct uses the following syntax:

```
<loop_label>: LOOP
    <sql statements>
```

```
        LEAVE <loop_label>;
END LOOP;
```

Moving the conditional logic into the code block makes it possible to implement multiple exit points within the loop, for example:

```
<loop_label>: LOOP
    <sql statements>
    LEAVE <loop_label>;
    <sql statements>
    LEAVE <loop_label>;
    .
    .
    .
END LOOP;
```

The LOOP statement also supports nested loops using the following syntax:

```
<loop_1_label>: LOOP
    <sql statements>

    <loop_2_label>: LOOP
        <sql_statments>
        LEAVE <loop_2_label>
    END LOOP;

    LEAVE <loop_1_label>;
END LOOP;
```

The following procedure accepts parameters named *count* and *max* and contains a loop that doubles *count* until it exceeds the maximum value:

```
DELIMITER //

CREATE PROCEDURE SingleLoop(IN count INT, IN max INT)
BEGIN
    count_loop: LOOP
        IF count > max THEN
            LEAVE count_loop;
        END IF;

        SELECT count;
        SET count = count * 2;
    END LOOP;
END //

DELIMITER ;
```

Use the following CALL statement to try out the procedure:

```
CALL SingleLoop(2, 10);
+-------+
| count |
+-------+
|     2 |
+-------+
1 row in set (0.01 sec)
```

```
+-------+
| count |
+-------+
|     4 |
+-------+
1 row in set (0.01 sec)

+-------+
| count |
+-------+
|     8 |
+-------+
1 row in set (0.01 sec)

Query OK, 0 rows affected (0.01 sec)
```

The next example demonstrates a nested LOOP construct that accepts a third parameter that controls the number of times count_loop executes:

```
DELIMITER //

CREATE PROCEDURE NestedLoop(IN count INT, IN max INT, IN reps INT)
BEGIN

    DECLARE outer_count INT DEFAULT 1;
    SET @saved_count = count;

    outer_loop: LOOP
        IF outer_count > reps THEN
            LEAVE outer_loop;
        END IF;

        inner_loop: LOOP
            IF count > max THEN
                LEAVE inner_loop;
            END IF;
            SELECT count;
            SET count = count * 2;
        END LOOP;

        SET count = @saved_count;
        SET outer_count = outer_count + 1;
    END LOOP;
END //

DELIMITER ;
```

In the NestedLoop() example, inner_loop is nested within outer_loop. Before outer_loop starts, the count parameter value is saved so that it can be restored at the end of each repetition of the inner loop.

The inner loop will run until the count parameter reaches the maximum value, at which point the LEAVE statement will exit the inner loop, passing control to the following line of the outer loop, where the saved initial count value is restored, and outer_count is incremented.

The outer loop will continue to execute inner_loop until the outer_count value exceeds the designated number of repetitions (as defined by the *reps* parameter), resulting in the following output:

```
CALL NestedLoop(2, 8, 2);
+-------+
| count |
+-------+
|     2 |
+-------+
1 row in set (0.01 sec)

+-------+
| count |
+-------+
|     4 |
+-------+
1 row in set (0.01 sec)

+-------+
| count |
+-------+
|     8 |
+-------+
1 row in set (0.01 sec)

+-------+
| count |
+-------+
|     2 |
+-------+
1 row in set (0.01 sec)

+-------+
| count |
+-------+
|     4 |
+-------+
1 row in set (0.00 sec)

+-------+
| count |
+-------+
|     8 |
+-------+
1 row in set (0.00 sec)

Query OK, 0 rows affected (0.00 sec)
```

When working with nested loops, the LEAVE statement does not have to reference the loop in which it is declared. We could, for example, use the LEAVE statement in the inner loop to exit from the outer loop, essentially exiting both loops in a single operation:

```
DROP PROCEDURE nestedloop;

DELIMITER //
```

```
CREATE PROCEDURE NestedLoop(IN count INT, IN max INT, IN reps INT)
BEGIN

    DECLARE outer_count INT DEFAULT 1;
    SET @saved_count = count;

    outer_loop: LOOP
        IF outer_count > reps THEN
            LEAVE outer_loop;
        END IF;

        inner_loop: LOOP
            IF count > max THEN
                LEAVE outer_loop;
            END IF;
            SELECT count;
            SET count = count * 2;
        END LOOP;

        SET count = @saved_count;
        SET outer_count = outer_count + 1;
    END LOOP;
END //

DELIMITER ;
```

When the procedure runs, the outer loop will only run once, irrespective of the value of the *reps* parameter:

```
CALL NestedLoop(2, 8, 100);
+-------+
| count |
+-------+
|     2 |
+-------+
1 row in set (0.01 sec)

+-------+
| count |
+-------+
|     4 |
+-------+
1 row in set (0.01 sec)

+-------+
| count |
+-------+
|     8 |
+-------+
1 row in set (0.01 sec)

Query OK, 0 rows affected (0.01 sec)
```

19.4 Conditional Statements in MariaDB

Programming is an exercise in applying logic and primarily involves writing code that makes decisions based on one or more criteria. Such decisions define which code gets executed and which is bypassed during execution. Control flow is common to most programming languages and, in the case of MariaDB, is provided by the IF and CASE statements, each of which will be covered in the remainder of this chapter:

19.4.1 The IF statement

The IF statement allows you to execute an SQL code block only when a specified condition is evaluated as true. The IF statement can be combined with the ELSEIF clause to test for multiple conditions and the ELSE clause to provide a default action if none of the conditions are evaluated to be true.

The basic syntax of an IF statement is as follows:

```
IF <condition_1> THEN
    <code to execute if the condition_1 is true>
ELSEIF <condition_2> THEN
    <code to execute if the condition_2 is true>
.
.
ELSE
    <code to execute if no conditions are met>
END IF;
```

The flow diagram in Figure 19-4 below provides a visual representation of an IF statement containing three ELSEIF conditions:

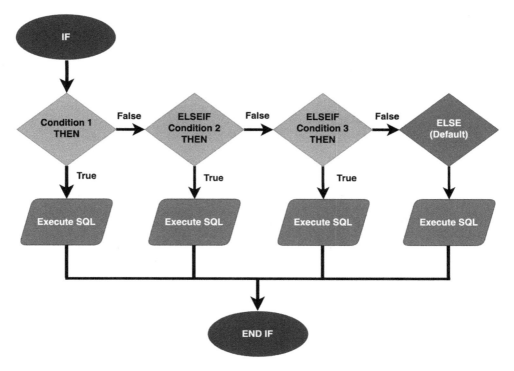

Figure 19-4

Suppose we need a way to identify an item's stock level in our product database. A procedure that uses an IF

149

statement to check stock levels based on the product id might read as follows:

```
DELIMITER //

CREATE PROCEDURE StockCheck(IN product_id INT, OUT stock_status VARCHAR(50))
BEGIN
    DECLARE product_name VARCHAR(25);
    DECLARE stock_quantity INT;

    SELECT quantity
    INTO stock_quantity
    FROM product
    WHERE id = product_id;

    IF stock_quantity = 0 THEN
        SET stock_status = 'Out of Stock';
    ELSEIF stock_quantity < 20  THEN
        SET stock_status = 'Low Stock';
    ELSEIF stock_quantity > 80 THEN
        SET stock_status = 'Excess Stock';
    ELSE
        SET stock_status = 'Product not found';
    END IF;
    END //

DELIMITER ;
```

If we call the StockCheck() procedure with a product id value, the stock_status variable will update to reflect the stock level of the corresponding product:

```
CALL StockCheck(4, @stock_status);

SELECT @stock_status;
+---------------+
| @stock_status |
+---------------+
| Low Stock     |
+---------------+
1 row in set (0.00 sec)
```

We can also test the default ELSE statement by providing a non-existent product id:

```
CALL StockCheck(100, @stock_status);

SELECT @stock_status;
+-------------------+
| @stock_status     |
+-------------------+
| Product not found |
+-------------------+
1 row in set (0.00 sec)
```

19.4.2 The CASE statement

The CASE statement provides functionality similar to IF .. ELSEIF constructs but uses a more concise format, making it easier to evaluate many conditions in a single statement. CASE constructs also provide a convenient way to integrate control flow directly into SQL queries.

There are two ways to use the CASE statement. The first method is ideal for use in stored routines, allows SQL statements to be executed for each matching condition, and uses the following syntax:

```
CASE <case_value>
    WHEN <value_1> THEN <sql code>
    WHEN <value_2> THEN <sql code>
    ELSE <sql code>
END CASE;
```

The diagram in Figure 19-5 illustrates the structure of the above CASE syntax:

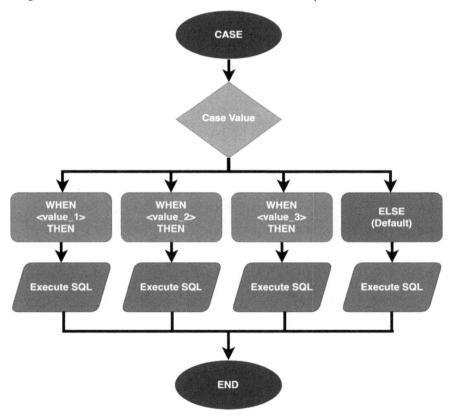

Figure 19-5

The second CASE variant returns a result for each condition instead of executing SQL statements and is ideal for integrating control flow directly into SQL queries. The syntax for this type of CASE expression reads as follows:

```
CASE
    WHEN <condition_1> THEN <result_1>
    WHEN <condition_2> THEN <result_2>
    ELSE <default_result>
END
```

Figure 19-6 outlines the flow of the result-based CASE constructs:

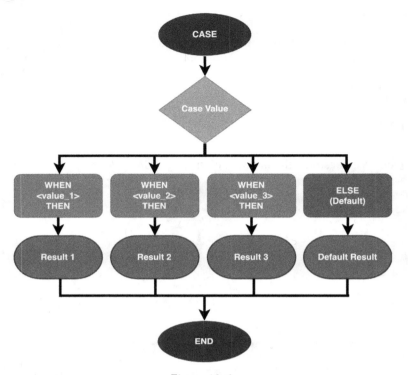

Figure 19-6

Execute the following SELECT statement to generate the stock status for each item in the product table using an embedded CASE statement:

```
SELECT name, quantity,
    CASE
        WHEN quantity = 0 THEN 'Out of Stock'
        WHEN quantity > 60 THEN 'Excess Stock'
        WHEN quantity <= 20 THEN 'Low Stock'
        ELSE 'Medium Stock'
    END AS 'stock_level'
FROM product;
```

name	quantity	stock_level
MacBook Pro M4 14-in	60	Medium Stock
MacBook Air M3	55	Medium Stock
Mac Mini M3	100	Excess Stock
Mac Studio	15	Low Stock
iPhone 17 Pro	30	Medium Stock
iPhone 17	30	Medium Stock
iMac	30	Medium Stock
NZXT Mid Tower	100	Excess Stock
Corsair Full Tower	15	Low Stock
Dell Model 4823	35	Medium Stock
Dell XPS Model 7823	16	Low Stock
Dell Dock Model [4807]	35	Medium Stock
One&One Touch 200	60	Medium Stock
One2One USB-A Hub	60	Medium Stock

```
| One4One USB-A Hub      |        60 | Medium Stock |
+-----------------------+----------+--------------+
15 rows in set (0.00 sec)
```

If you do not intend to use the routines from this chapter in the future, delete them using the following statements:

```
DROP PROCEDURE SquareNumbers;
DROP PROCEDURE Factorial;
DROP PROCEDURE SafeFactorial;
DROP PROCEDURE SingleLoop;
DROP PROCEDURE NestedLoop;
DROP PROCEDURE StockCheck;
```

19.5 Reference points

The main points covered in this chapter are as follows:

- **Overview**
    - Control flow enables dynamic decision-making and repetitive execution of SQL statements.
    - Includes looping constructs (WHILE, REPEAT, and LOOP) and conditional statements (IF and CASE) to structure logic.

- **Loops**
    - Use WHILE for precondition checks, REPEAT for guaranteed execution, and LOOP for custom termination logic.
    - Nested loops allow complex iterations and multiple exit points.

- **WHILE Loop**
    - Executes a block of SQL statements repeatedly as long as a condition is true.
    - Evaluates the condition before the loop starts, ensuring the loop does not run if the condition is initially false.

- **REPEAT Loop**
    - Guarantees at least one execution of the code block before the condition is checked.
    - Ideal for scenarios where the code must always run at least once before validation.

- **LOOP Statement**
    - Executes a block of code repeatedly without built-in conditions for termination.
    - Requires the LEAVE statement to terminate the loop.
    - Supports nested loops, where an inner loop can terminate the outer loop for more complex logic.

- **Conditional Statements**
    - Use IF for versatile decision-making logic with multiple branches.
    - CASE offers a compact, readable alternative, ideal for query-based conditions.

- **IF Statement**

- Tests conditions and executes specific SQL code based on evaluation.

- Supports multiple branches using `ELSEIF` and a default action with `ELSE`.

- Commonly used to perform logic such as evaluating stock levels in a database.

- **CASE Statement**

  - A concise alternative to `IF..ELSEIF` for evaluating multiple conditions.

  - Two forms:

    - Executes SQL code for each matching condition.

    - Returns results directly in SQL queries for embedded logic.

20. Error Handling in MariaDB

Like any programming environment, errors can occur when executing code on a MariaDB database. Some code is more susceptible to errors than others and usually arises from invalid data, logic errors, or miscalculations. Regardless of the cause, errors can cause code execution to terminate, potentially leaving the database in an indeterminate state. For this reason, it is important to identify the potential risks and develop defensive code to handle them. MariaDB provides extensive error-handling features that will allow you to respond gracefully to errors when they occur. This chapter will cover error handling in MariaDB using handlers, conditions, states, and exceptions.

20.1 Overview of MariaDB error handling

Error handling in MariaDB is configured using the CREATE HANDLER statement, which allows us to specify actions to be taken in response to specific errors or conditions. The three key elements of error handling in MariaDB are *handlers*, *conditions*, and *custom conditions*, and we need to understand these before we explore error handling in more detail:

- **Handlers** - Handlers define the code to execute when a specified error or condition occurs and are declared using the CREATE HANDLER statement.

- **Conditions** - Conditions are codes that indicate whether an operation was successful and, if unsuccessful, the type of problem encountered. These are either the SQLSTATE codes built into MariaDB or the custom conditions you specify.

- **Custom conditions** - Custom conditions allow you to handle issues within your application logic that MariaDB would not otherwise consider problems.

20.2 Deciphering SQLSTATE codes

When MariaDB encounters an error while executing a statement, it returns a SQLSTATE result code identifying the problem type. Otherwise, MariaDB returns a code indicating that the operation was successful.

SQLSTATE codes consist of five characters and are grouped using specific character sequences. The first two characters of a SQLSTATE code designate the class. A return value that begins with 00 indicates success, 01 a warning, and 02 a result that contains no data. All other class codes indicate that an exception occurred.

The remaining four characters represent the SQLSTATE subclass and identify the specific problem. For example, SQLSTATE code 00000 is returned when a task is successfully completed. Code 01002, on the other hand, is a warning that indicates a connectivity issue between the client and server, while code 46121 is an exception caused by an invalid column name reference.

The SQLSTATE classes are further divided into one of four categories: success (S), warning (W), and exception (X). For a complete list of the SQLSTATE codes used by MariaDB, refer to the following web page:

https://en.wikipedia.org/wiki/SQLSTATE

20.3 Opening the sample database

This chapter assumes that you have completed the steps in the previous chapters. If you haven't, you can import the current database snapshot using the sample files provided in the *"Start Here"* chapter.

To import the snapshot, open a terminal or command prompt, navigate to the directory containing the sample files, and run the following commands:

```
mariadb-admin -u demo -p drop sampledb
mariadb-admin -u demo -p create sampledb
mariadb -u demo -p sampledb < mariadb_error_handling.sql
```

Once the database is ready, open the MariaDB client and select the *sampledb* database:

```
USE sampledb
```

20.4 Declaring a handler

The DECLARE HANDLER statement allows you to define an action for a particular error or condition. MariaDB provides two types of handlers:

- **CONTINUE** - A continue handler allows the code to execute at the following statement after handling the error. Only use this option for non-critical conditions that do not prevent subsequent statements from completing successfully.

- **EXIT** - An EXIT handler stops the routine's execution after handling the error. This is typically used for critical errors where proceeding further could lead to incorrect results, data corruption, or other unintended consequences.

The syntax for creating a handler is as follows:

```
DECLARE <handler_type> HANDLER FOR <condition>
    <sql_statement>;
```

When using the above syntax to declare a handler, you will need to provide the following values:

- **handler_type**: Defines how to proceed after handling the error (CONTINUE or EXIT).

- **condition**: The type of error or condition to handle (SQLEXCEPTION, SQLWARNING, NOT FOUND, or SQLSTATE).

- **statement**: The SQL statement to be executed when the condition occurs.

To execute multiple statements within the handler body, enclose them in BEGIN and END statements:

```
DECLARE <handler_type> HANDLER FOR <condition>
BEGIN
    <sql_statements>
END;
```

20.5 Error handling with SQLEXCEPTION

The SQLEXCEPTION condition type catches all exception errors that occur within a routine. In an earlier chapter, we created a procedure to calculate factorials. Let's create a similar procedure that we can use to demonstrate exception handling. Within the MariaDB client, enter the following statements:

```
DELIMITER //

CREATE PROCEDURE SafeFactorial(IN num INT)
BEGIN
    DECLARE result INT DEFAULT 1;
```

```
    REPEAT
        SET result = result * num;
        SET num = num - 1;
    UNTIL num = 0
    END REPEAT;

    SELECT CONCAT('Factorial = ', result) AS Result;
END //

DELIMITER ;
```

Begin by calling the SafeFactorial() procedure with a valid parameter:

```
CALL SafeFactorial(10);
+--------------------+
| Result             |
+--------------------+
| Factorial = 3628800 |
+--------------------+
1 row in set (0.00 sec)
```

The output shows that the procedure completed the calculation and returned a result. One shortcoming of factorials is that they cannot handle negative numbers. To experience the effect of calculating the factorial of a negative number, run the following command:

```
CALL safefactorial(-10);
ERROR 1264 (22003): Out of range value for column 'result' at row 1
```

The error message describes the cause of the problem together with the corresponding SQLSTATE code (22003). From the first two characters (22), we can tell that this is an exception error, and if we look it up in the Wikipedia SQLSTATE list provided earlier, we will find the following entry:

SQLSTATE	Category	Class	Class Text	Subclass	Subclass Text
22003	X	22	data exception	003	numeric value out of range

Table 20-1

If the factorial calculation occurred within the code of an application client, we would need to catch this error and take remedial action to prevent the application from crashing. To do so, we must add a SQLEXCEPTION handler to the SafeFactorial() procedure. Implement this change by dropping the current procedure and redeclaring it as follows:

```
DROP PROCEDURE SafeFactorial;

DELIMITER //

CREATE PROCEDURE SafeFactorial(IN num INT)
BEGIN

DECLARE result INT DEFAULT 1;

    DECLARE EXIT HANDLER FOR SQLEXCEPTION
        SELECT 'Statement to handle the error goes here' AS ErrorMessage;

    REPEAT
```

```
            SET result = result * num;
            SET num = num - 1;
        UNTIL num = 0
        END REPEAT;

        SELECT CONCAT('Factorial = ', result) AS Result;
END //

DELIMITER ;
```

Future attempts to call the procedure with a negative value will execute the handler statement and exit:

```
CALL safefactorial(-10);
+----------------------------------------+
| ErrorMessage                           |
+----------------------------------------+
| Statement to handle the error goes here |
+----------------------------------------+
1 row in set (0.00 sec)
```

The SafeFactorial() procedure currently uses an EXIT handler to terminate the procedure after handling the error. Converting the handler to use CONTINUE instead of EXIT will demonstrate the risks of allowing execution to continue after an error has occurred. Drop and redeclare the procedure as follows:

```
DROP PROCEDURE SafeFactorial;

DELIMITER //

CREATE PROCEDURE SafeFactorial(IN num INT)
BEGIN

    DECLARE result INT DEFAULT 1;

    DECLARE CONTINUE HANDLER FOR SQLEXCEPTION
        SELECT 'Statement to handle the error goes here' AS ErrorMessage;

    REPEAT
        SET result = result * num;
        SET num = num - 1;
    UNTIL num = 0
    END REPEAT;

    SELECT CONCAT('Factorial = ', result) AS Result;
END //

DELIMITER ;
```

Call SafeFactorial() with a negative number once more and note that although the error message appears, control does not return to the command prompt. The problem is that allowing the execution to continue following the error has caused the REPEAT statement to loop infinitely. In other words, our SafeFactorial() procedure is no longer "safe."

The only way to exit from the procedure is to type Ctrl-C on the keyboard, an option that would not be available if a client application had called this routine:

```
CALL SafeFactorial(-10);
```

158

```
+---------------------------------------+
| ErrorMessage                          |
+---------------------------------------+
| Statement to handle the error goes here |
+---------------------------------------+
1 row in set (0.01 sec)

^C -- query aborted
ERROR 1317 (70100): Query execution was interrupted
```

In summary, only use CONTINUE handlers when doing so will not lead to critical issues in subsequent code.

20.6 Error handling with SQLWARNING and NOT FOUND

A SQLEXCEPTION condition handler will catch errors that are categorized as exceptions. The same technique can be used to create handlers specifically for warning (01) and no data (02) code classes. The following handler example will display a custom message for no data (NOT FOUND) class codes:

```
DECLARE CONTINUE HANDLER FOR NOT FOUND
    SELECT 'No matching record found' AS ErrorMessage;
```

Conditions may also be combined when creating a handler. The following handler catches exceptions and warnings:

```
DECLARE CONTINUE HANDLER FOR SQLEXCEPTION, SQLWARNING
    SELECT 'Warning or No data detected' AS ErrorMessage;
```

20.7 Handling specific errors with SQLSTATE

While adequate for many situations, the above examples handle errors based solely on the code class (exceptions, warnings, or no data). However, this "catch-all" approach doesn't allow different actions to be performed based on the code subclass or to ignore specific exception codes. For instance, it allows us to handle all exceptions but not to differentiate between a divide by zero exception (22012) and a client-server connection failure (08006). This distinction may be critical in deciding the actions to handle the problem.

To catch and handle specific types of error, we must use SQLSTATE handler conditions, the syntax for which is as follows:

```
DECLARE [CONTINUE | EXIT] HANDLER FOR SQLSTATE '<sqlstate_code>'
BEGIN
    <sql_statements>
END;
```

We can declare handlers for multiple conditions in a single routine by targeting specific error codes. The following procedure, for example, performs division and multiplication calculations on two TINYINT values and declares handlers to catch division by zero (22012) and out-of-range value (22003) error codes. The routine continues executing when a division by zero is detected and exits when a value is out of range:

```
DELIMITER //

CREATE PROCEDURE CalcDemo(x TINYINT, y TINYINT)
BEGIN

    DECLARE result TINYINT DEFAULT 1;

    DECLARE CONTINUE HANDLER FOR SQLSTATE '22012'
```

```
            SELECT 'Division by zero occurred. Continuing...' AS ErrorMessage;

        DECLARE EXIT HANDLER FOR SQLSTATE '22003'
            SELECT 'Out of range value occurred. Exiting...' AS ErrorMessage;

        SELECT x / y AS Division_Result;

        SET result = x * y;

        SELECT result AS Multiplication_Result;
    END //

    DELIMITER ;
```

An unsigned TINYINT value stores integers ranging from 0 to 255, so calling CalcDemo() with small, non-zero parameter numbers produces both division and multiplication results:

```
CALL CalcDemo(10, 2);
+-----------------+
| Division_Result |
+-----------------+
|          5.0000 |
+-----------------+
1 row in set (0.01 sec)

+----------------------+
| Multiplication_Result |
+----------------------+
|                   20 |
+----------------------+
1 row in set (0.01 sec)
```

The following CalcDemo() call will trigger the division by zero handler, display the corresponding message, and then continue execution to the multiplication:

```
CALL CalcDemo(10, 0);
+-----------------+
| Division_Result |
+-----------------+
|            NULL |
+-----------------+
1 row in set (0.01 sec)

+------------------------------------------+
| ErrorMessage                             |
+------------------------------------------+
| Division by zero occurred. Continuing... |
+------------------------------------------+
1 row in set (0.01 sec)

+----------------------+
| Multiplication_Result |
+----------------------+
|                    0 |
+----------------------+
```

```
1 row in set (0.00 sec)
```

Calling CalcDemo() with values that exceed 255 when multiplied will divide successfully but cause an out-of-range value exception. The out-of-range handler will output the corresponding message and exit the routine:

```
CALL CalcDemo(100, 10);
+-----------------+
| Division_Result |
+-----------------+
|         10.0000 |
+-----------------+
1 row in set (0.00 sec)


+----------------------------------------+
| ErrorMessage                           |
+----------------------------------------+
| Out of range value occurred. Exiting... |
+----------------------------------------+
1 row in set (0.00 sec)

Query OK, 0 rows affected (0.00 sec)
```

20.8 Custom error handling with SIGNAL

So far, we have looked at handling conditions generated internally by the server. MariaDB also provides a way to create custom conditions to handle errors that may occur in the logic of our own code. We might, for example, create a custom handler to validate a value based on criteria that would not be considered an error by MariaDB.

Consider a database table that stores product pricing and discount information. While the table is declared such that any integer value can be stored in the discount column, the application's business logic dictates that discounts must not exceed 20%. MariaDB allows us to create custom conditions consisting of a SQLSTATE code and error message text that can be invoked using the SIGNAL statement. The syntax for throwing a custom error is as follows:

```
SIGNAL SQLSTATE '<sqlstate_code>'
  SET MESSAGE_TEXT = '<message_text>';
```

The SQLSTATE code provided to the SIGNAL statement can be an existing code (ideally one that is similar to the custom error type) or a custom code consisting of five alphanumeric characters. The following routine uses a custom error code to validate a discount value parameter:

```
DELIMITER //

CREATE PROCEDURE ValidateDiscount(discount INT)
BEGIN

    IF discount > 20 THEN
        SIGNAL SQLSTATE 'MNOPQ'
            SET MESSAGE_TEXT = 'Discount cannot exceed 20%';
    END IF;

    SELECT 'Discount accepted' AS Status;
END //

DELIMITER ;
```

Error Handling in MariaDB

Use the MariaDB client to declare the above procedure, then call it with valid and invalid discount values:

```
CALL ValidateDiscount(15);
+-------------------+
| Status            |
+-------------------+
| Discount accepted |
+-------------------+
1 row in set (0.01 sec)

Query OK, 0 rows affected (0.01 sec)

CALL ValidateDiscount(30);
ERROR 1644 (MNOPQ): Discount cannot exceed 20%
```

If you do not intend to use the routines from this chapter in the future, delete them using the following statements:

```
DROP PROCEDURE CalcDemo;
DROP PROCEDURE ValidateDiscount;
DROP PROCEDURE SafeFactorial;
```

20.9 Reference points

The main points covered in this chapter are as follows:

- **Overview**

  - Errors in MariaDB may arise from invalid data, logic errors, or miscalculations.

  - Errors can terminate execution and leave the database in an indeterminate state.

  - Defensive coding and MariaDB's error-handling features enable graceful responses to errors.

- **Key Concepts**

  - Handlers: Define actions to execute when specific errors or conditions occur.

  - Conditions: Indicate operation success, failure, or specific issues using MariaDB's SQLSTATE codes.

  - Custom Conditions: Allow handling of application-specific logic errors not inherently flagged by MariaDB.

- **SQLSTATE Codes**

  - Five-character codes indicating operation status:

    - 00: Success.

    - 01: Warning.

    - 02: No data.

  - Other codes indicate exceptions.

  - Example: 22003 indicates "numeric value out of range."

- **Declaring a Handler**

  - Declare handlers using the following syntax:

```
DECLARE <handler_type> HANDLER FOR <condition>
    <sql_statement>;
```

- **Handler Condition Types**

  - `CONTINUE`: Continue execution after handling the error.

  - `EXIT`: Stop execution after handling the error.

- **Error Handling for Specific Conditions**

  - `SQLWARNING`: Catches warnings (01 class codes).

  - `NOT FOUND`: Catches "no data" conditions (02 class codes).

  - `SQLEXCEPTION`: Catches all exception errors.

  - Specific `SQLSTATE` Codes:

    - Example: Handling division by zero (22012) or out-of-range values (22003).

- **Custom Error Handling**

  - Create custom conditions for application-specific errors.

  - Trigger errors using `SIGNAL` statement:

    ```
    SIGNAL SQLSTATE '<sqlstate_code>'
        SET MESSAGE_TEXT = '<message_text>';
    ```

- **Best Practices**

  - Use `EXIT` handlers for critical errors to prevent incorrect results or infinite loops.

  - Use `CONTINUE` handlers cautiously to avoid cascading failures.

  - Combine specific error codes in handlers for fine-grained error management.

21. An Introduction to MariaDB Virtual Columns

Earlier in the book, we described table rows and columns as being like spreadsheets, where each cell is populated with static data retrieved from database storage. In this chapter, we will introduce a way to create *virtual columns* containing dynamic values generated based on calculations, expressions, or functions.

21.1 An overview of virtual columns

A typical table column contains the values retrieved from a database. In our example product table, the price column contains price values for each product. These values are static, and the only way to change them is to insert a new value into the table and then retrieve it again. In contrast, virtual columns (also called generated columns) can be added to tables to display dynamically generated values without being stored as fields in the database.

To extend our spreadsheet analogy, virtual columns are like spreadsheet cells that contain a formula instead of a fixed value. We could, for example, add a virtual column to our product table that displays the inventory value for each product by multiplying the price and quantity fields. One option might be to add a new column to the product table and then calculate and store the inventory value each time a product is added. However, this approach has several problems.

First, not only would the inventory value have to be calculated for each new record, but it would also need to be calculated retrospectively and stored for all existing records. More significantly, because the inventory values are static, they will not update automatically when a product's price or quantity changes. Changes to the price or quantity fields in a row would also require a recalculation and update of the inventory value. Finally, the inventory column occupies storage space that would not be needed if the total was calculated dynamically on demand instead of stored. Both of these problems can be avoided using virtual columns.

MariaDB supports two types of virtual columns:

- **Virtual** - Virtual values are generated dynamically each time the column is retrieved and do not occupy storage space.

- **Persistent** - Persistent values are generated and stored in the table whenever a row is inserted or updated. While persistent values can improve query performance for complex or frequently accessed values, they require additional storage space.

21.2 Creating virtual columns

Virtual columns can be added when a table is created or to existing tables using the VIRTUAL and PERSISTENT keywords. The syntax to add a virtual column when creating a table is as follows:

```
CREATE TABLE table_name (
    column_name definitions,
    column_name definitions,
    virtual_column_name definitions AS expression VIRTUAL | PERSISTENT,
    ...,
    PRIMARY KEY=(column_name)
```

```
);
```

To add a virtual column to an existing table, use the ALTER TABLE statement as follows:

```
ALTER TABLE table_name
ADD COLUMN virtual_column_name definitions AS expression VIRTUAL | PERSISTENT;
```

21.3 Opening the sample database

This chapter assumes that you have completed the steps in the previous chapters. If you haven't, you can import the current database snapshot using the sample files provided in the *"Start Here"* chapter.

To import the snapshot, open a terminal or command prompt, navigate to the directory containing the sample files, and run the following commands:

```
mariadb-admin -u demo -p drop sampledb
mariadb-admin -u demo -p create sampledb
mariadb -u demo -p sampledb < mariadb_virtual.sql
```

Once the database is ready, open the MariaDB client and select the *sampledb* database:

```
USE sampledb
```

21.4 A virtual column example

As an example, we will add a virtual column to the product table that dynamically calculates the inventory total as described earlier in the chapter. Run the following ALTER TABLE to add the virtual column:

```
ALTER TABLE product
ADD COLUMN inventory DECIMAL(10,2) AS (price * quantity) VIRTUAL;
```

Once the virtual column has been added, review the table using the DESCRIBE statement:

```
DESCRIBE product;
+-------------+---------------+------+-----+---------+-------------------+
| Field       | Type          | Null | Key | Default | Extra             |
+-------------+---------------+------+-----+---------+-------------------+
| id          | int(11)       | NO   | PRI | NULL    | auto_increment    |
| name        | varchar(25)   | NO   |     | NULL    |                   |
| description | varchar(50)   | YES  |     | NULL    |                   |
| price       | decimal(6,2)  | YES  |     | NULL    |                   |
| quantity    | smallint(6)   | YES  |     | NULL    |                   |
| supplier_id | int(11)       | YES  | MUL | NULL    |                   |
| inventory   | decimal(10,2) | YES  |     | NULL    | VIRTUAL GENERATED |
+-------------+---------------+------+-----+---------+-------------------+
7 rows in set (0.001 sec)
```

As shown above, the inventory column contains generated virtual values. To identify how the virtual column is generated, use the SHOW CREATE TABLE statement:

```
SHOW CREATE TABLE\G
*************************** 1. row ***************************
       Table: newproduct
Create Table: CREATE TABLE 'newproduct' (
  'id' int(11) NOT NULL AUTO_INCREMENT,
  'name' varchar(25) NOT NULL,
  'description' varchar(50) DEFAULT NULL,
  'price' decimal(6,2) DEFAULT NULL,
```

```
'quantity' smallint(6) DEFAULT NULL,
'supplier_id' int(11) DEFAULT NULL,
'inventory' decimal(10,2) GENERATED ALWAYS AS ('price' * 'quantity') VIRTUAL,
PRIMARY KEY ('id'),
KEY 'supplier_id' ('supplier_id')
) ENGINE=InnoDB AUTO_INCREMENT=17 DEFAULT CHARSET=utf8mb4 COLLATE=utf8mb4_
uca1400_ai_ci
1 row in set (0.000 sec)
```

Next, perform a query to test that the virtual column functions as expected:

```
SELECT name, inventory FROM newproduct;
+-----------------------+-----------+
| name                  | inventory |
+-----------------------+-----------+
| MacBook Pro M4 14-in  | 149999.40 |
| MacBook Air M3        |  82499.45 |
| Mac Mini M3           |  99999.00 |
.
.
.
+-----------------------+-----------+
15 rows in set (0.001 sec)
```

Virtual column expressions can reference other virtual columns within the same table. For example, add a persistent virtual column to the product database to display a discounted inventory value for each product as follows:

```
ALTER TABLE product
ADD COLUMN discounted DECIMAL(10,2) AS (inventory * 0.8) PERSISTENT;
```

Use the DESCRIBE statement to review the table schema:

```
DESCRIBE product;
+-------------+---------------+------+-----+---------+-------------------+
| Field       | Type          | Null | Key | Default | Extra             |
+-------------+---------------+------+-----+---------+-------------------+
| id          | int(11)       | NO   | PRI | NULL    | auto_increment    |
| name        | varchar(25)   | NO   |     | NULL    |                   |
| description | varchar(50)   | YES  |     | NULL    |                   |
| price       | decimal(6,2)  | YES  |     | NULL    |                   |
| quantity    | smallint(6)   | YES  |     | NULL    |                   |
| supplier_id | int(11)       | YES  | MUL | NULL    |                   |
| inventory   | decimal(10,2) | YES  |     | NULL    | VIRTUAL GENERATED |
| discounted  | decimal(10,2) | YES  |     | NULL    | STORED GENERATED  |
+-------------+---------------+------+-----+---------+-------------------+
8 rows in set (0.001 sec)
```

Finally, run a SELECT statement to test the new column:

```
SELECT name, inventory, discounted FROM product;
+-----------------------+-----------+------------+
| name                  | inventory | discounted |
+-----------------------+-----------+------------+
| MacBook Pro M4 14-in  | 149999.40 |  149989.40 |
| MacBook Air M3        |  82499.45 |   82489.45 |
| Mac Mini M3           |  99999.00 |   99989.00 |
```

```
.
.
+-----------------------+----------+-----------+
15 rows in set (0.000 sec)
```

Before proceeding to the next chapter, use the following statement to remove the virtual columns from the product table:

```
ALTER TABLE product DROP COLUMN inventory;
ALTER TABLE product DROP COLUMN discounted;
```

21.5 Reference points

The main points covered in this chapter are as follows:

- **Overview**

  - Traditional table columns store static data retrieved from the database.

  - Virtual columns (or generated columns) contain dynamic values calculated using expressions, functions, or other columns.

  - Example: A virtual column could calculate an inventory value (price × quantity) without storing it.

- **Benefits of Virtual Columns**

  - Avoids manual updates: Values recalculate automatically when referenced columns change.

  - Saves storage: Virtual columns (non-persistent) don't occupy disk space.

  - Reduces redundancy: Eliminates the need to manually update derived values (e.g., inventory totals).

- **Types of Virtual Columns in MariaDB**

  - VIRTUAL:

    - Dynamically calculated on retrieval.

    - No storage used.

  - PERSISTENT (STORED):

    - Calculated on insert/update and stored.

    - Occupies storage but improves query performance for complex calculations.

- **Creating Virtual Columns**

  - During table creation:

    ```
    CREATE TABLE table_name (
        column_name definitions,
        virtual_column AS (expression) VIRTUAL | PERSISTENT
    );
    ```

  - Adding to an existing table:

    ```
    ALTER TABLE table_name
    ADD COLUMN virtual_column AS (expression) VIRTUAL | PERSISTENT;
    ```

- **Verifying Virtual Columns**

  - `DESCRIBE table_name` - Shows column metadata (e.g., VIRTUAL GENERATED).

  - `SHOW CREATE TABLE table_name` - Displays the expression used for generation.

- **Removing Virtual Columns**

  - Use ALTER TABLE to drop virtual columns:

    ```
    ALTER TABLE <table name> DROP COLUMN <column name>;
    ```

- **Key benefits**

  - Virtual columns automate calculations and reduce data redundancy.

  - VIRTUAL = on-demand (no storage).

  - PERSISTENT = stored (faster reads).

  - Useful for derived values (e.g., totals, discounts, computed metrics).

22. Automation with MariaDB Triggers

When working with databases, operations often need to be performed in response to table data changes. For instance, if a customer is deleted from one table, their purchase history may need to be automatically removed from the table that contains customer orders. While it would, theoretically, be possible to write code in a stored routine to achieve this automation, it is far more efficient to use MariaDB triggers.

This chapter introduces MariaDB triggers, explains how to use them, and discusses their limitations.

22.1 An overview of MariaDB triggers

Triggers automatically execute blocks of SQL code in response to changes to a database table, such as deleting, inserting, or updating rows. These triggers are configured to execute before or after an event occurs. For instance, you could use a trigger to validate column values before a row is inserted into a table or to add a row to an audit log table after a row has been deleted.

22.2 The syntax for creating triggers

Triggers are declared in MariaDB using the CREATE TRIGGER statement combined with clauses defining the circumstance under which the trigger will activate. The CREATE TRIGGER statement uses the following syntax:

```
CREATE TRIGGER <trigger_name>
    [BEFORE | AFTER] [INSERT | UPDATE | DELETE]
    ON <table_name>
    FOR EACH ROW
    BEGIN
        <trigger_body>
    END;
```

The elements of the above syntax can be summarized as follows:

- **trigger_name** - The name of the trigger. This name must be unique within the scope of the database.

- **BEFORE | AFTER** - Defines whether the trigger execution occurs before or after the event.

- **INSERT | UPDATE | DELETE** - Specifies the event that will activate the trigger.

- **table_name** - The table on which the specified event will activate the trigger.

- **FOR EACH ROW** - Indicates that the trigger operates at the row level.

- **trigger_body** - The SQL statements to execute when the trigger is activated.

22.3 Accessing trigger event data

Triggers activate in response to changes in table data and execute the SQL code in the trigger body in response. A typical trigger body will act based on the data changes that activated the trigger. To continue our previous example, a trigger to log row deletions might need to include information about the deleted row. In the case of an UPDATE operation, the trigger body may need access to both the original and replacement data values.

In the trigger code, access to the event data is available via the OLD and NEW trigger extension variables using dot notation to reference the column name. For instance, consider an UPDATE event that changes the customer name column of a table row. Within the trigger code, the old and new customer_name values would be referenced as follows:

```
OLD.customer_name
NEW.customer_name
```

In most cases, the event data within the trigger body is readable and writable. This allows us to identify and change the values before they are applied to the tables via the corresponding insertion or update operation.

22.4 Triggers in action

This chapter assumes that you have completed the steps in the previous chapters. If you haven't, you can import the current database snapshot using the sample files provided in the *"Start Here"* chapter.

To import the snapshot, open a terminal or command prompt, navigate to the directory containing the sample files, and run the following commands:

```
mariadb-admin -u demo -p drop sampledb
mariadb-admin -u demo -p create sampledb
mariadb -u demo -p sampledb < mariadb_triggers.sql
```

Once the database is ready, open the MariaDB client and select the *sampledb* database:

```
USE sampledb
```

22.4.1 An AFTER INSERT example

As an initial example, we will create a trigger to log when a row is added to the supplier database. The log table will be called supplier_log and consist of a primary key, the name of the database user, the supplier name, and the event type and date. Using the MariaDB client, create the supplier_log table as follows:

```
CREATE TABLE supplier_log (
    id INT AUTO_INCREMENT PRIMARY KEY,
    username VARCHAR(35),
    supplier_name VARCHAR(25),
    event_type VARCHAR(25),
    event_date DATE
);
```

With the supplier log table added to the database, the next step is to create the trigger:

```
DELIMITER //

CREATE TRIGGER after_supplier_insert
AFTER INSERT ON supplier
FOR EACH ROW
BEGIN
    INSERT INTO supplier_log (username, supplier_name, event_type, event_date)
    VALUES (USER(), NEW.company, 'INSERT', CURDATE());
END //

DELIMITER ;
```

The trigger body contains a semicolon delimiter, so we have to temporarily change the delimiter to // while entering the trigger code. We use the USER() and CURDATE() functions within the code body to identify the database user's name and the current date, respectively.

Test the trigger by inserting a new row into the supplier table:

```
INSERT INTO supplier (
    company,
    address)
VALUES (
    'The Big Box',
    'Durham, NC'
);
```

After inserting the row, run the following statement to confirm that the addition was recorded in the log table:

```
SELECT * FROM supplier_log;
+----+----------------+--------------+------------+------------+
| id | username       | supplier_name | event_type | event_date |
+----+----------------+--------------+------------+------------+
|  1 | root@localhost | The Big Box  | INSERT     | 2025-01-10 |
+----+----------------+--------------+------------+------------+
1 row in set (0.01 sec)
```

22.4.2 A BEFORE INSERT example

The BEFORE clause performs actions before changes are made to a database table. This allows us to perform actions such as validating or transforming the data before it is written to the table or preventing a deletion from proceeding under specific conditions. The following trigger, for example, converts the address field to uppercase when new records are inserted into the supplier table:

```
DELIMITER //

CREATE TRIGGER before_supplier_insert
BEFORE INSERT ON supplier
FOR EACH ROW
BEGIN
    SET NEW.address = UPPER(NEW.address);
END //

DELIMITER ;
```

Next, add a new row to the supplier table, then run a SELECT statement to check that the address was converted to upper case:

```
INSERT INTO supplier (
    company,
    address
)
VALUES (
    'Acme Networks',
    'boston, ma'
);

SELECT * FROM supplier WHERE company = 'Acme Networks';
+----+----------------+------------+
| id | company        | address    |
+----+----------------+------------+
```

```
| 10 | Acme Networks | BOSTON, MA |
+----+---------------+------------+
1 row in set (0.00 sec)
```

22.4.3 A BEFORE DELETE example

The BEFORE DELETE trigger is useful for ensuring that certain conditions are met before rows are deleted from a table. The following trigger uses a SIGNAL statement to prevent rows from being deleted from the supplier table:

```
DELIMITER //

CREATE TRIGGER before_supplier_delete
BEFORE DELETE ON supplier
FOR EACH ROW
BEGIN
    SIGNAL SQLSTATE '45000'
        SET MESSAGE_TEXT = 'Deletions are not allowed in the supplier table';
END //

DELIMITER ;
```

Test the trigger by attempting to delete the Acme Networks row from the supplier table:

```
DELETE FROM supplier WHERE company LIKE 'Acme Networks';
ERROR 1644 (45000): Deletions are not allowed in the supplier table
```

22.5 Displaying trigger information

Information about the triggers defined within a database can be displayed using the SHOW TRIGGERS statement. The following statement lists all of the active triggers for the current database:

```
SHOW TRIGGERS\G
*************************** 1. row ***************************
            Trigger: before_supplier_delete
              Event: DELETE
              Table: supplier
          Statement: BEGIN
    SIGNAL SQLSTATE '45000'
        SET MESSAGE_TEXT = 'Deletions are not allowed in the supplier table';
END
             Timing: BEFORE
            Created: 2025-01-16 09:51:32.30
           sql_mode: ONLY_FULL_GROUP_BY,STRICT_TRANS_TABLES,NO_ZERO_IN_
DATE,NO_ZERO_DATE,ERROR_FOR_DIVISION_BY_ZERO,NO_ENGINE_SUBSTITUTION
            Definer: root@localhost
character_set_client: utf8mb4
collation_connection: utf8mb4_0900_ai_ci
  Database Collation: utf8mb4_0900_ai_ci
.
.
```

Note the use of the \G modifier in the above example. The result set generated by the SHOW TRIGGERS statement contains wide output lines that are best viewed using vertical formatting.

To limit the list of triggers to specific tables, combine the SHOW TRIGGERS statement with the LIKE clause, using either the full table name or wildcard matching to select multiple tables, for example:

```
SHOW TRIGGERS LIKE 'suppl%' \G
```

22.6 Deleting triggers

Triggers are deleted using the DROP TRIGGER statement, the syntax for which is as follows:

```
DROP TRIGGER <trigger_name>;
```

To avoid unexpected behavior later, run the following statements to remove the supplier_log table and the triggers created in this chapter:

```
DROP TABLE supplier_log;
DROP TRIGGER after_supplier_insert;
DROP TRIGGER before_supplier_insert;
DROP TRIGGER before_supplier_delete;
```

22.7 Limitations of triggers

Before learning about MariaDB events in the next chapter, we need to outline the limitations of MariaDB triggers, beginning with recursion. Triggers are non-recursive, meaning that they cannot activate themselves. Triggers also cannot start, commit, or rollback transactions. Finally, excessive use of triggers on databases with high transaction rates can result in performance degradation. Try to avoid using triggers as a "quick fix" for a problem that could be addressed more efficiently elsewhere.

22.8 Reference points

The main points covered in this chapter are as follows:

- **Overview**

    - Triggers automatically execute SQL code in response to changes in a table (INSERT, UPDATE, DELETE).

    - More efficient than using stored routines for automation.

- **Creating Triggers**

    - Syntax:

    ```
    CREATE TRIGGER <trigger_name>
        [BEFORE | AFTER] [INSERT | UPDATE | DELETE]
        ON <table_name>
        FOR EACH ROW
        BEGIN
            <trigger_body>
        END;
    ```

- **Trigger Components**

    - BEFORE | AFTER: Defines when the trigger runs relative to the event.

    - INSERT | UPDATE | DELETE: Specifies the event type.

    - FOR EACH ROW: Indicates the trigger operates at the row level.

- **Accessing Trigger Event Data**

    - OLD.column_name: Accesses previous row values before an update or delete.

    - NEW.column_name: Accesses new values being inserted or updated.

Automation with MariaDB Triggers

- **Managing Triggers**

  - Show all triggers in the current database:

    ```
    SHOW TRIGGERS\G
    ```

  - Show triggers for a specific table:

    ```
    SHOW TRIGGERS LIKE 'suppl%'\G
    ```

- **Deleting Triggers**

  - Remove a trigger using:

    ```
    DROP TRIGGER <trigger_name>;
    ```

- **Limitations of Triggers**

  - Triggers are **non-recursive** (they cannot activate themselves).

  - Cannot start, commit, or rollback transactions.

  - Excessive use in high-transaction databases may impact performance.

  - Avoid using triggers as a shortcut for problems that could be solved more efficiently elsewhere.

23. Scheduling Tasks with MariaDB Events

The previous chapter introduced MariaDB triggers and explored how they execute code automatically in response to table data changes. While triggers help automate tasks, they are not designed to handle scheduled tasks or operations that do not depend on changes in table data. MariaDB events fill this gap by allowing us to schedule repetitive tasks like data cleanups, backups, or routine updates based on dates, times, and intervals.

This chapter will introduce MariaDB events, explain how they work, and provide practical examples.

23.1 An introduction to MariaDB events

MariaDB events execute SQL statements at specified times or intervals and typically automate tasks such as generating reports, deleting old data and logs, and monitoring and logging database activity.

Unlike triggers, which respond to table operations such as INSERT, UPDATE, DELETE, events are time-based and execute independently of any specific database activity or user actions. Table 23-1 outlines the difference between triggers and events:

Feature	Triggers	Events
Activation	Execution in response to table events (INSERT, UPDATE, DELETE).	Execution based on a time schedule.
Scope	Applies to specific tables.	Operates at the database level.
Timing	Triggered immediately during or after a table operation.	Executes at a specified time or interval.

Table 23-1

23.2 Enabling the MariaDB event scheduler

Events are controlled, managed, and executed by the MariaDB event scheduler process, which can be turned on and off via the *event_scheduler* global variable. The event scheduler is not activated by default when MariaDB is installed, and you can check the current status using the following statement:

```
SHOW VARIABLES LIKE 'event_scheduler';
+-----------------+-------+
| Variable_name   | Value |
+-----------------+-------+
| event_scheduler | ON    |
+-----------------+-------+
1 row in set (0.06 sec)
```

If the event scheduler is off, use the following statement to enable it before proceeding with the examples in this chapter:

```
SET GLOBAL event_scheduler = ON;
```

23.3 Creating Events

Events are created using the CREATE EVENT statement, the basic syntax for which is as follows:

```
CREATE EVENT <event_name>
ON SCHEDULE [AT <timestamp> | EVERY <interval>]
DO
    <sql_statement>;
```

The elements of the above syntax can be summarized as follows:

- **event_name** - The event name which must be unique within the database scope.

- **ON SCHEDULE** - Defines when the event will execute using one of the following options:

  - **AT** *<timestamp>* - Schedules the event to run once at a specific date and time.

  - **EVERY** *<interval>* - Schedules the event to repeat at regular intervals (e.g., every hour).

- **DO** - The SQL statement or block of statements to execute.

Note that the BEGIN and END keywords must be used when executing more than one statement in the DO block:

```
CREATE EVENT <event_name>
ON SCHEDULE [AT <timestamp> | EVERY <interval>]
DO
BEGIN
    <sql_statements>
END;
```

23.4 Opening the sample database

This chapter assumes that you have completed the steps in the previous chapters. If you haven't, you can import the current database snapshot using the sample files provided in the *"Start Here"* chapter.

To import the snapshot, open a terminal or command prompt, navigate to the directory containing the sample files, and run the following commands:

```
mariadb-admin -u demo -p drop sampledb
mariadb-admin -u demo -p create sampledb
mariadb -u demo -p sampledb < mariadb_events.sql
```

Once the database is ready, open the MariaDB client and select the *sampledb* database:

```
USE sampledb
```

23.5 Adding the event_tests table

Before we look at some event examples, we need to add a table called event_tests to our sampledb database. This table will consist of id, description, and timestamp columns and will be used to verify that the example events are working. Use the statement below to create the table:

```
CREATE TABLE event_tests
(
  id int NOT NULL AUTO_INCREMENT,
  description char(20) NOT NULL,
  timestamp TIMESTAMP NOT NULL,
```

```
    PRIMARY KEY (id)
);
```

23.6 Creating a one-time event

One-time events are the simplest event type and are created by specifying when the code must execute using the following TIMESTAMP format:

```
YYYY-MM-DD hh:mm:ss
```

For example, to schedule an event to occur at 2:35pm on January 16, 2027, the CREATE EVENT statement might read as follows:

```
CREATE EVENT do_something
ON SCHEDULE AT '2027-01-16 14:35:00'
DO
    <sql_statement>;
```

While it is possible to use the timestamp format to schedule an event, it is also a common requirement to schedule a one-time event relative to the current date and time. For example, we might need to schedule an event to execute in one hour, at the same time tomorrow, or at this time exactly one week, month, or year in the future. While these calculations may seem daunting, they can easily be performed by referencing the CURRENT_TIMESTAMP variable and adding an INTERVAL:

```
CURRENT_TIMESTAMP + INTERVAL <number> <time_unit>
```

In the above syntax, CURRENT_TIMESTAMP contains the system data and time of the server on which MariaDB is running, *<time_unit>* is the unit of time (MINUTE, HOUR, DAY, WEEK, MONTH, etc.), and *<number>* is the number of time units to be added.

The following statement, for example, schedules an event to occur in one minute. When the event triggers, it inserts a row into the event_tests table consisting of a description and the date and time the event executed:

```
CREATE EVENT one_time_demo
ON SCHEDULE AT CURRENT_TIMESTAMP + INTERVAL 1 MINUTE
DO
    INSERT INTO event_tests VALUES (
        NULL,
        'One-time event',
        CURRENT_TIMESTAMP()
);
```

Run the above statement and wait for one minute before checking the event_tests table:

```
SELECT * FROM event_tests;
+----+----------------+---------------------+
| id | description    | timestamp           |
+----+----------------+---------------------+
|  1 | One-time event | 2025-01-16 13:35:00 |
+----+----------------+---------------------+
1 row in set (0.04 sec)
```

23.7 Creating recurring events

A recurring event repeats at specified intervals until it is canceled or, if one is provided, an end date is reached. By default, the first recurring event will trigger after the specified time interval has elapsed. Alternatively, scheduling can be deferred by providing a start timestamp. The CREATE EVENT statement uses the following syntax to declare recurring events:

```
CREATE EVENT <event_name>
ON SCHEDULE EVERY <number> <time_unit>
STARTS <start_timestamp>
ENDS <end_timestamp>
DO
    <sql_statement>;
```

Use the statement below to create a recurring event that adds a row to the event_tests table every minute until 5 minutes have elapsed:

```
CREATE EVENT recurring_demo
ON SCHEDULE EVERY 1 MINUTE
ENDS CURRENT_TIMESTAMP + INTERVAL 5 MINUTE
DO
    INSERT INTO event_tests VALUES (
    NULL,
    'Recurring event',
    CURRENT_TIMESTAMP()
);
```

Run the following statement occasionally to verify that records are being added to event_tests table by the recurring event and that insertions stop after 5 minutes:

```
SELECT * FROM event_tests;
+----+----------------+---------------------+
| id | description    | timestamp           |
+----+----------------+---------------------+
|  1 | One-time event | 2025-01-16 14:21:24 |
|  2 | Recurring event | 2025-01-16 14:50:42 |
|  3 | Recurring event | 2025-01-16 14:52:42 |
|  4 | Recurring event | 2025-01-16 14:54:42 |
|  5 | Recurring event | 2025-01-16 14:56:42 |
|  6 | Recurring event | 2025-01-16 14:58:42 |
+----+----------------+---------------------+
6 rows in set (0.00 sec)
```

23.8 Viewing event details

Details of active events can be viewed using the SHOW EVENTS statement as outlined below:

```
SHOW EVENTS\G
*************************** 1. row ***************************
                   Db: sampledb
                 Name: recurring_demo
              Definer: root@localhost
            Time zone: SYSTEM
                 Type: RECURRING
           Execute at: NULL
       Interval value: 1
       Interval field: MINUTE
               Starts: 2025-01-16 14:50:42
                 Ends: 2025-01-16 15:00:40
               Status: ENABLED
           Originator: 1
```

```
character_set_client: utf8mb4
collation_connection: utf8mb4_0900_ai_ci
  Database Collation: utf8mb4_0900_ai_ci
1 row in set (0.03 sec)
```

To display information about a specific event, use the SHOW CREATE EVENT statement, referencing the event name:

```
SHOW CREATE EVENT one_time_demo\G
*************************** 1. row ***************************
               Event: one_time_demo
            sql_mode: ONLY_FULL_GROUP_BY,STRICT_TRANS_TABLES,NO_ZERO_IN_
DATE,NO_ZERO_DATE,ERROR_FOR_DIVISION_BY_ZERO,NO_ENGINE_SUBSTITUTION
           time_zone: SYSTEM
        Create Event: CREATE DEFINER='root'@'localhost' EVENT 'one_time_demo'
ON SCHEDULE AT '2025-01-16 15:05:55' ON COMPLETION NOT PRESERVE ENABLE DO
INSERT INTO event_tests VALUES (
        NULL,
        'One-time event',
        CURRENT_TIMESTAMP()
)
character_set_client: utf8mb4
collation_connection: utf8mb4_0900_ai_ci
  Database Collation: utf8mb4_0900_ai_ci
1 row in set (0.00 sec)
```

23.9 Preserving events

Unless instructed otherwise, the scheduler will delete events after they finish executing. As a demonstration, recreate the *one_time_demo* event and use the SHOW EVENTS statement to verify it is running. Listing the events after the 1-minute interval has elapsed will show that the event has been deleted.

To retain an event for future use, the CREATE EVENT statement must include the ON COMPLETION clause with the PRESERVE option. Use the statement below to recreate the *one_time_demo* event with preservation enabled:

```
CREATE EVENT one_time_demo
ON SCHEDULE AT CURRENT_TIMESTAMP + INTERVAL 1 MINUTE
ON COMPLETION PRESERVE
DO
    INSERT INTO event_tests VALUES (
        NULL,
        'One-time event',
        CURRENT_TIMESTAMP()
);
```

After the event finishes, it will be disabled and preserved by the event scheduler:

```
SHOW EVENTS\G
*************************** 1. row ***************************
                  Db: sampledb
                Name: one_time_demo
             Definer: root@localhost
           Time zone: SYSTEM
                Type: ONE TIME
          Execute at: 2025-01-17 09:38:35
```

```
        Interval value: NULL
        Interval field: NULL
                Starts: NULL
                  Ends: NULL
                Status: DISABLED
             Originator: 1
  character_set_client: utf8mb4
  collation_connection: utf8mb4_0900_ai_ci
    Database Collation: utf8mb4_0900_ai_ci
1 row in set (0.01 sec)
```

Two event properties need to be changed to reuse this event. The first issue is that the event is currently disabled, so it needs to be enabled before it will run again. In addition, the event is configured to execute at a date and time that is now in the past. Therefore, in addition to enabling the event, we will also need to schedule it to run at a date and time in the future. These and many other event properties can be changed using the ALTER EVENT statement.

23.10 Altering event properties

The ALTER EVENT statement allows us to modify the properties of existing events using similar syntax to the CREATE EVENT statement. Using ALTER EVENT, we can perform tasks such as enabling, disabling, and renaming events, changing scheduling settings, turning preservation on and off, and replacing the SQL statements in the DO code block.

Below is the basic syntax used by the ALTER EVENT statement:

```
ALTER EVENT <event_name>
  ON SCHEDULE [AT <timestamp> | EVERY <interval>]
  ON COMPLETION [NOT] PRESERVE
  RENAME TO <new_event_name>
  [ENABLE | DISABLE | DISABLE ON {REPLICA | SLAVE}]
  COMMENT '<comment_string>'
  DO
     <sql_statement>;
```

When using ALTER EVENT, we only need to reference the event properties that are changing. Properties that are not referenced in the statement will retain their current values.

Continuing our previous example, we can re-enable our one_time_demo event with a 1-minute interval using the following ALTER EVENT statement:

```
ALTER EVENT one_time_demo
ON SCHEDULE AT CURRENT_TIMESTAMP + INTERVAL 1 MINUTE
ENABLE;
```

In addition to re-enabling preserved events, changes can be made to running events. To see this in action, use the following statement to re-create a slightly modified version of our recurring_demo event:

```
CREATE EVENT recurring_demo
ON SCHEDULE EVERY 1 MINUTE
ENDS CURRENT_TIMESTAMP + INTERVAL 10 MINUTE
ON COMPLETION PRESERVE
DO
   INSERT INTO event_tests VALUES (
   NULL,
   'Recurring event',
```

```
    CURRENT_TIMESTAMP()
);
```

After one minute, run a query on the event_tests table to verify that the event is executing:

```
SELECT * FROM event_tests;
+----+--------------------+--------------------+
| id | description        | timestamp          |
+----+--------------------+--------------------+
.
.
.
| 46 | Recurring event    | 2025-01-17 10:48:37 |
+----+--------------------+--------------------+
46 rows in set (0.00 sec)
```

While the event continues to execute, use the statement below to decrease the interval to 30 seconds and provide a new DO statement:

```
ALTER EVENT recurring_demo
ON SCHEDULE EVERY 30 SECOND
DO
    INSERT INTO event_tests VALUES (
    NULL,
    'Altered event',
    CURRENT_TIMESTAMP()
);
```

Recheck the test table to verify that the event occurs every 30 seconds and includes the modified description text:

```
SELECT * FROM event_tests;
+----+--------------------+--------------------+
| id | description        | timestamp          |
+----+--------------------+--------------------+
|  1 | One-time event     | 2025-02-07 14:19:37 |
|  2 | Recurring event    | 2025-02-07 14:19:52 |
|  3 | Recurring event    | 2025-02-07 14:21:52 |
.
.
| 46 | Recurring event    | 2025-01-17 10:48:37 |
| 47 | Altered event      | 2025-01-17 10:48:46 |
| 48 | Altered event      | 2025-01-17 10:49:16 |
| 49 | Altered event      | 2025-01-17 10:49:46 |
+----+--------------------+--------------------+
49 rows in set (0.00 sec)
```

23.11 Deleting events

Events are removed from the event scheduler using the DROP EVENT statement. With the practical sections of this chapter completed, take this opportunity to delete event_tests table and the two example events:

```
DROP EVENT one_time_demo;
DROP EVENT recurring_demo;
DROP TABLE event_tests;
```

23.12 Reference points

The main points covered in this chapter are as follows:

- **Overview**

  - MariaDB events allow tasks to be scheduled for automatic execution at predefined times.

  - Used for automating repetitive processes such as backups, data cleanups, and routine updates.

- **Enabling the MariaDB Event Scheduler**

  - The MariaDB event scheduler is responsible for executing scheduled events.

  - Checking and modifying its status ensures that scheduled tasks run as expected.

    ```
    SHOW VARIABLES LIKE 'event_scheduler';
    SET GLOBAL event_scheduler = ON;
    ```

- **Creating MariaDB Events**

  - Events are scheduled either for a specific time or at recurring intervals.

  - Events can be configured to run once or to repeat at regular intervals such as minutes, hours, or days.

- **One-Time Events**

  - These events execute only once at a specified date and time.

  - By default, they are removed after execution unless explicitly preserved.

  - Syntax:

    ```
    CREATE EVENT event_name
    ON SCHEDULE AT 'YYYY-MM-DD HH:MM:SS'
    DO
        SQL_statement;
    ```

- **Recurring Events**

  - Recurring events are designed to execute repeatedly at defined time intervals.

  - They continue running indefinitely or until a specified end time is reached.

  - Syntax:

    ```
    CREATE EVENT event_name
    ON SCHEDULE EVERY interval TIME_UNIT
    DO
        SQL_statement;
    ```

- **Viewing and Managing Events**

  - The list of scheduled events can be viewed using the SHOW EVENTS statement.

  - View details of a specific using SHOW CREATE EVENT statement.

  - Events can be modified, enabled, or disabled without deleting them.

- **Preserving and Altering Events**

- Events are deleted after execution unless `ON COMPLETION PRESERVE` is specified.

- Preserved events can be re-enabled and rescheduled to run at a future time.

- Modify an existing event using `ALTER EVENT`.

- **Disabling and Deleting Events**

  - Disabling an event prevents it from running while keeping it stored in the database:

    ```
    ALTER EVENT event_name DISABLE;
    ```

  - Deleting an event permanently removes it from the system:

    ```
    DROP EVENT event_name;
    ```

- **Triggers vs. Events**

  - Triggers execute in response to table modifications (`INSERT`, `UPDATE`, `DELETE`), while events execute based on a time schedule.

  - Triggers apply to specific tables, whereas events operate at the database level.

  - Triggers execute immediately after a table modification, while events run at predefined intervals.

24. Configuring MariaDB using the my.cnf File

MariaDB has built-in settings that define the server's behavior and performance. It uses these values by default unless custom configuration settings override them. Custom configuration settings are declared in the MariaDB *my.cnf* file, which the MariaDB server reads at startup. This chapter will explore the my.cnf file and outline some of the main configuration options. Although we will refer to the my.cnf file in this chapter, the file is named my.ini on Windows systems.

24.1 Introducing the my.cnf file

The my.cnf file is the primary configuration file for MariaDB, containing settings that modify how the MariaDB server performs and operates and is typically located in one of the following directories, depending on the host operating system and MariaDB installation:

- **Linux** - /etc/my.cnf, /etc/mysql/my.cnf, or /usr/local/mysql/etc/my.cnf

- **Windows** - C:\ProgramData\MariaDB\data\my.ini

- **Custom Installations** - The my.cnf file can also be placed in other locations and may be specified on the command line at MariaDB startup.

When the MariaDB server starts, it will search for the my.cnf file in a predefined set of locations. These locations and the order in which they are searched can be identified by running the mariadb --help command and looking for the following information:

```
Default options are read from the following files in the given order:
/etc/my.cnf /etc/mysql/my.cnf /usr/local/mysql/etc/my.cnf ~/.my.cnf
```

MariaDB uses the built-in default settings if the my.cnf file is missing or incorrectly configured.

24.2 The my.cnf file structure

The configuration file organization differs between Linux and Windows. On Windows, the configuration options for MariaDB are defined in a single file named my.ini which, by default, contains the following settings:

```
[mysqld]
datadir=C:/Program Files/MariaDB 11.7/data
port=3306
innodb_buffer_pool_size=1013M
[client]
port=3306
plugin-dir=C:\Program Files\MariaDB 11.7/lib/plugin
```

On Linux, however, the default my.cnf file is more likely to contain a combination of settings and 'includedir' statements that import settings from other configuration files. Consider, for example, the default my.cnf file for MariaDB on Ubuntu:

\#

Configuring MariaDB using the my.cnf File

```
# This group is read both by the client and the server
# use it for options that affect everything
#
[client-server]
# Port or socket location where to connect
# port = 3306
socket = /run/mysqld/mysqld.sock

# Import all .cnf files from configuration directory
!includedir /etc/mysql/conf.d/
!includedir /etc/mysql/mariadb.conf.d/
```

In the above example, the my.cnf file includes all the configuration files located in the following directories:

```
/etc/mysql/conf.d/
/etc/mysql/mariadb.conf.d/
```

The configuration files located in the conf.d directory are global settings that apply to both MariaDB and MySQL servers. In other words, in an environment where MariaDB and MySQL are running on the same database, configuration settings that are to apply to both should be placed in this directory. The mariadb.conf.d directory, on the other hand, should be used for configuration settings that are only to be applied to MariaDB.

The configuration file layout differs between Linux distributions, so start with my.cnf file and follow any 'includedir' statements to identify other configuration file dependencies.

The configuration file is divided into sections called *option groups*, each beginning with a group header enclosed in square brackets ([ ]). Each group contains configuration directives that apply to a specific MariaDB or MySQL component. For example, to find out which configuration groups are read by the MariaDB client, run mariadb --help and locate the help section that lists the groups that are read:

```
mariadb --help
.
.
The following groups are read: mysql mariadb-client client client-server
client-mariadb
.
.
```

From the above output we can see the five option groups that the client will read when it is launched.

Similarly, to identify the groups that apply to the MariaDB server, run the mariadbd executable as follows:

```
mariadbd --verbose --help
.
.
The following groups are read: mysqld server mysqld-11.7 mariadb mariadb-11.7
mariadbd mariadbd-11.7 client-server galera
.
.
```

Each group controls different aspects of MariaDB. Table 24-1 provides a list of commonly used option groups and their purpose:

Option Group	Description
[mysqld]	Options applying to both MariaDB and MySQL servers.

[mariadb]	Options applying to MariaDB servers only.
[mariadb-client]	Options for the mariadb client only.
[client]	Options applying to all MariaDB and MySQL client programs (mysql, mariadb, mysqldump, mariadb-dump, etc.)
[client-server]	Options applying to all MariaDB clients and the MariaDB Server.
[client-mariadb]	Options applying to all MariaDB client programs.

Table 24-1

24.3 Key my.cnf parameters

The my.cnf file supports a wide range of parameters that control different aspects of MariaDB's behavior. Fortunately, only settings that differ from the default value must be included in the file. Below are some of the more commonly used parameters, grouped by category:

24.3.1 General server settings

These settings define the basic behavior of the MariaDB server.

```
[mysqld]
port = 3306
bind-address = 127.0.0.1
max_connections = 200
skip_name_resolve = 1
```

- **port** - Specifies the port MariaDB listens on (the default port 3306).

- **bind-address** - Defines the network interface MariaDB should listen on (127.0.0.1 restricts access to the local machine).

- **max_connections** - Limits the number of simultaneous client connections.

- **skip_name_resolve** - Disables DNS resolution for client connections, improving performance.

24.3.2 Performance tuning

Performance optimization usually involves adjustments to memory, caching, and query execution settings. The following are examples of performance-related configuration options for the InnoDB storage engine:

```
[mysqld]
query_cache_size = 64M
query_cache_type = 1
innodb_buffer_pool_size = 1G
innodb_log_file_size = 256M
thread_cache_size = 16
```

- **query_cache_size** - Sets the size of the query cache, which stores query results for faster retrieval.

- **query_cache_type** - Enables (1) or disables (0) query caching.

- **innodb_buffer_pool_size** - Defines the memory allocated to InnoDB's buffer pool (should be 50-80% of total server RAM).

- **innodb_log_file_size** - Determines the size of each InnoDB redo log file.

- **thread_cache_size** - Caches client threads to improve performance when handling multiple connections.

24.3.3 Storage engine configuration

MariaDB storage engine performance can be optimized through the my.cnf file. The available options are storage engine-specific. The following settings relate to the InnoDB engine:

```
[mysqld]
default_storage_engine = InnoDB
innodb_flush_log_at_trx_commit = 1
innodb_file_per_table = 1
```

- **default_storage_engine** - Defines the default storage engine (InnoDB is the preferred choice for most applications).

- **innodb_flush_log_at_trx_commit** - Controls transaction log flushing.

- **innodb_file_per_table** - Stores each table in a separate .ibd file instead of a shared tablespace.

24.3.4 Logging and debugging

MariaDB provides extensive logging options for debugging and monitoring via the following options:

```
[mysqld]
log_error = /var/log/mysql/error.log
slow_query_log = 1
slow_query_log_file = /var/log/mysql/slow.log
long_query_time = 2
```

- **log_error** - Specifies the file where MariaDB logs errors.

- **slow_query_log** - Enables slow query logging (1 for enabled, 0 for disabled).

- **slow_query_log_file** - Specifies the file for slow query logs.

- **long_query_time** - Defines the threshold (in seconds) for slow queries.

24.3.5 Security settings

Security is a critical aspect of MariaDB configuration. Two key security options are as follows:

```
[mysqld]
skip-networking
secure-file-priv = /var/lib/mysql-files
```

- **skip-networking** - Disables remote connections for added security.

- **secure-file-priv** - Restricts the directory for file operations like LOAD DATA INFILE.

24.4 Changing the client prompt

The prompt displayed by the MariaDB client can be changed adding the prompt parameter to the [mariadb-client] option group, for example:

```
[mariadb-client]
prompt=\N [\h]>\_
```

Refer to the *"The MariaDB Client"* chapter for a listing of special characters available for customizing the prompt.

24.4.1 Applying my.cnf file changes

Changes to the my.cnf file will not take effect until the MariaDB server is restarted. On Linux, run the following command within a terminal window to perform a server restart:

```
sudo systemctl restart mariadb.service
```

On Windows, open a PowerShell session with administrator privileges and run the following commands where

```
net stop MariaDB
net start MariaDB
```

Once the server has restarted, connect using the MariaDB client and use the SHOW VARIABLES statement to check that any overridden settings are reflected in the running server instance:

```
SHOW VARIABLES LIKE 'innodb_buffer_pool_size';
+-------------------------+-----------+
| Variable_name           | Value     |
+-------------------------+-----------+
| innodb_buffer_pool_size | 334227128 |
+-------------------------+-----------+
1 row in set (0.00 sec)
```

24.5 Reference points

The main points covered in this chapter are as follows:

- **Overview**

  - The my.cnf file customizes MariaDB server behavior.

  - Settings control general configurations, performance tuning, storage engines, logging, and security.

  - MariaDB uses default configuration settings unless overridden by the my.cnf file.

  - The my.cnf file (my.ini on Windows) defines server behavior and performance settings.

- **my.cnf File Locations**

  - **Linux**: /etc/my.cnf, /etc/mysql/my.cnf, /usr/local/mysql/etc/my.cnf

  - **macOS**: /etc/my.cnf, /etc/mysql/my.cnf, /usr/local/mysql/etc/my.cnf, ~/.my.cnf

  - **Windows**: C:\ProgramData\MySQL\MySQL Server <version>\my.ini

- **my.cnf File Structure**

  - Configuration sections:

    - [**mysqld**] -> MariaDB and MySQL server settings

    - [**mariadb**] -> MariaDB server settings

    - [**client**] -> MariaDB and MySQL client settings

    - [**mariadb-client**] -> MariaDB client settings

- **Key my.cnf Parameters**

  - **General Server Settings**

Configuring MariaDB using the my.cnf File

- **port** -> Defines MariaDB listening port (default: 3306).

- **bind-address** -> Restricts server access to specific network interfaces.

- **max_connections** -> Limits the number of concurrent client connections.

- **skip_name_resolv** -> Disables DNS lookups for performance improvement.

- **Performance Tuning**

  - **query_cache_size** -> Caches query results for faster retrieval.

  - **innodb_buffer_pool_size** -> Defines memory allocation for InnoDB (50-80% of RAM).

  - **innodb_log_file_size** -> Defines size of InnoDB transaction log files.

- **Storage Engine Configuration**

  - **default_storage_engine** -> Defines default table storage engine (InnoDB recommended).

  - **innodb_flush_log_at_trx_commit** -> Ensures ACID compliance (1) or better performance (0/2).

  - **innodb_file_per_table** -> Stores each table in a separate .ibd file.

- **Logging and Debugging**

  - **log_error** -> Defines error log file location.

  - **slow_query_log** -> Enables logging of slow queries.

  - **long_query_time** -> Defines threshold for slow queries (in seconds).

- **Security Settings**

  - **skip-networking** -> Disables remote MariaDB access.

  - **secure-file-priv** -> Restricts file operations to a secure directory.

- **Applying my.cnf Changes**

  - Restart MariaDB for changes to take effect:

  - Linux:

```
sudo systemctl restart mariadb
```

  - Windows (PowerShell):

```
net stop <version>
net start <version>
```

25. An Introduction to mariadb-admin

Administering a MariaDB database involves many tasks, including monitoring server status, managing users, and maintaining database tables. Although several tools, such as MariaDB Workbench and phpMyAdmin, allow you to administer MariaDB using a graphical user interface, tools like *mariadb-admin* provide a quick and convenient way to perform tasks from the command line. The mariadb-admin tool can also be called from within scripts to automate administrative tasks.

In this chapter, we will introduce mariadb-admin and explain how you can use it to administer MariaDB databases.

25.1 Setting up mariadb-admin

The mariadb-admin tool is provided as part of the MariaDB Server installation and will be located in the same directory as the *mariadb* client tool. You can verify that mariadb-admin is included in your path by opening a terminal or command-prompt window and typing the following command:

```
mariadb-admin --version
```

If mariadb-admin is in your path, you will see output similar to the following containing version information:

```
mariadb-admin from 11.7.2-MariaDB, client 10.0 for Linux (x86_64)
```

If the tool is not found, follow the steps in the chapter *"The MariaDB Client"* to add the MariaDB tools to your PATH environment variable.

Many tasks you will perform using mariadb-admin will require root user access or a user account with appropriate permissions.

25.2 Basic mariadb-admin syntax

Unlike the MariaDB client, mariadb-admin is not an interactive tool where you can enter sequences of commands in a shell environment. Instead, mariadb-admin operates transactionally, meaning you provide instructions directly on the command line when you invoke the tool. Once the task is completed, mariadb-admin exits and returns you to the command prompt.

The general syntax for using mariadb-admin is as follows:

```
mariadb-admin [options] command [command_options]
```

The command-line argument categories can be summarized as follows:

- **options** - Global settings like the username (-u) and password (-p) for authentication, or the host (-h) for remote server connections.

- **command** - The specific operation you want to perform (e.g., status, shutdown, create).

- **command_options** - Additional parameters specific to the chosen command.

An Introduction to mariadb-admin

For example, to check the status of the server as the demo user, you would run the following command:

```
mariadb-admin -u demo -p status
```

After the root password has been entered, status information similar to the following will appear:

```
Uptime: 176854  Threads: 2  Questions: 346  Slow queries: 0  Opens: 160  Flush
tables: 3  Open tables: 81  Queries per second avg: 0.001
```

To display a list of all of the command line options supported by mariadb-admin, run it with the --help argument:

```
mariadb-admin --help
```

The help information will make it clear that mariadb-admin can perform various administrative tasks. While a detailed overview of all of these capabilities is beyond the scope of this book, we will cover many of the more common uses in the remainder of this chapter.

25.3 Checking server status

Several options are available to check various server status properties. As we saw previously, we can request the overall server status as follows:

```
mariadb-admin -u demo -p status
Uptime: 177747  Threads: 2  Questions: 348  Slow queries: 0  Opens: 160  Flush
tables: 3  Open tables: 81  Queries per second avg: 0.001
```

The MariaDB server operates as a collection of background processes rather than a single entity. These processes start and stop depending on the volume and nature of the incoming requests. A server managing hundreds of requests per minute will have more active background processes than an idle server. However, having too many active processes can affect the server's performance.

You can view the list of currently running processes using the mariadb-admin tool with the processlist command:

```
mariadb-admin -u root -p processlist
+----+-------+-----------+----+---------+-----+------+-----------------+
| Id | User  | Host      | db | Command |Time |State | Info            |
+----+-------+-----------+----+---------+-----+------+-----------------+
| 5  | event | localhost |    | Daemon  | 177 | Wait |                 |
| 14 | root  | localhost |    | Query   | 0   | init | show processlist |
+----+-------+-----------+----+---------+-----+------+-----------------+
```

25.4 Shutting down the server

The server can be stopped from the command line using the shutdown option as follows:

```
mariadb-admin -u demo -p shutdown
```

The above command will gracefully shut down the server and close all active connections. Although the start command can be used to launch the server, this is best performed using a service manager such as systemctl on Linux or a Windows Service.

25.5 Resetting user passwords

The password assigned to root or any other user can be changed using the mariadb-admin password command. The following command changes the password for the root account:

```
mariadb-admin -u demo -p password 'new_password'
```

The tool will prompt for the current password before applying the new one. If you know the current password for a user, you can change it to a new password as follows:

```
mariadb-admin -u <username> -p password 'new_password'
```

You will be prompted to enter the user's current password when the above command runs. If you do not know the password, you will need to make the change using the ALTER USER statement, as outlined in the *"MariaDB Users, Privileges, and Security"* chapter.

25.6 Flushing privileges and logs

When making changes to a database configuration, it may be necessary to perform a flush operation before the changes take effect. For example, if user privileges need to be reloaded, run the following command:

```
mariadb-admin -u demo -p flush-privileges
```

To reload the privilege tables in addition to any other configuration files or settings that need to be refreshed, use the reload command:

```
mariadb-admin -u demo -p reload
```

Similarly, you can clean up the server log files as follows:

```
mariadb-admin -u demo -p flush-logs
```

25.7 Creating and dropping databases

To create a new database from the command line, run mariadb-admin with the create command:

```
mariadb-admin -u demo -p create new_database
```

To delete a database, use the following drop command:

```
mariadb-admin -u demo -p drop new_database
```

25.8 Viewing server variables

To see a list of server variables defined on the server and their values, run mariadb-admin as follows:

```
mariadb-admin -u demo -p variables
```

25.9 Connecting to remote servers

The mariadb-admin tool does not need to run on the same system as the MariaDB server. In fact, it is more likely that you will use the tool to administer database servers remotely. To manage a MariaDB server on a remote system, use the -h option to specify the hostname or IP address:

```
mariadb-admin -u demo -p -h 133.787.2.101 create new_database
```

25.10 Reference points

The main points covered in this chapter are as follows:

- **Overview**

  - A command-line tool for administering MariaDB databases, enabling tasks like monitoring, managing users, and maintaining database tables.

  - Launched from the command line or used in scripts to automate tasks.

An Introduction to mariadb-admin

- Provided as part of the MariaDB Server installation and located in the same directory as the MariaDB client.

- Use `mariadb-admin --version` to confirm the tool is installed and accessible in your system's PATH.

- **Setup**

  - Many commands require root access or a user account with the necessary privileges.

- **Basic Syntax**

  - `mariadb-admin [options] command [command_options]`

    - **options:** Authentication or connection settings (e.g., username, password, host).

    - **command:** Specific administrative task (e.g., status, shutdown).

    - **command options**: Additional parameters for the chosen command.

  - Executes a command and exits, unlike interactive tools such as the MariaDB client.

- **Checking Server Status**

  - `mariadb-admin -u root -p status`

  - Includes uptime, threads, questions, open tables, and queries per second.

- **Viewing Active Processes**

  - `mariadb-admin -u root -p processlist`

  - Lists running processes, their states, and related information.

- **Server Shutdown**

  - `mariadb-admin -u root -p shutdown`

  - Gracefully stops the server and terminates all active connections.

- **Resetting Passwords**

  - `mariadb-admin -u <username> -p password 'new_password'`

  - Requires the current password for verification.

  - Use the `ALTER USER` statement if the password is unknown.

- **Flushing Privileges**

  - `mariadb-admin -u root -p flush-privileges`

  - Reloads privilege tables to apply recent changes.

- **Flushing Logs**

  - `mariadb-admin -u root -p flush-logs`

  - Cleans up server log files.

- **Reloading Configuration**

- `mariadb-admin -u root -p reload`
- Reloads privilege tables and refreshes server settings.

- **Viewing Server Variables**

  - `mariadb-admin -u root -p variables`
  - Lists server variables and their current values.

- **Remote Administration**

  - Use the -h option to connect to a MariaDB server on a remote host.
  - `mariadb-admin -u root -p -h <host> create new_database`

- **Additional Commands**

  - Help Information: Use `mariadb-admin --help` to display all available commands and options.

26. Backing up and Restoring Databases

There are many ways in which data can be lost or become inaccessible, with hardware failures and malware attacks being key examples. As a database administrator, you need to ensure that database data is backed up and that you know how to restore it in the event of a data loss.

This chapter will explore some of the tools for mitigating these risks by backing up and restoring MariaDB databases.

26.1 An overview of database backups

A database server instance manages several elements, including user accounts and privileges, databases and tables, events, and stored routines, all of which must be restored from backup in the event of a data loss.

MariaDB supports logical and physical backups. A logical backup saves the database structure and corresponding data in an SQL script file. When executed, these SQL statements rebuild the database structure and re-populate it with the original data. On the other hand, a physical backup makes copies of the underlying database files managed by the MariaDB server.

Logical backups work best with smaller databases and are particularly useful when migrating databases between servers. Physical backups should be used in environments involving large databases that need to be restored quickly.

Backups are categorized as full, incremental, and differential. A full backup contains a copy of the entire database, while an incremental backup contains only the changes made since the last full or incremental backup. To restore a database using this technique, the most recent full backup is first restored, and then each incremental backup is applied sequentially until the database is fully restored.

A differential backup retains all the changes to a database since the last full backup. Differential backups have faster restore times than incremental backups but take longer to create and use more storage space.

26.2 Logical backups with mariadb-dump

The mariadb-dump utility is a command-line tool for creating logical backups. Based on the command-line options you provide, mariadb-dump can back up all the databases on a server, specific databases, or individual database tables.

Table 26-1 lists the command-line syntax for some common mariadb-dump backup operations.

Operation	Syntax
Entire database	`mariadb-dump -u <user> -p <database>`
Multiple databases	`mariadb-dump -u <user> -p --databases <database1> <database2> ..`
All databases	`mariadb-dump -u <user> -p --all-databases`

Individual tables	`mariadb-dump -u -p <database> <table1> <table2>` `..`

Table 26-1

A full listing of mariadb-dump command-line options is available via the --help option:

```
mariadb-dump --help
```

When mariadb-dump runs, it sends the SQL output to the terminal or command-prompt window in which it is running. To save the SQL script, the output must be redirected to a file using the '>' operator, for example:

```
mariadb-dump -u demo -p --database MySalesDB > salesdb_backup.sql
```

To restore data from a backup, the mariadb client is used with the '<' input redirection operator using the following syntax options:

Operation	Syntax
Restore a single database backup	`mariadb -u <user> -p database_name < backupfile.sql`
Restore multiple databases	`mariadb -u <user> -p < backupfile.sql`
All databases	`mariadb-dump -u <user> -p --all-databases`
Restore tables	`mariadb -u <user> -p database_name < backupfile.sql`

Table 26-2

26.3 Logical backup examples

With the basics of logical backups covered, it is time to try out some example backup scenarios, beginning with a backup of the entire sampledb database. In a command-prompt or terminal window, execute the following mariadb-dump command-line and enter the password for the demo user when prompted:

```
mariadb-dump -u demo -p sampledb > sampledb_backup.sql
```

Once the backup is complete, the sampledb_backup.sql file will contain an SQL script that recreates the entire database. Open the file in an editor and take some time to explore the contents. For example, the script file will include the following statement to re-create the customer table:

```
.
.
DROP TABLE IF EXISTS 'customer';
/*!40101 SET @saved_cs_client     = @@character_set_client */;
/*!40101 SET character_set_client = utf8mb4 */;
CREATE TABLE 'customer' (
  'id' int(11) NOT NULL AUTO_INCREMENT,
  'name' char(30) NOT NULL,
  'address' varchar(60) DEFAULT NULL,
  'email' varchar(25) NOT NULL,
  PRIMARY KEY ('id','name'),
  KEY 'idx_composite' ('name','email')
) ENGINE=InnoDB DEFAULT CHARSET=utf8mb4 COLLATE=utf8mb4_uca1400_ai_ci;
/*!40101 SET character_set_client = @saved_cs_client */;
.
.
```

Instead of overwriting the sampledb database, we will restore the backup into a temporary database called restoredb. Open the MariaDB client and create the database using the following statement:

```
CREATE DATABASE restoredb;
```

Next, return the command prompt and restore the backup as follows:

```
mariadb -u demo -p restoredb < sampledb_backup.sql
```

Using the client, check that the database was restored using the following statements:

USE restoredb

SHOW TABLES;
```
+--------------------+
| Tables_in_restoredb |
+--------------------+
| customer           |
| euro_supplier      |
| join_demo          |
| product            |
| supplier           |
+--------------------+
5 rows in set (0.000 sec)
```

SELECT * FROM supplier;
```
+----+--------------+---------------------+
| id | company      | address             |
+----+--------------+---------------------+
|  1 | Apple        | Cupertino, CA       |
|  2 | Dell         | Round Rock, TX      |
|  3 | NZXT         | City of Industry, CA |
|  4 | Corsair      | Milpitas, CA        |
|  5 | Nvidia       | Santa Clara, CA     |
|  9 | The Big Box  | Durham, NC          |
| 10 | Acme Networks | BOSTON, MA         |
+----+--------------+---------------------+
7 rows in set (0.000 sec)
```

The following example will demonstrate how to backup and restore individual tables. Before performing the backup, drop and recreate the restoredb database:

```
DROP DATABASE restoredb;
CREATE DATABASE restoredb;
```

For this example, we will backup the product and supplier tables from the sampledb database, and restore them into the restoredb database. Use the following command to perform the backup operation:

```
mariadb-dump -u demo -p sampledb product supplier > table_backup.sql
```

Next, use the MariaDB client to recreate the tables in the restoredb database:

```
mariadb -u demo -p restoredb < table_backup.sql
```

Return to the MariaDB client and verify that the restoration was successful:

USE restoredb

```
SHOW TABLES;
+--------------------+
| Tables_in_restoredb |
+--------------------+
| product             |
| supplier            |
+--------------------+
2 rows in set (0.000 sec)
```

```
SELECT * FROM supplier;
+----+--------------+----------------------+
| id | company      | address              |
+----+--------------+----------------------+
|  1 | Apple        | Cupertino, CA        |
|  2 | Dell         | Round Rock, TX       |
|  3 | NZXT         | City of Industry, CA |
|  4 | Corsair      | Milpitas, CA         |
|  5 | Nvidia       | Santa Clara, CA      |
|  9 | The Big Box  | Durham, NC           |
| 10 | Acme Networks | BOSTON, MA          |
+----+--------------+----------------------+
7 rows in set (0.000 sec)
```

26.4 Physical backups with mariadb-backup

MariaDB physical backups can be performed using the mariadb-backup tool. This tool is installed with the MariaDB Server on Windows systems if the "Backup utilities" option is selected during installation. If mariadb-backup is not installed, re-run the MariaDB MSI Installer, click the "Change" button, enable the backup utilities option, and proceed with the installation.

To install mariadb-backup on Linux, use the command below that matches your Linux distribution:

Red Hat-based systems:

```
sudo dnf install mariadb-backup
```

Ubuntu/Debian systems:

```
sudo apt install mariadb-backup
```

26.4.1 Full physical backups

The syntax for creating a full physical backup of the database server instance using mariadb-backup is as follows:

```
mariadb-backup --backup --user=<user> --password=<password> --target-dir=/path/
to/backup
```

In the above syntax, specify the MariaDB user account and corresponding password to be used for the backup and provide a path to an empty or non-existent directory into which the backup files will be placed.

Restoring from a physical backup is a multi-step process, the first of which is to prepare the backup. Note that the following commands will require superuser or administrator privileges using sudo on Linux or a command prompt running as administrator on Windows:

```
mariadb-backup --prepare --target-dir=/path/to/backup
```

Next, stop the MariaDB server and move the current data directory to a temporary location. The default data location is */var/lib/mysql* on Linux and *C:\Program Files\MariaDB <version>\data* on Windows. Once the data directory has been moved, the backup can be restored as follows:

```
mariadb-backup --copy-back --target-dir=/path/to/backup
```

Once the backup has been restored, restart the MariaDB server. If the server fails to start on Linux, you may need to change the permissions of the data directory so that it can be read by the server using the following command:

```
sudo chown -R mysql:mysql /var/lib/mysql/
sudo systemctl start mariadb
sudo rm -rf /var/lib/mysql-old
```

Once the instance is restored, delete the temporary copy of the original data directory before using the MariaDB client to check that the restoration was successful.

26.4.2 Incremental physical backups

Incremental backups using mariadb-backup begin with a full backup, as outlined above. For example:

```
mariadb-backup --backup --user=<user> --password=<password> \
    --target-dir=/path/to/full/backup
```

Once the full backup has been saved, an incremental backup is created by referencing the full backup as the base directory and providing a new directory to contain the incremental files:

```
mariabackup --backup --user=<user> --password=<password> \
    --target-dir=/path/to/incremental/backup1 \
    --incremental-basedir=/path/to/full/backup
```

For each subsequent incremental backup, repeat the above step, but referencing the previous incremental backup as the incremental base directory:

```
mariabackup --backup --user=<user> --password=<password> \
    --target-dir=/path/to/incremental/backup2 \
    --incremental-basedir=/path/to/incremental/backup1
```

To restore a server instance from incremental backups, begin by preparing the base full backup:

```
mariabackup --prepare --target-dir=/path/to/full/backup
```

Next, prepare each incremental backup, providing the incremental directory and the full base directory:

```
mariabackup --prepare \
    --target-dir=/var/mariadb/backup \
    --incremental-dir=/path/to/incremental/backup1

mariabackup --prepare \
    --target-dir=/var/mariadb/backup \
    --incremental-dir=/path/to/incremental/backup2
    .
    .
```

Once the full and incremental backups are prepared, the following command will restore the backup:

```
mariabackup --copy-back \
    --target-dir=/var/mariadb/backup/
```

26.5 Reference Points

The main points covered in this chapter are as follows:

- **Importance of Database Backups**

  - Protects against data loss from hardware failures, malware, or corruption.

  - Ensures recovery readiness for critical databases.

- **Types of Database Backups**

  - **Logical Backups:**

    - Save database structure and data as SQL scripts.

    - Ideal for small databases and cross-server migrations.

    - Created using mariadb-dump.

  - **Physical Backups:**

    - Copy raw database files (e.g., InnoDB tablespaces).

    - Faster for large databases but server-specific.

    - Created using mariadb-backup.

- **Backup Strategies**

  - Full Backup: Complete copy of the database.

  - Incremental Backup: Only stores changes since the last backup (full or incremental).

  - Differential Backup: Stores changes since the last full backup (faster restore than incremental).

  - Logical Backups with mariadb-dump

- **Backup Commands**

  - Entire database:

    ```
    mariadb-dump -u <user> -p <database> > backup.sql
    ```

  - Multiple databases:

    ```
    mariadb-dump -u <user> -p --databases db1 db2 > backup.sql
    ```

  - All databases:

    ```
    mariadb-dump -u <user> -p --all-databases > backup.sql
    ```

  - Specific tables:

    ```
    mariadb-dump -u <user> -p <database> <table1> <table2> > backup.sql
    ```

- **Restoring Logical Backups**

  - Single database:

    ```
    mariadb -u <user> -p <database> < backup.sql
    ```

- Multiple databases:

```
mariadb -u <user> -p < backup.sql
```

- **Full Physical Backup**

  - Create backup:

```
mariadb-backup --backup --user=<user> --password=<password> --target-dir=/
path/to/backup
```

  - Prepare backup:

```
mariadb-backup --prepare --target-dir=/path/to/backup
```

  - Restore backup:

```
mariadb-backup --copy-back --target-dir=/path/to/backup
```

- **Incremental Physical Backups**

  - Initial full backup:

```
mariadb-backup --backup --user=<user> --password=<password> --target-dir=/
path/to/full_backup
```

  - First incremental backup:

```
mariadb-backup --backup --user=<user> --password=<password> --target-dir=/
path/to/incr_backup1 --incremental-basedir=/path/to/full_backup
```

  - Subsequent incremental backups:

```
mariadb-backup --backup --user=<user> --password=<password> --target-dir=/
path/to/incr_backup2 --incremental-basedir=/path/to/incr_backup1
```

- **Restoring Incremental Backups**

  - Prepare full backup:

```
mariadb-backup --prepare --target-dir=/path/to/full_backup
```

  - Apply incremental backups:

```
mariadb-backup --prepare --target-dir=/path/to/full_backup --incremental-
dir=/path/to/incr_backup1
```

  - Final restore:

```
mariadb-backup --copy-back --target-dir=/path/to/full_backup
```

- **Key Takeaways**

  - Logical backups (SQL scripts) are portable but slower for large databases.

  - Physical backups (file copies) are faster but server-dependent.

  - Incremental backups save space but require sequential restoration.

  - Test backups regularly to ensure recoverability.

27. Installing MySQL Workbench

The preceding chapters relied on the text-based MariaDB client to enter and execute SQL statements and view results. While this interactive environment offers a quick and lightweight way to perform small database administration tasks, more intuitive and user-friendly options are available. One such option is MySQL Workbench. MySQL Workbench is one of several applications and web-based tools that provide a graphical user interface, allowing many tasks to be performed visually. Before we look at the main features of MySQL Workbench, this chapter will provide the steps to install it on Windows, macOS, and Linux-based systems.

27.1 Downloading MySQL Workbench

MySQL Workbench can be downloaded from the MySQL Developer website at the following URL:

https://dev.mysql.com/downloads/workbench/

Use the menu at the top of the download page to select the operating system (marked A in Figure 27-1) and version (B) menus to match your system version and processor architecture. Finally, click the Download button (C) next to the matching installation file:

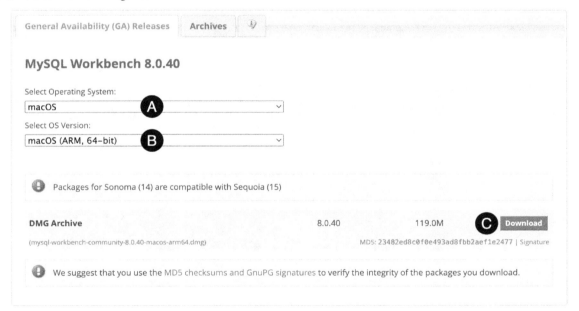

Figure 27-1

When prompted, either sign in with an Oracle web account or select the "No thanks, just start my download" option to proceed anonymously. Finally, save the file to your local filesystem. Once the download is complete, follow the instructions below for your operating system.

27.2 Installation on Windows

MySQL Workbench for Windows is available as a Microsoft Software Installer (.MSI) file. Using Windows Explorer, navigate to where you downloaded the MSI file and double-click it to begin the installation. Once the

Installing MySQL Workbench

installer has loaded, the screen shown in Figure 27-2 will appear:

Figure 27-2

Click the Next button to review and accept the licensing terms before moving on to the Setup Type screen shown below:

Figure 27-3

After completing the installation, the screen displayed in Figure 27-4 will appear. Ensure the "Launch MySQL Workbench now" option is checked, then click the Finish button to start Workbench:

Figure 27-4

27.3 Installation on macOS

To complete the installation on macOS, locate the downloaded disk image (.dmg) file and double-click it to open it in a Finder window:

Figure 27-5

Within the Finder window, select the MySQL Workbench icon and drag it into the Applications folder. To start Workbench, open the macOS Finder and locate it in the Applications folder. Take this opportunity to drag and drop it onto your dock for easier access in the future. Click on the Workbench icon in the dock to launch the tool.

27.4 Installation on RPM-based Linux distributions

MySQL Workbench for Red Hat Linux-based systems (including RHEL, Fedora, CentOS, AlmaLinux, and Rocky Linux) is provided as a Red Hat Package Manager (RPM) file named using the following convention:

Installing MySQL Workbench

```
mysql-workbench-community-<version>.<os>.<arch>.rpm
```

For example, the RPM file for MySQL Workbench 8.0.40 for Red Hat Enterprise Linux 9 on 64-bit x86 systems is named as follows:

```
mysql-community-client-9.1.0-1.el9.x86_64.rpm
```

Before installing MySQL Workbench, we need to install other packages on which it depends. The first steps are enabling the CodeReady Linux Builder (CRB) and installing the Extra Packages for Enterprise Linux (EPEL) repository, which contains several required packages. Open a terminal window and enter the following commands, entering your password when prompted to do so:

```
crb enable
sudo dnf install \
    https://dl.fedoraproject.org/pub/epel/epel-release-latest-9.noarch.rpm \
    https://dl.fedoraproject.org/pub/epel/epel-next-release-latest-9.noarch.rpm
```

Next, use the command below to install the package dependencies:

```
dnf install libzip unixODBC mesa-libGL-devel gtk2-2.24.33-8.el9proj
```

To complete the installation, change directory to the location of the downloaded RPM file and run the following command, replacing the *<version>*, *<os>*, and *<arch>* values with those matching your file:

```
sudo rpm -ihv mysql-workbench-community-8.0.40-1.el9.x86_64.rpm
```

Once the installation is complete, execute the following command at the shell prompt:

```
mysql-workbench
```

Alternatively, MySQL Workbench can be launched from within the desktop environment, for example, within the applications screen of the GNOME desktop.

27.5 Installation on Ubuntu

At the time of writing, Ubuntu's latest long-term support (LTS) edition is 24.04, and the current version of MySQL Workbench is 8.0.411. Unfortunately, these two versions are incompatible, so if you are running Ubuntu 24.04 and the latest version of MySQL Workbench is still 8.0.41, you may need to download version 8.0.38 to complete the installation. To download this older version, run the following command in a terminal window:

```
wget https://cdn.mysql.com/Downloads/MySQLGUITools/mysql-workbench-
community_8.0.38-1ubuntu24.04_amd64.deb
```

To begin the installation, change directory to the folder containing the downloaded package file, replacing *<package filename>* with the name of the file you downloaded:

```
sudo dpkg -i <package filename>.deb
```

During the installation, the installer may report dependency problems like the following:

```
dpkg: dependency problems prevent configuration of mysql-workbench-community:
 mysql-workbench-community depends on libatkmm-1.6-1v5 (>= 2.28.4); however:
  Package libatkmm-1.6-1v5 is not installed.
 mysql-workbench-community depends on libglibmm-2.4-1t64 (>= 2.66.7); however:
  Package libglibmm-2.4-1t64 is not installed.
 mysql-workbench-community depends on libgtkmm-3.0-1t64 (>= 3.24.9); however:
  Package libgtkmm-3.0-1t64 is not installed.
```

```
mysql-workbench-community depends on libmysqlclient21 (>= 8.0.11); however:
 Package libmysqlclient21 is not installed.
mysql-workbench-community depends on libodbc2 (>= 2.3.1); however:
 Package libodbc2 is not installed.
mysql-workbench-community depends on libproj25 (>= 8.2.0); however:
 Package libproj25 is not installed.
mysql-workbench-community depends on libsigc++-2.0-0v5 (>= 2.8.0); however:
 Package libsigc++-2.0-0v5 is not installed.
mysql-workbench-community depends on libzip4t64 (>= 0.10); however:
 Package libzip4t64 is not installed.
```

If you see dependency errors, run the following command to resolve them:

```
sudo apt -f install
```

Once the installation is complete, execute the following command at the shell prompt:

```
mysql-workbench
```

Alternatively, launch MySQL Workbench using the application launcher screen of the GNOME desktop.

27.6 Reference points

The main points covered in this chapter are as follows:

- **Overview**

  - MySQL Workbench provides a graphical user interface (GUI) for managing MariaDB databases.

  - Offers a more intuitive alternative to the MariaDB command-line client.

  - Available for Windows, macOS, and Linux.

- **Downloading MySQL Workbench**

  - Download from the MySQL Developer website:

    - *https://dev.mysql.com/downloads/workbench/*

  - Select the appropriate operating system and version before downloading.

- **Windows Installation**

  - Download the MSI installer file.

  - Double-click the MSI file to start installation.

  - Click Next to accept the license agreement.

  - Select the setup type and complete the installation.

  - Ensure the 'Launch MySQL Workbench now' option is checked and click Finish.

- **macOS Installation**

  - Download the .dmg file.

  - Open the DMG file in Finder.

  - Drag MySQL Workbench to the Applications folder.

Installing MySQL Workbench

- Launch Workbench from the Applications folder.

- (Optional) Drag the Workbench icon to Dock for easier access.

- **Installation on RPM-based Linux**

  - Enable required repositories:

    ```
    crb enable
    sudo dnf install \
     https://dl.fedoraproject.org/pub/epel/epel-release-latest-9.noarch.rpm \
     https://dl.fedoraproject.org/pub/epel/epel-next-release-latest-9.noarch.
    rpm
    ```

  - Install dependencies:

    ```
    dnf install libzip unixODBC mesa-libGL-devel gtk2-2.24.33-8.el9proj
    ```

  - Install MySQL Workbench:

    ```
    sudo rpm -ihv mysql-workbench-community-8.0.40-1.el9.x86_64.rpm
    ```

- **Installation on Ubuntu**

  - If using Ubuntu 24.04, download version 8.0.38 of MySQL Workbench:

    ```
    wget https://cdn.mysql.com/Downloads/MySQLGUITools/mysql-workbench-
    community_8.0.38-1ubuntu24.04_amd64.deb
    ```

  - Install the package:

    ```
    sudo dpkg -i mysql-workbench-community_8.0.38-1ubuntu24.04_amd64.deb
    ```

  - If dependency errors occur, resolve them with:

    ```
    sudo apt -f install
    ```

  - Launch Workbench

    ```
    mysql-workbench
    ```

  - Alternatively, open from GNOME Applications Menu.

28. MySQL Workbench Administration

This chapter explains how to use MySQL Workbench to administer and monitor MariaDB server instances. MySQL Workbench also offers features for creating and modifying database models, and a SQL Editor environment for interactively executing SQL statements and creating SQL scripts. The next chapter will cover these topics in more detail.

28.1 Creating a server connection

MySQL Workbench uses a tabbed panel approach to presenting information. On the initial startup, only the Home tab shown in Figure 28-1 is displayed:

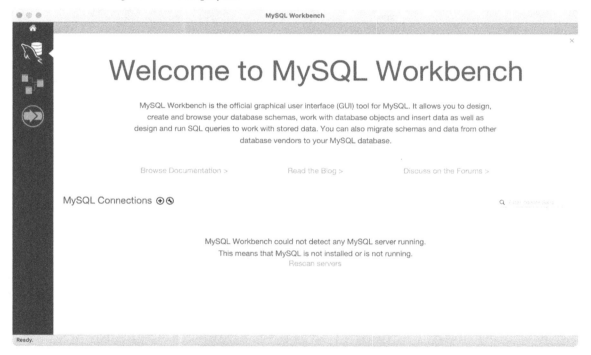

Figure 28-1

MySQL Workbench can administer both local and remote MariaDB server instances. Before any administrative tasks can be performed, however, a connection to the target server must first be established. In the above figure, Workbench has scanned the local system and failed to detect an active MariaDB server, so no connections are listed.

If, on the other hand, a local MariaDB server is detected, it will be added automatically to the "MySQL Connections" list marked A in Figure 28-2:

Figure 28-2

To create a new connection, click the + button (marked B above) to display the Setup New Connection dialog shown below:

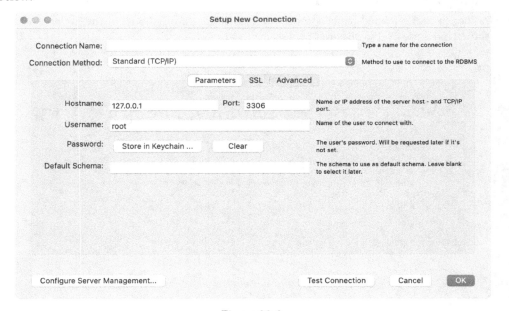

Figure 28-3

The connection dialog is used to create connections to remote and local servers. The minimum configuration requirements to establish a remote connection are as follows:

- **Connection name** - The name by which the connection will be referenced in MySQL Workbench.

- **Connection method** - The network protocol used to communicate with the server.

- **Hostname** - The hostname or IP address of the system on which the MariaDB server is running. If the server is running locally, this can be set to 127.0.0.1.

- **Port** - The TCP port on which the MariaDB server instance will listen for connection requests. The standard port number for MariaDB connections is 3306.

- **Username** - The database user that will be logged into the database when the connection is established.

- **Password** - The database user's password. If the password is not entered in this dialog, Workbench will request it each time the connection is established.

Note that the database user account specified above must be granted appropriate privileges to connect from a remote host, details of which were covered in the *"MariaDB Users, Privileges, and Security"* chapter.

Once you have entered the connection details, click the Test Connection button to verify that the connection is configured correctly, entering the database user password if prompted:

Figure 28-4

If the test is successful, close the result dialog above, then click OK in the Setup New Connection dialog to save the connection. On returning to the home screen, the new connection should be listed as shown in Figure 28-5:

Figure 28-5

To connect to a server, click on the connection icon on the home screen and wait while Workbench communicates with the MariaDB server instance.

28.2 The MySQL Workbench user interface.

Once a server connection has been established, the window shown in Figure 28-6 will appear:

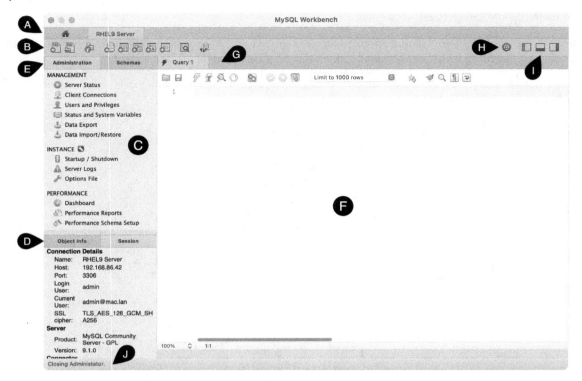

Figure 28-6

The top-level tab bar (marked A above) contains a tab to return to the home screen. MySQL Workbench can maintain concurrent connections to multiple servers, each appearing alongside the Home tab.

The toolbar (B) contains shortcuts to commonly performed tasks, including creating databases, tables, and stored routines and opening new tabs for performing queries. The sidebar panel (C) contains links to panels for administering the currently selected MariaDB server. Use tab bar E to switch the sidebar between Administration and Schema views and tab bar D to toggle between information about the currently selected object and connection session.

When a link is selected from the sidebar, a corresponding tabbed panel will be added to the content area (F). Use the tab bar marked G to navigate between open panels.

The settings button (H) displays the Preferences dialog, where you can customize Workbench to your requirements. The panel buttons (I) toggle the appearance of the navigation sidebar, Action Output, and Context Help/Snippets panels.

Finally, the status bar (J) displays status messages reflecting the success or otherwise of Workbench activities.

28.3 Managing servers with MySQL Workbench

The navigation sidebar is divided into Management, Instance, and Performance categories. The management section includes the following options:

28.3.1 Server status

The Server Status panel provides an overall view of the status of the currently connected server. The left-hand section of the panel lists information about the server, such as the version, locations of files and directories, disk space usage, and the features that have been enabled:

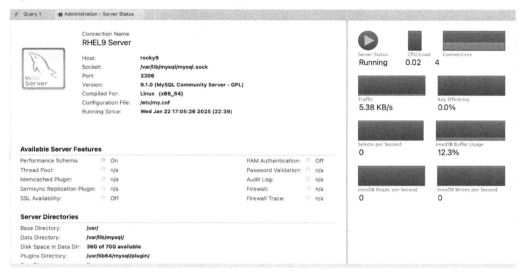

Figure 28-7

The right-hand section displays real-time graphs indicating whether the server is running, the CPU load on the host system, network traffic, and database activity.

28.3.2 Client connections

The Client Connections panel monitors active database connections and allows specific connections or queries to be terminated:

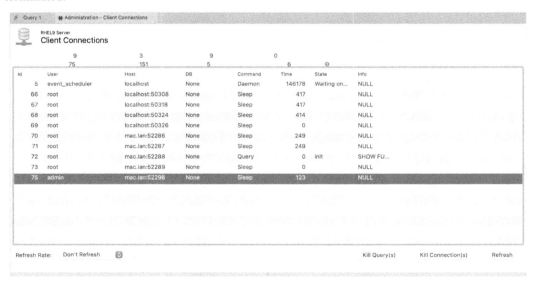

Figure 28-8

To terminate a connection or query, select the connection in the list and click either the Kill Query(s) or Kill Connection(s) button. By default the list must be updated manually using the Refresh button. To configure automatic refreshing, select an interval from the Refresh Rate menu.

28.3.3 Users and privileges

In the *"MariaDB Users, Privileges, and Security"* chapter, we learned how to add and remove users and grant privileges using SQL statements. MySQL Workbench provides a visual alternative for managing users that makes it easy to make changes and view the current settings:

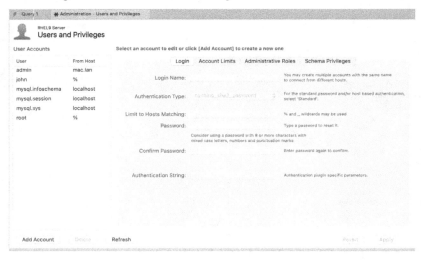

Figure 28-9

The Users and Privileges panel displays all users with database access and allows users to be added and deleted. Viewing and modifying user privileges, including account limits, administrative roles, and table access privileges for individual users, is as simple as turning checkboxes on and off and clicking a few buttons.

28.3.4 Status and system variables

MariaDB server instances contain many variables that store state information and define server behavior. The Status and System Variables panel groups these variables into categories that can be browsed and searched:

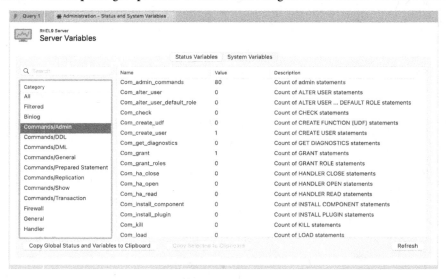

Figure 28-10

28.4 Importing and exporting data

MySQL Workbench provides several options for exporting and importing data. For example, data from specific databases and tables can be exported to dump files and imported into other servers.

Figure 28-11

28.5 Performance monitoring

The performance dashboard (Figure 28-12) displays real-time statistics relating to network traffic, server status, and database storage engine activity:

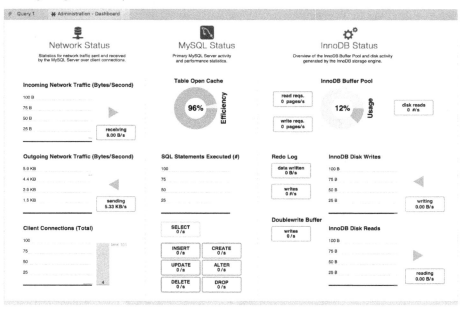

Figure 28-12

Use the Performance Reports option to display fine-grained details on low-level server activity, such as the memory usage for every event, I/O statistics on individual files, or wait times listed by user:

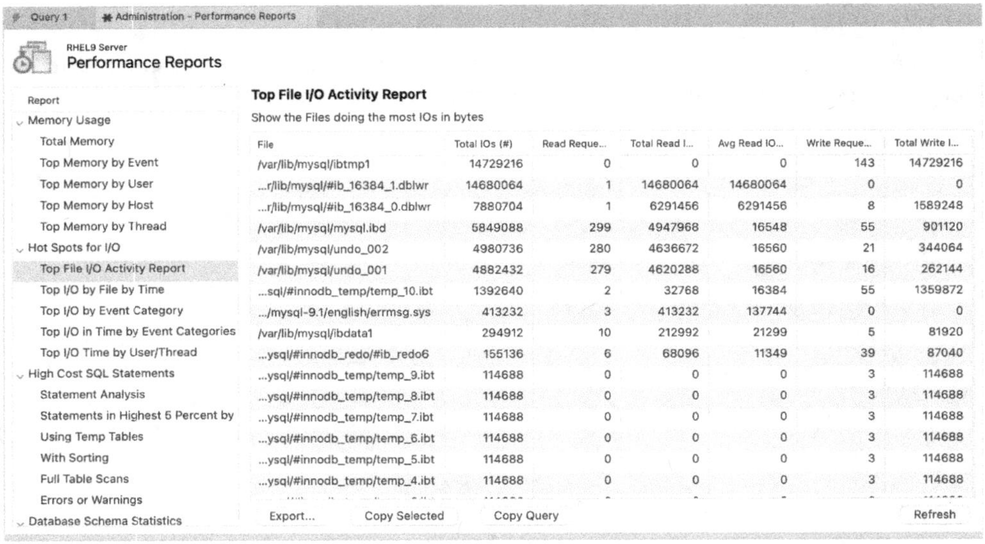

MySQL Workbench Administration

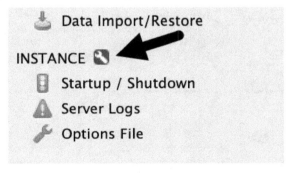

Figure 28-13

28.6 Instance management

The MySQL Workbench features covered so far involve performing tasks while logged into the MariaDB server. However, some administrative tasks, such as starting and stopping the server instance, can only be performed outside the MariaDB server environment. To perform these tasks, MySQL Workbench needs to know how to log into the operating system on which MariaDB is running, the operating system type, and the location of the tools and scripts required to start and shut down the MariaDB server instance.

To configure the instance administration features of MySQL Workbench, begin by clicking the settings button next to the instance category title, as indicated in Figure 28-14:

Figure 28-14

When setting up instance management, the first requirement is to provide the details required to log into the system on which the MariaDB server is running. Within the Manage Server Settings dialog, select the Remote Management tab and configure the settings to enable Workbench to establish a secure connection to the host system. When specifying a username for the connection, choose a user with adequate permissions to start and stop the MariaDB server. For example, if the MariaDB server is running on a Linux host, the user account will most likely need sudo permission:

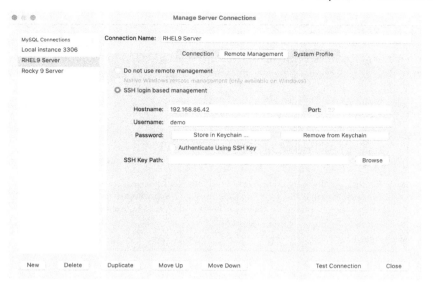

Figure 28-15

The next step is selecting the operating system type so MySQL Workbench knows how to start and stop the server. To configure the operating system details, select the System Profile tab in the Manage Server Connections dialog and set the System Type and Installation Type menus to match the host system:

Figure 28-16

Within the system profile dialog, configure the following settings:

- **Configuration File:** /etc/my.cnf

- **Configuration File Section:** mysqld

- **Start MySQL:** systemctl start mariadb.service

- **Stop MySQL:** systemctl stop mariadb.service

After entering the system profile information, click the Test Connection button to confirm that MySQL Workbench can access the host system successfully.

When remote management has been configured, select the Startup / Shutdown option in the navigation sidebar and, in the resulting panel, click the Stop Server button (highlighted in Figure 28-17) to shut down the current MariaDB server instance:

Figure 28-17

Review the output in the Startup Message Log to confirm the shutdown was successful before clicking the Start Server button to restart the server.

28.7 Reference points

The main points covered in this chapter are as follows:

- **Overview**

  - MySQL Workbench is a powerful GUI tool for managing MariaDB databases.

  - Supports local and remote MariaDB server administration.

  - Provides tools for performance monitoring, user management, and database security.

  - Allows instance management, including remote server start and stop.

- **Creating a Server Connection**

  - MySQL Workbench detects local MariaDB servers automatically.

  - Remote and local servers can be added manually.

  - Required details for new connections include:

    - Connection name, hostname/IP, port (default: 3306), username, and password.

  - Saved connections appear on the Home tab for easy access.

- **The MySQL Workbench User Interface**

  - Uses a tabbed panel approach for multiple server connections.

  - Key UI components:

  - Home tab for managing connections.

  - Toolbar for creating databases, tables, and stored procedures.

- Sidebar for Administration and Schema views.

- Status bar for real-time server activity and success/error messages.

- Managing Servers with MySQL Workbench

- **Server Status**

  - Displays MariaDB server version, directories, disk usage, and enabled features.

  - Real-time monitoring of CPU usage, network traffic, and database activity.

- **Client Connections**

  - Monitors active database connections and queries.

  - Allows terminating specific queries or connections.

  - Auto-refresh can be enabled to update the connection list.

Users and Privileges

  - Provides a graphical interface for managing database users and privileges.

  - Users can be added, removed, and granted privileges using checkboxes.

  - Allows easy management of administrative roles and table access.

Status and System Variables

  - Displays MariaDB server system variables and their values.

  - Variables are categorized and can be searched for easy navigation.

- **Importing and Exporting Data**

  - MySQL Workbench allows exporting databases and tables to dump files.

  - Data can be imported into another MariaDB server instance from dump files.

- **Performance Monitoring**

  - The Performance Dashboard provides real-time network and server statistics.

  - Performance Reports offer in-depth analysis of memory, I/O, and wait times.

- **Instance Management**

  - Enables starting and stopping MariaDB server instances remotely.

  - Requires setting up remote management credentials.

  - Uses SSH or native OS tools for server control.

  - Startup and shutdown logs help track server status.

29. MySQL Workbench Queries and Models

The previous chapters taught us how to install MySQL Workbench and connect to MariaDB server instances. We also explored some of its management features, including user and privilege management, data import and export, and performance monitoring. This chapter will focus on executing SQL queries, creating scripts, and working with models in MySQL Workbench.

29.1 Introducing the SQL Editor

Once a connection has been established to a MariaDB server, Workbench will open a SQL Editor panel, as shown in Figure 29-1 below:

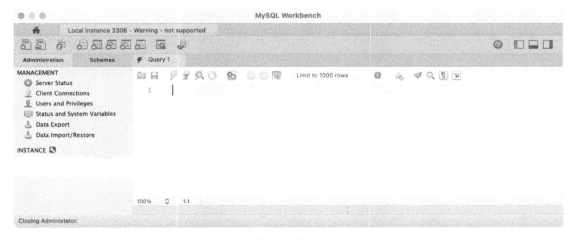

Figure 29-1

Multiple SQL Editor panels may be open simultaneously, each with its own tab within the tab bar location above the editor toolbar. To open new editor sessions, select the *File -> New Query Tab* menu option or click the first button in the main toolbar:

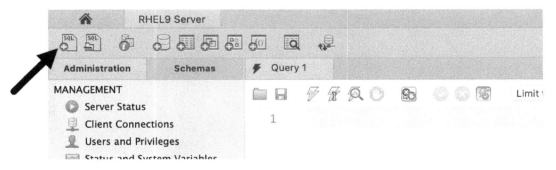

Figure 29-2

MySQL Workbench Queries and Models

The SQL Editor panel allows lines of SQL statements to be entered and executed using the buttons displaying lightning bolts in the toolbar. The leftmost "lightning" button executes either the currently selected statements or all the statements if none are selected, while the second button executes the statement on which the cursor is positioned.

If you have not already done so, start MySQL Workbench and connect to your server instance. Once connected, type the following statements into the "Query 1" editor panel:

Figure 29-3

Unlike the MariaDB client prompt, the USE statement must be terminated (;) when used within the SQL Editor environment. After entering the statements, click the leftmost of the two execute buttons in the toolbar to run the code. After execution, two additional panels will appear with the editor. The Action Output panel (Figure 29-4) records a list of actions executed in the editor, including the action type and the server response:

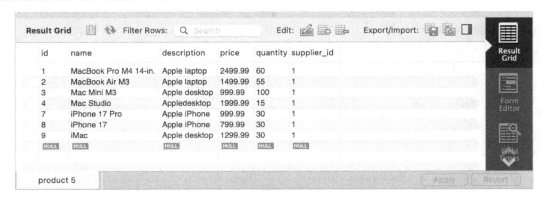

Figure 29-4

Click the Action Output menu in the title bar to display text output and action history.

When a query returns a result set, Workbench will also display the Result Grid panel shown below containing the extracted row and column values:

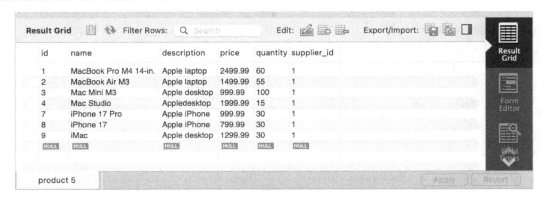

Figure 29-5

The result grid can be used to edit the retrieved data and update the database table. As an example, double-click on the price column of the Mac Studio product so that it highlights, change the value to 1499.99, and press the enter key:

id	name	description	price	quantity	supplier_id
1	MacBook Pro M4 14-in.	Apple laptop	2499.99	60	1
2	MacBook Air M3	Apple laptop	1499.99	55	1
3	Mac Mini M3	Apple desktop	999.99	100	1
4	Mac Studio	Appledesktop	1499.99	15	1
7	iPhone 17 Pro	Apple iPhone	999.99	30	1
8	iPhone 17	Apple iPhone	799.99	30	1
9	iMac	Apple desktop	1299.99	30	1
NULL	NULL	NULL	NULL	NULL	NULL

Figure 29-6

After making the change, click the Apply button at the bottom of the result grid panel to update the table. The dialog shown in Figure 29-7 will preview the update statement:

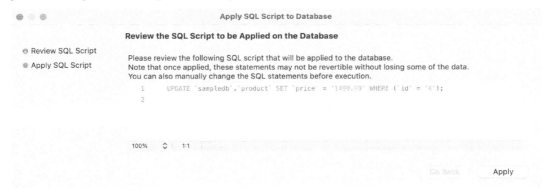

Figure 29-7

Click Apply to perform the update, then return to the result grid and click on the refresh toolbar button indicated below to update the result set with the new price:

Figure 29-8

The sequence of SQL statements entered into the SQL Query panel may be saved as a script by selecting the *File -> Save Script* menu option or clicking the save button in the toolbar. Saved scripts are loaded into the SQL Editor using the *File -> Open SQL Script…* menu option or the corresponding toolbar button.

29.2 Creating a database model

One of the most powerful features of the MySQL Workbench tool is the ability to design and manage database models. A database model is a blueprint for a database structure, including the schema, users, privileges, scripts, and routines. Once a model has been defined, Workbench generates and executes it on the connected MariaDB server to create a physical database. In addition to allowing new models to be designed, the workbench tool also includes reverse engineering capabilities, allowing models to be generated from existing databases.

Start MySQL Workbench and select the *File -> New Model* menu option to create a new model. The model panel will appear with an entry added to the top-level tab bar labeled MySQL Model:

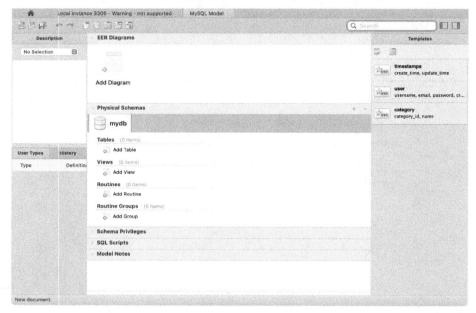

Figure 29-9

An initial schema named mydb is created as a basis for the model (keeping in mind that the term schema is synonymous with database). Double-click on the mydb tab in the Physical Schemas section and, in the resulting properties panel, change the name of the schema to orderdb before pressing the enter key:

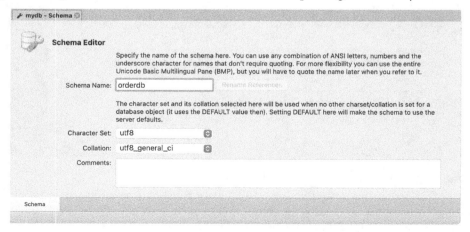

Figure 29-10

Close the schema property panel by clicking the small "x" in the Schema tab. Having given our schema a name, we can now add a table to the model by double-clicking the Add Table button in the Tables section of the Physical Schemas panel. In the table editor, change the table name to order (marked A in Figure 29-11), then select the Columns tab (B) to begin adding columns to the table. Next, click the <click to edit> column entry (C):

Figure 29-11

By default, Workbench will create a non-null primary key named idorder. For this exercise, we will keep this column, though in practice, this can be changed to meet your requirements:

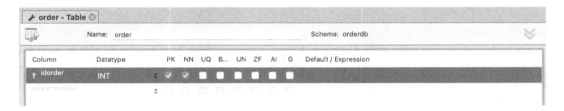

Figure 29-12

Select <click to edit> in the second line, name the column product, and accept the default value of VARCHAR for the data type. Repeat these steps to add a date column of type DATETIME and a quantity column of type INTEGER. Each of these should be declared as non-null by checking the boxes in the NN column:

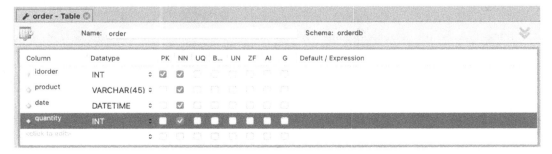

Figure 29-13

Before proceeding, save your progress using the *File -> Save Model* menu option.

29.3 Adding a user to the model

To add a user to the database, unfold the Schema Privileges section of the Physical Schemas panel and double-click on the Add User item:

Figure 29-14

Name the user account order_admin in the User panel and enter a password using the fields marked A in the figure below. From the list of available roles (B), select the table.modify and table.insert roles, using the arrow buttons (C) to assign them to the assigned roles column (D):

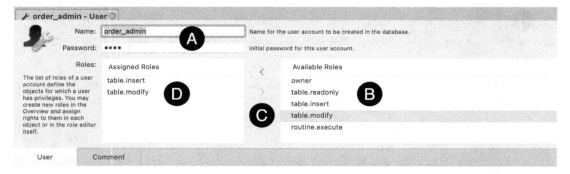

Figure 29-15

Although not required for this example, models may also contain scripts, routines, and views.

Save your progress once again using the *File -> Save Model* menu option.

29.4 Generating the database creation script

Having created a model, the next step is to generate an SQL script from the model to execute on a server to create the database. To achieve this, select the *Database -> Forward Engineer...* menu option. In the resulting dialog, select the server using the Stored Connections menu or enter the server details if they have not previously been saved.

Click Continue to access the database options screen. Unless you have specific requirements, leave the default selections unchanged and continue to the next screen to select the objects to be included in the script. Enable the MySQL Table Objects and MySQL User Objects options before clicking Continue:

Select Objects to Forward Engineer

To exclude objects of a specific type from the SQL Export, disable the corresponding checkbox. Press Show Filter and add objects or patterns to the ignore list to exclude them from the export.

☑ Export MySQL Table Objects
1 Total Objects, 1 Selected
Show Filter

☐ Export MySQL View Objects
0 Total Objects, 0 Selected
Show Filter

☐ Export MySQL Routine Objects
0 Total Objects, 0 Selected
Show Filter

☐ Export MySQL Trigger Objects
0 Total Objects, 0 Selected
Show Filter

☑ Export User Objects
1 Total Objects, 1 Selected
Show Filter

Figure 29-16

The next screen will display the generated script. Review the script to ensure it matches your database requirements:

Figure 29-17

Assuming the script appears as expected given the initial model from which it has been generated, click Continue to execute the script on the destination server or use the *File...* button to save the script if it is to be used later, perhaps within the SQL Editor or MariaDB client.

The success or otherwise of the execution will then be reported in the following screen. Assuming a successful operation, the new database will now be present on the designated database server:

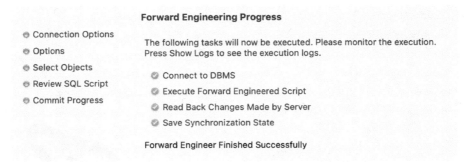

Figure 29-18

Close the Forward Engineering dialog and, using MySQL Workbench SQL editor or MariaDB client, log in using the order_admin user and verify that the database and table have been created:

```
SHOW COLUMNS FROM orderdb.order;
+----------+-------------+------+-----+---------+-------+
| Field    | Type        | Null | Key | Default | Extra |
+----------+-------------+------+-----+---------+-------+
| idorder  | int         | NO   | PRI | NULL    |       |
| product  | varchar(45) | NO   |     | NULL    |       |
| date     | datetime    | NO   |     | NULL    |       |
| quantity | int         | NO   |     | NULL    |       |
+----------+-------------+------+-----+---------+-------+
4 rows in set (0.01 sec)
```

29.5 Generating EER diagrams

Enhanced entity relationship (EER) diagrams visually represent the relationships between the tables in a database model and are helpful when designing or understanding complex database structures. An EER diagram can be generated from an existing MySQL Workbench model by opening the saved model file and selecting the *Model -> Create Diagram from Catalog Objects* menu option. The diagram generated for our orderdb model will appear as shown in Figure 29-19:

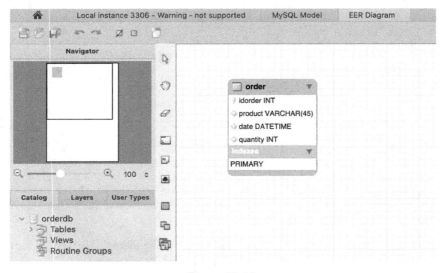

Figure 29-19

In addition to generating EER diagrams from a model file, MySQL Workbench can create diagrams by reverse engineering existing databases. To demonstrate reverse engineering, close the current model and diagram tabs and select the *Database -> Reverse Engineer...* menu option. Step through the screens in the Reverse Engineer Database dialog, providing the credentials to connect to your database server and retrieve the schema list. When prompted, select the sampledb database schema as shown below:

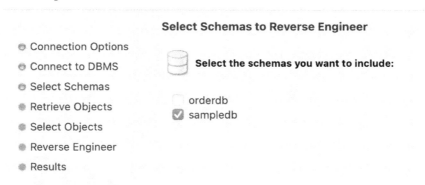

Figure 29-20

Continue through the screens until the object selection options appear. MySQL Workbench can import table, view, routine, and trigger objects. For this exercise, select only the Import MySQL Table Objects option. To avoid having to manually place the tables onto the diagram after it has been generated, make sure that the "Place imported objects on a diagram" checkbox is selected otherwise you will need to manually place the tables on the diagram after it has been generated:

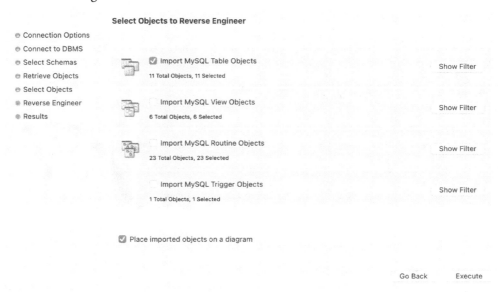

Figure 29-21

After making the object selections, click execute and close the dialog after importing the objects. Once the database has been reverse-engineered, the EER diagram will appear:

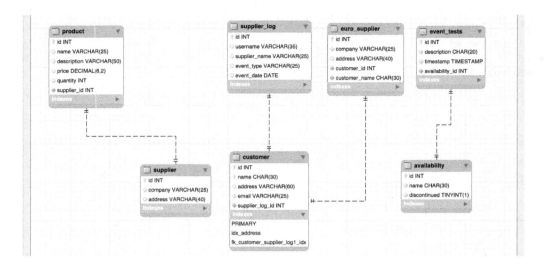

Figure 29-22

The diagram view is an interactive environment where tables can be moved and removed from the diagram and text added to label diagram elements. Double-clicking on a table will display the table editor (outlined in Figure 29-13 above), allowing changes to be made to the model.

In addition to the EER diagram, Workbench has also generated a model file for the reverse-engineered database. The model will appear in a new "MySQL Model" tab where changes can be made and applied to the database using the earlier steps.

Take some time to explore the EER diagram and save the model before exiting MySQL Workbench.

29.6 Reference points

The main points covered in this chapter are as follows:

- **Overview**

  - MySQL Workbench allows users to execute SQL queries, create scripts, and manage database models.

  - Supports both interactive query execution and structured database modeling.

  - Provides tools for database creation, forward engineering, and reverse engineering.

- **Introducing the SQL Editor**

  - SQL Editor is opened when a connection to a MariaDB server is established.

  - Multiple query tabs can be opened for executing SQL statements.

  - Execute queries using toolbar buttons (lightning icons).

  - Results are displayed in the Result Grid panel, allowing for direct data modification.

  - Changes in the Result Grid must be applied and refreshed manually.

  - SQL scripts can be saved and loaded for later execution.

- **Creating a Database Model**

- MySQL Workbench allows designing database structures using models.

- Models contain schemas, tables, users, privileges, scripts, and routines.

- Reverse engineering can generate models from existing databases.

- New models are created using the *File -> New Model* menu option.

- Schemas and tables can be defined using a visual editor.

- **Adding Tables and Users**

  - Tables are added to models using the Physical Schemas panel.

  - Columns can be configured with specific data types and constraints.

  - Users can be added with assigned privileges and roles.

- **Generating a Database Creation Script**

  - Models are transformed into SQL scripts using the Forward Engineering feature.

  - Generated scripts can be executed on a MariaDB server to create the database structure.

  - Users can review and modify scripts before execution.

  - Successful execution results in a fully configured database.

- **Generating EER Diagrams**

  - Enhanced Entity-Relationship (EER) diagrams provide a visual representation of database models.

  - Workbench can generate diagrams from model files or reverse-engineered databases.

  - Tables and relationships are displayed interactively.

  - Users can modify the diagram layout and make database changes through the diagram interface.

- **Reverse Engineering an Existing Database**

  - MySQL Workbench can generate models from existing databases using reverse engineering.

  - The process retrieves schema objects and generates a model representation.

  - Users can edit the reverse-engineered model and apply changes to the database.

30. Database Administration with phpMyAdmin

So far, we have explored MariaDB database administration using the MariaDB client command-line environment and graphical user interface-based MySQL Workbench application. A third option, and the topic of this chapter, is a web-based interface. This chapter will introduce phpMyAdmin, one of several popular web-based tools for managing MariaDB databases.

30.1 Introducing phpMyAdmin

phpMyAdmin is a free tool that provides a graphical user interface for managing MariaDB databases. Unlike the MariaDB client and MySQL Workbench tools, which must be installed on each client computer, phpMyAdmin is hosted by a web server typically running on the same system as the MariaDB server. This centralization allows the phpMyAdmin interface to be accessed from any web browser without the need to install additional software.

phpMyAdmin is available for several operating systems, including Windows and most Linux distributions, including Red Hat-based distributions, Ubuntu, and Debian. The installation steps on Ubuntu and Debian differ based on the operating system version, so for the purposes of this chapter, we cover installing phpMyAdmin on Red Hat-derived systems.

30.2 Setting up a web server on Red Hat-based Linux distributions

Before installing phpMyAdmin, the first step is to install and configure a web server on the system hosting the MariaDB server instance. Open a terminal window, log into the host system, and run the following command to check if the Apache web server is installed and running:

```
sudo systemctl status httpd
```

If the web server is installed and running, the output from systemctl will read in part:

```
httpd.service - The Apache HTTP Server
    Loaded: loaded (/usr/lib/systemd/system/httpd.service; disabled; preset:
d>
   Drop-In: /usr/lib/systemd/system/httpd.service.d
            └─php-fpm.conf
    Active: active (running) since Mon 2025-01-27 10:50:23 EST; 3h 29min ago
      Docs: man:httpd.service(8)
  Main PID: 251590 (httpd)
```

If the service is reported as inactive (dead), run the following command to start the web server:

```
sudo systemctl start httpd
```

Alternatively, if systemctl reports that the httpd service is not found, install it using the following command:

```
dnf install httpd
```

After the installation finishes, run the following command to open firewall ports 80 and 443 to allow remote access to the web server. This step is not required if the web browser will be running locally on the server:

Database Administration with phpMyAdmin

```
firewall-cmd --zone=public --permanent --add-service=http
firewall-cmd --zone=public --permanent --add-service=https
```

Next, start the httpd service as follows:

```
sudo systemctl start httpd
```

If required, the web server can be configured to start automatically when the system boots using the following command:

```
sudo systemctl enable httpd
```

30.3 Testing the web server

If you can access the server's desktop environment, open a web browser and enter http://127.0.0.1 in the address bar (127.0.0.1 is the loop-back network address that tells the system to connect to the local machine). If everything is set up correctly, the browser should load a test page like the one in Figure 30-1:

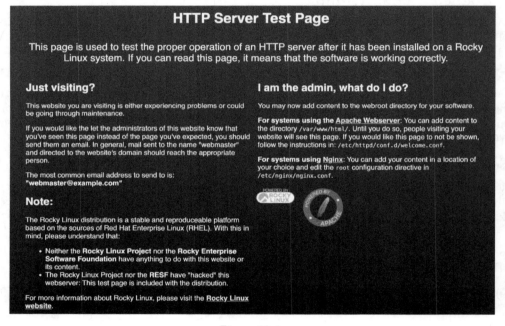

Figure 30-1

If the desktop environment is unavailable, connect from another system on the same local network as the server or use the external IP address assigned to the system if it is hosted remotely.

30.4 Installing phpMyAdmin

The easiest way to install phpMyAdmin on Red Hat-based servers (such as CentOS, Fedora, AlmaLinux, and Rocky Linux) is via the Extra Packages for Enterprise Linux (EPEL) repository. If you did not install EPEL in the MySQL Workbench chapter, you can do so now using the following commands:

```
crb enable
sudo dnf install \
    https://dl.fedoraproject.org/pub/epel/epel-release-latest-9.noarch.rpm \
    https://dl.fedoraproject.org/pub/epel/epel-next-release-latest-9.noarch.rpm
```

With the EPEL repository added, run the following command to install phpMyAdmin:

```
sudo dnf install phpmyadmin
```

Once the packages are installed, the next step is to configure the phpMyAdmin security settings.

30.5 Securing phpMyAdmin access

Access to phpMyAdmin is gained by entering a database username and password. By default, phpMyAdmin will only allow connections from browsers running on the local system (in other words, the system on which phpMyAdmin is installed). These security settings can be viewed and modified in the *phpMyAdmin.conf* file located in the */etc/httpd/conf.d* directory and read as follows:

```
<Directory /usr/share/phpMyAdmin/>
   AddDefaultCharset UTF-8

   Require local
</Directory>

<Directory /usr/share/phpMyAdmin/setup/>
   Require local
</Directory>
```

Access is controlled by placing restrictions on phpMyAdmin directories using the standard Apache <Directory> directive. These restrictions can be based on various factors, such as IP addresses and subnets. For instance, the following setting permits access from 192.168.86.21:

```
   .
   .
Require ip 192.168.86.21
   .
   .
```

Alternatively, the following configuration allows access from all addresses on the specified subnet:

```
   .
   .
Require ip 192.168.86.0/24
   .
   .
```

Though not necessarily recommended, the following example removes all access restrictions:

```
   .
   .
Require all granted
   .
   .
```

If your web server is accessible to external systems via a public IP address, ensure that your site is secured using SSL (HTTPS) before changing the phpMyAdmin access settings and consider enabling two-factor authentication from within the phpMyAdmin settings screen outlined in the next chapter.

Once the changes to the *phpMyAdmin.conf* file are complete, restart the web server to apply the new configuration:

```
sudo systemctl restart httpd
```

30.6 Opening phpMyAdmin

Test that phpMyAdmin is correctly installed and configured by opening a browser window and navigating to http://<*server*>/phpmyadmin, where <*server*> is replaced with the server's IP address, hostname, or URL.

If the installation was successful, the following page will load:

Figure 30-2

Complete the login process by entering the username and password of a database user and clicking the log-in button.

30.7 Troubleshooting

When logging in to the phpMyAdmin console, the following error may occur:

```
mysqli::real_connect(): (HY000/2002): Permission denied
```

There are generally two possible causes for this. One is that the MariaDB server is not running on the system. Use the following command to verify that the server is active:

```
sudo systemctl status mariadb
```

If the MariaDB server is inactive, start it as follows and try again to log in:

```
sudo systemctl start mariadb
```

If this does not resolve the problem, it may be caused by SELinux enforcement. Check the status of SELinux by running the sestatus command:

```
sudo sestatus
SELinux status:                 enabled
SELinuxfs mount:                /sys/fs/selinux
SELinux root directory:         /etc/selinux
Loaded policy name:             targeted
Current mode:                   enforcing
```

```
Mode from config file:          enforcing
Policy MLS status:              enabled
Policy deny_unknown status:     allowed
Memory protection checking:     actual (secure)
Max kernel policy version:      33
```

If the status indicates that SELinux is enabled, use the following steps to disable it:

1. Edit the */etc/selinux/config* file and modify it as follows:

```
.
.
SELINUX=permissive
.
.
```

2. Run the following command to modify the kernel setting:

```
sudo grubby --update-kernel ALL --args selinux=0
```

3. Reboot the system.

Test that you are now able to log into the phpMyAdmin console. If you decide to re-enable SELinux, you can do as follows:

1. Edit the */etc/selinux/config* file and modify it as follows:

```
.
.
SELINUX=enforcing
.
.
```

2. Run the following command to modify the kernel setting:

```
grubby --update-kernel ALL --remove-args selinux
```

3. Reboot the system.

30.8 Reference points

The main points covered in this chapter are as follows:

- **Overview**

  - phpMyAdmin is a web-based MariaDB administration tool.

  - It provides a graphical user interface for managing MariaDB databases.

  - Allows database administrators to manage databases using a browser without installing additional client applications.

- **Installation and Setup**

  - phpMyAdmin requires a web server, typically Apache.

  - It can be installed on Linux distributions via package managers such as *dnf* for Red Hat-based systems.

  - Security settings can be configured in the *phpMyAdmin.conf* file to restrict access to specific IP addresses.

- The firewall must be configured to allow HTTP and HTTPS traffic for remote access.

- **Security and Access Control**

  - By default, phpMyAdmin restricts access to the local system.

  - Administrators can modify the `Require` directive in Apache configuration to allow access from other IP addresses.

  - For security, phpMyAdmin should be accessed via HTTPS and should have strong authentication mechanisms.

- **Logging into phpMyAdmin**

  - Access phpMyAdmin via *http://<server>/phpmyadmin* where *<server>* is the IP address or hostname of the MariaDB server.

  - Users must enter a valid MariaDB username and password to log in.

Chapter 31

31. A Guided Tour of phpMyAdmin

With phpMyAdmin installed and accessible in a web browser, this chapter will briefly overview its main features. Topics covered include the phpMyAdmin user interface, the key tools available for database administration, and how to perform tasks such as creating databases, managing tables, executing SQL queries, and importing/exporting data.

31.1 The phpMyAdmin home screen

The phpMyAdmin interface is designed to be intuitive and to make it easy to administer and manage MariaDB databases. After signing in, phpMyAdmin will display the home page illustrated in Figure 31-1 below:

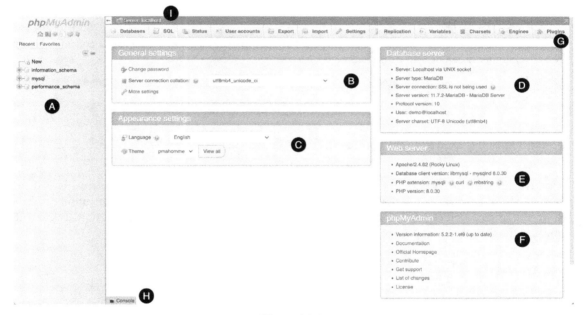

Figure 31-1

The home screen consists of the following areas:

- **A - Navigation panel** - The navigation panel includes a toolbar beneath the phpMyAdmin logo containing quick links to common activities such as returning to the home page, accessing online help, and logging out. The hierarchy tree provides an overview of the databases and tables managed by the MariaDB server, including tables, columns, and indexes. Use the + button to unfold sections of the tree for more detail.

- **B - General settings** - Provides access to basic settings such as configuring two-factor authentication, password changes, and the behavior of phpMyAdmin features.

- **C - Appearance settings** - Includes options to change the user interface language and choose from a range of theme options.

- **D - Database server** - Lists information about the database server, including server and connection type,

A Guided Tour of phpMyAdmin

MariaDB version, and the current user.

- **E - Web server** - Displays details about the web server on which phpMyAdmin is running, including server type and version and information about the PHP version and extensions.

- **F - phpMyAdmin** - Contains the phpMyAdmin version and a list of useful links for documentation, support, and licensing details.

- **G - Toolbar** - This toolbar contains navigation tabs for all the main phpMyAdmin features. The options are context-sensitive, and change based on the current screen.

- **H - Console** - Displays the console panel where SQL statements can be typed and executed.

- **I - Navigation bar** - Much like a website, phpMyAdmin is structured as a hierarchy of pages. In fact, you can use your web browser's back and forward buttons to navigate through your phpMyAdmin screen history. As you navigate deeper into the phpMyAdmin page hierarchy, the navigation bar maintains a record of your path, allowing you to jump back to specific pages by clicking the links provided.

31.2 Using the console

Clicking the Console button (marked H in Figure 31-1 above) displays a panel containing a command prompt where SQL statements can be typed and executed:

Figure 31-2

Enter statements into the console and press Ctrl+Enter to execute them. To execute the statements as they are entered, select the Options link and enable the option to execute queries on enter. The execution results will appear in the main panel. Figure 31-3, for example, shows the results from running the SHOW DATABASES statement in the console:

Figure 31-3

31.3 Managing databases

The Databases screen (Figure 31-4) lists the databases managed by the server and allows new ones to be created:

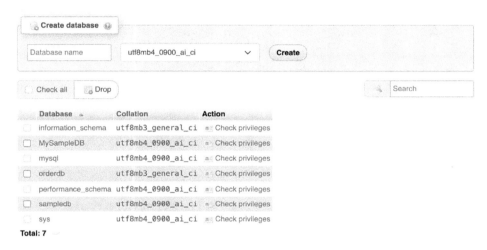

Figure 31-4

Click on a database to navigate to the Structure screen, which contains a list of the tables belonging to the database:

Figure 31-5

The structure screen also includes tabs to manage stored routines, events, triggers, and table privileges. To modify the structure of a table, locate it in the list and click on the Structure link to display the table structure editor shown below:

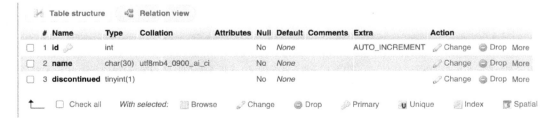

To review and edit individual table records, return to the Structure page and select the Browse link for a table to display the following screen:

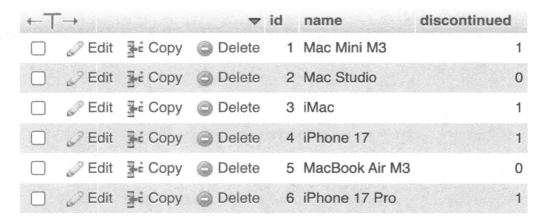

				id	name	discontinued
☐	🖉 Edit	⅓ᴱ Copy	⊖ Delete	1	Mac Mini M3	1
☐	🖉 Edit	⅓ᴱ Copy	⊖ Delete	2	Mac Studio	0
☐	🖉 Edit	⅓ᴱ Copy	⊖ Delete	3	iMac	1
☐	🖉 Edit	⅓ᴱ Copy	⊖ Delete	4	iPhone 17	1
☐	🖉 Edit	⅓ᴱ Copy	⊖ Delete	5	MacBook Air M3	0
☐	🖉 Edit	⅓ᴱ Copy	⊖ Delete	6	iPhone 17 Pro	1

Figure 31-6

31.4 Running SQL queries

In addition to the console, phpMyAdmin includes a SQL editor for entering and executing queries. Selecting the SQL tab in the toolbar will open the editor. Enter SQL statements into the editor and execute them by clicking the Go button:

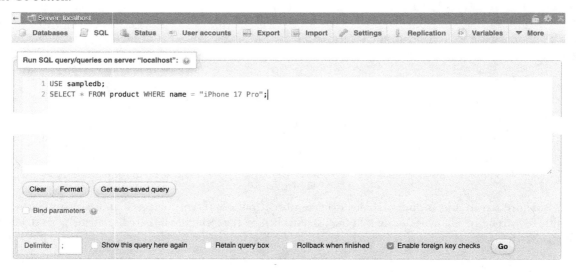

Figure 31-7

31.5 Monitoring server status

The Status page displays information relating to the performance of the MariaDB server. Options are available to list running processes, generate query statistics, browse variables, and monitor the server in real time. The state page also includes an advisor feature that identifies performance issues and recommends solutions. Figure 31-8 shows the status page in Monitor mode:

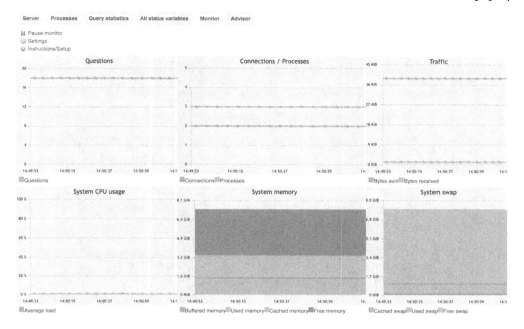

Figure 31-8

31.6 User accounts

As the name suggests, the user accounts screen is where database user management tasks are performed, including adding and deleting users, locking accounts, and modifying privileges:

User accounts overview

	User name	Host name	Password	Global privileges	Grant	Action		
☐	admin	mac.lan	Yes	USAGE	No	Edit privileges	Export	Lock
☐	john	%	Yes	USAGE	No	Edit privileges	Export	Lock
☐	mysql.infoschema	localhost	Yes	SELECT	No	Edit privileges	Export	Unlock
☐	mysql.session	localhost	Yes	SHUTDOWN, SUPER	No	Edit privileges	Export	Unlock
☐	mysql.sys	localhost	Yes	USAGE	No	Edit privileges	Export	Unlock
☐	root	%	Yes	ALL PRIVILEGES	Yes	Edit privileges	Export	Lock

Figure 31-9

31.7 Importing and exporting data

The import and export screens save database data to files that can be imported on other servers. Options are available to save all the server's databases or make custom selections based on individual databases and tables.

31.8 Working with database diagrams

phpMyAdmin includes a database designer tool that displays database relationships in diagram form and allows new tables and relationships to be created. To access the designer, select a database from the navigation panel (marked A in Figure 31-1 above). When the Structure screen appears, select the Designer tab from the toolbar to display the database diagram:

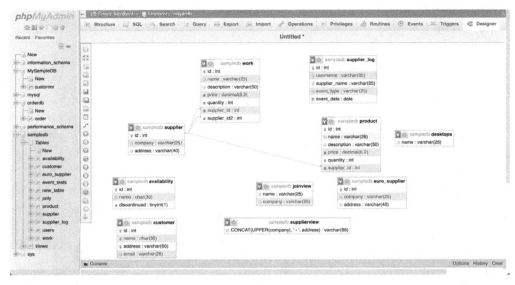

Figure 31-10

Click and drag items to move them, and use the vertical toolbar on the left-hand edge of the diagram panel to create and edit tables and establish new relationships.

This chapter has covered many phpMyAdmin features, but in this book's context, it is impossible to cover them all in detail. Now that you are familiar with the user interface, take some time to explore phpMyAdmin.

31.9 Reference points

The main points covered in this chapter are as follows:

- **Home Screen Overview**

  - Navigation panel provides access to databases and tables.

  - General and appearance settings allow customization of the interface.

  - Displays database server, web server, and phpMyAdmin version details.

  - The console allows SQL queries to be executed interactively.

- **Managing Databases and Tables**

  - The Databases screen lists all databases managed by the MariaDB server.

  - Users can create new databases and modify table structures.

  - The table editor allows changes to columns, indexes, and constraints.

  - Records in tables can be browsed and edited from the Structure page.

- **Running SQL Queries**

  - SQL queries can be executed using the console or the SQL editor.

  - The SQL editor provides a structured environment to enter and run queries.

  - Results from queries are displayed in real time within the interface.

- **Monitoring MariaDB Server Performance**
  - The Status page displays real-time server performance statistics.
  - Users can monitor running processes, query statistics, and database activity.
  - The performance advisor suggests optimizations based on server activity.

- **Managing User Accounts and Privileges**
  - User accounts can be created, modified, or deleted through phpMyAdmin.
  - Privileges and access levels can be configured for individual users.
  - Users can be locked or restricted from certain databases and tables.

- **Importing and Exporting Data**
  - phpMyAdmin supports importing and exporting databases in various formats.
  - Databases can be backed up and restored using export and import features.
  - Options exist to export entire databases or specific tables selectively.

- **Database Diagrams and Schema Management**
  - The Designer tool visually represents database relationships.
  - Users can create new tables and establish foreign key relationships graphically.
  - Database structures can be adjusted through drag-and-drop functionality.

Index

Symbols

@ 130
% 88
< 78
<= 78
<> 78
!= 78
= 78
>= 78
\G delimiter 26

A

ADD 53
AFTER 54, 171
AGAINST 124
aggregate functions 72
  column alias 74
ALTER EVENT 182
ALTER TABLE 53, 101
ALTER USER 32
AND 82
ARCHIVE storage engine 43
AS 74
AT 178
auto-commit 63
autocommit variable 63
AUTO_INCREMENT 41, 48

B

backups 199
  differential 199
  full 199
  incremental 199, 203
  logical 200
  physical 202

BEFORE 171
BEGIN 64, 129
BETWEEN AND 78
bind-address 189

C

CASE 150
  WHEN clause 151
CHANGE 55
COALESCE() 109
column
  ADD 53
  adding 53
  changing data type 56
  deleting 56
  modifying 55
  renaming 55
columns 4
  data types 4
  generated 165
  virtual 165
COMMIT 64
Common Table Expressions 137
comparison operators 78
composite index 125
CONCAT() 101
CONTAINS SQL 132
CONTINUE 156
Control flow 141
  CASE statement 150
  conditional logic 149
  ELSEIF clause 149
  IF statement 149
  LEAVE clause 144
  looping 141
  LOOP statement 144
  REPEAT loop 143
  WHEN clause 151
  WHILE loop 141

251

Index

Index

Index

escaping 91

    match by text position 95

    metacharacters 91

    special characters 91

    text replacement 96

regular index 124

RENAME TABLE 55

REPEAT 143

RETURN 132

RETURNS 132

right join 105

ROLLBACK 64

row

    adding 47

    adding multiple 49

rows 5

    remove all from table 42

S

schema 4

secondary index 124

SELECT 49, 67

    filtering results 77, 81

    limiting results 69

    retrieve single column 67

    retrieving multiple columns 68

    sorting 70

SELECT DISTINCT 70

SELECT INTO 130

SET 61

SET GLOBAL 36

SET PASSWORD 32

show all 40

SHOW COLUMNS FROM 53

SHOW CREATE EVENT 181

SHOW DATABASES 40

SHOW EVENTS 180

SHOW GRANTS 32

SHOW INDEX 126

SHOW TRIGGERS 174

SHOW WARNING 39

SIGNAL 161

Simple Password Check 35

skip_name_resolve 189

slow_query_log 190

slow_query_log_file 190

SMALLINT data type 56

sorting results 70

spatial index 126

special characters 91

SQL

    overview 5

SQL Editor 225

SQLEXCEPTION 156

SQLSTATE 155, 157

    handler conditions 159

    result codes 155

SQLWARNING 159

START TRANSACTION 64

Storage engines 42

    ARCHIVE 43

    CSV 43

    InnoDB 43

    MEMORY 43

    show default engine 43

Stored routines 129

    functions 129

    procedures 129

Structured Query Language 5

subqueries 84

SUM() 72

systemctl 8

    start 8

    status 8

    stop 8

T

Table

    adding columns 53

    adding rows 49

    altering 53

    changing column type 56

    column renaming 55

    columns 4

Index

www.ingramcontent.com/pod-product-compliance
Lightning Source LLC
LaVergne TN
LVHW080114070326
832902LV00015B/2578